'It is what it is: the weekly musings of a man who adored the rackety world of racing, given an afterlife as much because of who he was as for his gentle, funny, self-deprecating, occasionally dyspeptic descriptions of the sport of kings and quasi-criminals.'
Stephen Moss, *Guardian*

'*Freud on Course* reveals a personality seemingly at odds with the curmudgeonly reputation: curious and amused, enjoying adventure, relishing good things ... Freud died at his typewriter, a half-written column in front of him ... This book is full of life.'
Nicholas Clee, *Daily Mail*

'Anyone unamused by this book should consider therapy themselves.'
Simon Redfern, *Independent*

'A marvellous testament to his acerbic wit, appetite for the absurd and oblique take on the world.'
***Eclipse* magazine**

*This book is dedicated in Clement's memory
to his three racing friends Bob Solomon,
Charlie Wilson and Andy Wright, with whom
he shared so many delights and disasters
on the track.*

FREUD
ON COURSE

THE RACING LIVES OF
CLEMENT FREUD

edited by
SEAN MAGEE

with a Foreword by
BROUGH SCOTT

RACING POST

This paperback edition published in 2010 by Racing Post Books
Compton, Newbury, Berkshire RG20 6NL

First published in 2009

A catalogue record for this book is available from the British Library.

ISBN 978-1-905156-72-6

Designed by John Schwartz

Printed in the UK by CPI Bookmarque, Croydon

Cover photograph: Sir Clement Freud with Four Legs Good, 2000
(copyright © Racing Post/Edward Whitaker)

CONTENTS

I WAS ASKED the other day what I would like folk to say as they passed my body laid out in an open coffin for final inspection. I should like at least one of them to say: 'I think I saw him move.'

CLEMENT FREUD
21 FEBRUARY 2009

FOREWORD

BY BROUGH SCOTT

AT CLEMENT FREUD'S funeral his son Matthew said that of all his father's incarnations it was the writing that brought us closest to the man. These pages are proof that writing about racing brought him closest of all.

For wherever he was in the world Clement Freud liked to go to the races. Best of all he liked to write about it as if he were sending a postcard home to friends and family. 'In this land,' he wrote about a visit to Gulfstream Park in Florida, 'go where you will, what you miss is youth. The waitresses are old, the tote clerks are old and for entertainment in what we would call the members' restaurant an old man sits at a keyboard while his uncle, wearing an impressive red and white striped shirt, sings "It Had To Be You" – an odd choice for chanting septuagenarians, but there you go.'

An afternoon at the races gave him people, bets, jokes, hope, drink, disaster and the occasional wads-of-money moments of triumph, all before the long train home. It gave him the chance to satisfy his appetite for the absurd and his love of detail, not to mention the obligatory indulgence in food, a mix which worked so well that we had long wanted him to write this book. He had been producing columns about racing since the early 1960s and for the last ten years he had penned a weekly one for us at *Racing Post* which all surveys showed appealed to a bigger and wider audience than anyone else in the paper, present company very much included. This February he finally agreed, and while Sean Magee and I went round to the Marylebone flat in anticipation we had no idea of the treasure trove that awaited us.

In his immaculately ordered study with its pictures of the many ages of Freud – from infant to patriarch via soldier to restaurateur to performer to journalist to jockey to politico to knight of the realm – there was a long bookcase in the corner stuffed with rows and rows of tall albums, into which were pasted every article he had ever written.

Here was confirmation of Matthew's judgement. However many other roles he may have excelled at, nothing matched the width and the colour and the timing and the wit of his writing. Racing allowed him to do it to the end. On the day before he died he had been at Exeter, had lunched well in the restaurant, bet successfully and left the track with a large wad in his back pocket. He knew a heart operation was looming but was determined to live and chronicle life in the way he had made all his own, and whose vigour and clarity and straight-faced fun stayed with him right to the end.

The day after Clement's passing his daughter Emma thought to turn on his computer. He had been found dead at his desk, and in the ensuing activity nobody had noticed that the computer had gone into hibernation. He had a *Racing Post* article due, and these are the exact words he was writing as the night closed in:

Bob is younger than I am, not that there are too many people who fail to come under that category. I had made a speech at a convention in Monte Carlo some 40 years ago, his wife asked whether I would have dinner with them that evening, I replied 'why on earth?' and she said 'We shall drink a magnum of 1961 Chateau Leoville-Las Cases.' So I accepted and we became friends and in God's good time

Not bad for last thoughts ten days shy of your 85th birthday. How exactly Bob and his wife and the magnum of Chateau Leoville Las Cases came back into Clement's life is a secret he has taken away with him. The delight of this book is finding quite how much intrigue and laughter he has left behind.

PREFACE

BY SEAN MAGEE

ALL THE PIECES in this book were first published in the *Racing Post*, with the exception of section 3, 'The Jockey', which originally appeared as a chapter in Clement Freud's autobiography *Freud Ego* (2001).

By the time of Clement's sudden death in April 2009 we had agreed the overall shape and structure, as well as certain principles of editing. The original pieces would be tinkered with only in the lightest way, to avoid too much repetition and inconsistency and to correct mistakes. And he was adamant that the opinions, likes and dislikes expressed at the time should not be diluted through the filter of hindsight, whatever may have happened since they were first written. Thus his judgement in 1999 that at Plumpton racecourse 'they treat punters with contempt', or his complaint the same year that there was nowhere to sit at Bangor-on-Dee, were to remain, whatever improvements might have been made since the pieces were published.

We also agreed that to try to explain contemporary references in pieces written years ago or record what happened next – for example, the fate of Gary Wiltshire's ante-post vouchers in 2004 – would be as tedious and disruptive for the readers as for the compilers.

The task of putting together a volume of Clement Freud's writing on racing was made infinitely easier by his own diligence in preserving what he had written, with – as Brough Scott notes in his Foreword – every single article systematically pasted into albums, and I am especially grateful for the ready assistance of Clement's long-time friend and regular co-owner Andy Wright, who not only has helped preparation of this volume in a variety of ways, but kept spirits up with a emailed stream of jokes to fill the void left in Saturday morning's *Racing Post*. Thanks also to Julian Brown and James de Wesselow at Racing Post Books and to John Schwartz at SoapBox, who designed the book.

Clement Freud's *Racing Post* articles from August 1998 to April 2009 fill eight of those large albums. A ninth was prepared and labelled, but its pages remain blank.

1

THE NOVICE

6 A trickle of ice-cold sweat ran down the back of my neck **9**

BENNY LYNCH AND A BAPTISM OF FIRE
6 OCTOBER 1999

I STARTED GAMBLING at the age of eight, at a bent roulette table in my Devon boarding school. Prior to that I had had no experience of money, for ours was not a household in which children bought sweets or were dispatched to get penn'orths of chips.

Then suddenly, in those salad days of pre-puberty, I received a weekly stipend of sixpence. As the maximum bet on a single number at the Saturday night roulette school was a halfpenny, I had ammunition for 12 major shots on the green baize.

I don't recall losing, which I must have done a lot, but, goodness, the wins remain etched in the memory. Payouts of one shilling and fivepence ha'penny and the camaraderie of fellow gamblers that went with it; the language of the table – *plein*, *cheval*, *deuxieme*, *douzaine* – that made me feel as if I had become a member of a secret society of greater attraction and immediacy than the Ovalteenies.

I read the *Sporting Times* in the school library, wallowed in the racing terms and longed for the day that ponies and monkeys would become part of my lifestyle. In Walberswick on the Suffolk coast, where my parents had a holiday house, I studied the runners and riders in my father's *News Chronicle*.

Mr Rogers ran the village garage and took bets, illegally, at his back door. Racing results were announced after the six o'clock evening news; one had to await the next day's papers to get the odds. My first big winner came in at 13-2. Oh, the joy of knowing you had backed a winner – and the wondrous wait to learn the extent of the coup.

Rogers was a miserable old sod who called me 'buoy', which is Suffick for 'boy'. Once, when a tuppence each-way bet came up and I had raced to his door to collect, he looked at me over his glasses and asked: 'How old are you, buoy?' I told him I was about a day older than when he had taken my money.

The cause of Mr Rogers' wretchedness was the first Wednesday of June, 1932. On that day, the Walls ice-cream man who came across each summer morning on the ferry from Southwold pushed his tricycle up the street, went into The Bell for an Adnam's ale and told the assembled company that his governor's horse would win the Derby. He then sold Snofrutes for one penny and choc-ices for twice that sum on the village green, adjourned to The Anchor for a second drink and repeated his information.

Rogers, wearing his 'garage' hat, had driven someone to the afternoon train at Ipswich station. On his return, his wife said: 'Good news – I've taken over 50 bets.' All were on April The Fifth, owned and trained by Tom Walls the actor, who had no connection with the ice cream company. Rogers never smiled again.

At my Devon school, lessons were optional and I did not go a lot. A friend's father took us to Buckfastleigh racecourse where there were bookmakers and tic-tac men, Tote windows and people asking each other what they knew (at school, people only told you what you did not know). I became hooked.

I worked in the Dartington pottery making teapot spouts at fourpence an hour to finance my gaming. Later, I stayed with a friend whose mother, bored by small boys, sent us to Lewes races with her chauffeur and a £5 note: four years' pocket money. It was like having a short spell in heaven, and earth became a poorer place for it. When you have placed a tens-shilling bet on the Tote double, the thrill of a penny each-way is diminished.

A disgraced Suffolk cleric took me to my first greyhound race meeting. This happened in a field between Beccles and Bungay where the hare was activated by a man on a bicycle.

On the race-sheet the dogs were called Spot and Blackie and Ognib, but my mentor recognised them from their daytime jobs at the licensed tracks of Lowestoft and Yarmouth. We won and got drunk, and I embarked on what was considered a disreputable way of life. Gambling was never far from my thoughts; drinking was in attendance.

As a ten-shillings-a-week cook at the Dorchester Hotel, most afternoons were spent at Stamford Bridge dogs: reverse forecasts, shillings on the nose, watch the tic-tac men and pretend you understand.

Betting was fun; losing did not matter greatly while winning was cause for celebration. The criterion for whether or not one should embark on a gambler's life is, simply: do you mind losing more than you enjoy winning? If the answer is in the affirmative, find another hobby.

After the war, I worked for a year in a hotel in Cannes and spent most evenings in the casino, luxuriating in the sound of spinning roulette wheels, clunking chips, shuffling cards and the occasional heavy thud as another failed gambler jumped from the fifth-floor balcony to land on the marble terracing below.

I placed bets on 24, then 5 and 16 lest the ball narrowly missed my number. I met a girl who said 'the final sevens' and I backed 7, 17 and 27 because I loved her. My next girlfriend was into zero and its neighbours and I had a period backing 28 and 29 *en cheval*. There came a time when every number had, at one time, been my number and, as the ball fell, I asked myself in disbelief, how could I not have backed it?

In the summer of 1949 I managed a North Devon seaside hotel, spent my day off at a bookmakers in Barnstaple, ate local shellfish, adopted rum and lime and ice and soda as my drink and stuck a bet.

Stuck a bet; three words which represent the most acute agony I had suffered, then years of nightmares. A customer of quality who had arrived with wife, children, chauffeur and nanny came to

me one June afternoon and said: 'Freud, d'ye have a bookmaker?'
I did.

He said: 'Put me £100 on Benny Lynch for the Gold Cup. You'll
get 100-1.' The reason for the 100-1 was that Benny Lynch was
Alycidon's pacemaker and, even at 100-1, a pacemaker is a plum
bad bet. I put the £100 in my pocket – 20 crinkly white fivers, eight
weeks' pay. Reward for being knowledgeable about racing, I told
myself.

This was the pre-TV age and I listened to the race on the BBC
Light Programme. 'The pacemaker is in the lead,' said the laid-
back commentator. Then, half a minute later: 'Benny Lynch is 15
lengths ahead and shows no sign of slowing down.' Shortly after
that, he opined that 'the lead is down to ten lengths but he doesn't
look like getting caught.'

Ruin stared me in the face. £10,000 was 15 years' salary. For
£10,000 you could buy a 200-acre farm in Suffolk. It was 20 times
the average reason for jumping off Beachy Head. A trickle of ice-
cold sweat ran down the back of my neck.

By the time Alycidon was declared the winner, I had ceased to
care; had lost my bottle. I never spent 'winnings' with less
enjoyment; I understood how Mr Rogers felt and forgave him his
boorishness. I also decided to take gambling more seriously than
I had.

2
THE OWNER

❛ My wife, an innocent woman, asks whether I might not clean up even more comprehensively were I to abandon horse ownership and take up solitaire ❜

FLYING THE COLOURS IN DREAMWORLD
27 OCTOBER 1999

THEY HAVE SOMETHING about them, owners do. St Paul wrote to the Corinthians (who never seemed to write back) about faith, hope and charity, 'and the greatest of these is charity'.

So on racecourses there are entrances marked Silver Ring, Tattersalls, Members and 'Owners and Trainers', and the greatest of these is Owners and Trainers. They who pass through that gate stand out over their peers. People sidle up to them and ask, 'Will it win?', just as if the owner had any idea, or would tell them if he had. Owners are sought out by journalists to give interviews when their horses win, and sometimes when they don't, and when I became a sports columnist I decided that by not being an owner, I might be missing something.

In 1964 at Folkestone, after the seller, I was standing watching a tubed, pin-fired, gelded four-year-old called Bullfrog, who ran in blinkers, limp around the winner's enclosure as the auctioneer called: 'Who'll start me off at £100?' And among the sea of static hands, resolute chins and unmoving eyebrows, I raised my racecard.

'Must be worth more than a hundred, bound to pick up a few more little races. Do I hear guineas?', asked the auctioneer. He did not.

So I walked up to Mr Johnson Houghton, trainer of the winner and said: 'Dry your tears, lighten your countenance, I would like you to continue to train him.'

'Actually I was rather pleased to get shot of him,' said the man, 'but if you want me to go on training the old bugger, all right then.'

I filled in the appropriate forms, and asked if the trainer would like me to call on Bullfrog regularly and should I bring carrots, also when he might run again? And Mr J H, who is a gentleman, said: 'Do come if you'd like to and I'll ring you when he next runs. And do you have colours?'

I registered colours and had them made up, and about a fortnight later was informed that Bullfrog had been entered to run in a seller at Hurst Park.

'Is he fit and well and likely to win?', I asked.

'Well, since Folkestone he has coughed a couple of times, his shins are a bit sore, but he is working not much worse than before; hard to tell because I don't have too many horses he can work with.'

On the day of his first race in my silks, I bought the morning editions of all three London evening papers, mostly to see my name in print as 'owner', and noticed that Busy Bee in the *Evening News* had napped him: 2.30 Bullfrog.

I rang the paper, asked for racing and requested to speak to Mr Bee.

'Who?'

'Busy Bee.'

'We all do Busy Bee,' said the man on the phone. 'What ar'ya after?'

I explained that I was the owner of the horse, that my trainer had been only lukewarm in his enthusiasm and wondered whether they knew anything that had been withheld from me? The man rang off.

I went to Hurst Park, walked through the Owners' Entrance, met the trainer, entered the parade ring at 2.20, shook hands with my jockey and asked what he thought of my colours – which were orange and black and new and shiny.

And he said, 'They're a bit flashy all right, if you're trying. Me, I'd have gone for grey with light brown sleeves.'

Bullfrog tried and did not win, went lame and soon after that I sold him at a slight loss. I had been an owner for two months.

Nevertheless, like someone who has joined a club and thinks it economical to keep going there to get his money's worth, I had these colours and thought it extravagant to have no horse to go with them. So I went on buying horses.

I liked finding them names, enjoyed seeing my colours carried in races, had the occasional win and much fun. Winter Fair, Grunty Fen, Weareagrandmother and Nagnagnag were probably my most successful horses, though I might have won the Ebor with Escarole if Willie Carson had not given him a breather when in the lead four furlongs out; he told me after the race: 'He didn't need the breather. I should have kept him going.' Oh well.

Uri Geller came to open a fete in my constituency, said he would not buy a raffle ticket because he always won and people didn't like that. He was bullied into buying one ticket, one out of 2,500, and won. I showed him a sales catalogue, he chose a horse and we called her Spoonbender and owned her in partnership. Uri came up with some quite impressive reasons why she always ran so badly.

It is 35 years since Bullfrog. The orange and black colours have been in constant, if infrequent, use, and are currently awaiting the recovery from sniffles by Digup St Edmunds in Venetia Williams' yard.

Owners recoup 22 per cent of their racing costs and I think I am about par for the course. Owning a winner multiplies the enjoyment by a factor of hundreds; seeing the horse you own put down is much worse than losing the heaviest of bets.

It took me years to find out that owning horses is about dreams, and until a horse's first run there is no upper limit to the dream; the Derby, Champion Hurdle, Grand National are all within range. Only when the horse has appeared on a racecourse is the dream confined and even then, Red Rum began life in two-year-old sellers, Group 1 winners have been claimed for a few thousand pounds. Somewhere over the rainbow skies *are* blue.

The longer before the horse runs, the greater the scope for reverie.

*

Clement Freud's most comprehensive chronicle of the expectations and frustrations of owning racehorses is the series 'An Owner's Tale', published in the Racing Post *in summer 2000 about his filly Four Legs Good.*

FOUR LEGS GOOD, TWO LEGS MAD?

4 JUNE 2000

THERE ARE OWNERS who make racing pay – just as there are pawnbrokers who offer customers glasses of sloe gin before advancing money on wristwatches, and parking-meter attendants content to let you park on a double yellow line while you go to the dentist. Rare breeds, though.

Thousands upon thousands of people own or part-own a racehorse, and if you ask them the reasons, these are diverse: to get closer to racing; to impress the neighbours; to be able to get into racetracks for free and to drink in the owners' and trainers' bar; to become 'one of us' when they were previously 'one of them'. Bad reasons all.

You buy a Thoroughbred so that you can dream. Each year, a few dozen horses comprehensively outperform their peers, and if the Maktoums do not already own these, they will want to buy them. For this purpose, they wield cheques with noughts the way we have mice. We want to dream of telling them the horse is not for sale and see it prove at Epsom and Ascot that we made the right decision.

In the early 1990s when the great swindle began, a moronic politician announced that 'the lottery is a good gamble.'

On that basis, buying a yearling is a terrific gamble: the odds against winning the lottery are 14 million to one. The odds against buying a decently bred yearling who will make you a millionaire arc less than 10,000-1. A gambler would be foolish not to avail himself of such an opportunity, though it should be borne in mind that the upkeep of a lottery ticket is zilch, while keeping a yearling diminishes your fortune by £1.50 an hour. Since you began reading this article, Mr Giles Bravery (of whom more later) has benefited by about 4p, and the clock is ticking and will continue to tick, world without end.

I have owned racehorses since the early 1960s. I had felt being an owner would be helpful to writing about the sport (wrong) and that I might meet people I would not otherwise encounter (right) which would be uplifting (sometimes).

The closest I got to owning a Group One winner was in 1976 when Paul Kelleway invited me to choose a yearling from those he had bought and I picked the one in the next box to Swiss Maid.

As fortune has recently graced me with a smile, I decided to embark upon the purchase of another racehorse.

While deliberating about a trainer, I saw a TV interview with the man who trained Torgau, winner of last season's Cherry Hinton Stakes. He was smallish, youngish, agreeably pissed, and he radiated such high octane, contagious joy that I wanted to be part of it. I found his telephone number, gave him a few days to get over his hangover and arranged a meeting.

We got on well. He put away his cigarettes while I was in fuming distance, gave me a tour of his stables at the unfashionable end of Hamilton Road, Newmarket, and introduced his wife who bakes good cakes and his six-year-old son who may become a marathon runner. The upshot of the encounter was that I gave him a £30,000 limit to buy a filly, and agreed the all-in training and vetting and travelling and shoeing fee at north of £30 a day – but not nearly as far north as would have been the case with Messrs Cecil or Stoute.

In God's good time, Mr Bravery went to Ireland and bought a Be My Guest filly out of a Habitat mare – which is old-fashioned breeding. Had this been a human rather than an equine, you would be thinking the Army or the church rather than NASDAQ.

I met the filly in November. She was small, brown, handsome with a long, white blaze down her face and four white feet; friendly with it.

'Is she an early sort?', I asked.

It turned out that other owners have early sorts. 'This one would be likely to run in May or June,' said the trainer, which sounds so very much more acceptable than 'you will have spent £9,000 on training bills before she enters a starting stall in earnest.'

We needed a name. Be My Guest/Habitat made me consider Shoplifter, but Shoplifter is (a) a rotten name for a nice horse and (b) had already gone. At length, after consultation with my team of Andy (ten per cent), Charlie (ten per cent) and trainer Giles (ten per cent), and in view of the colour of her feet, we agreed Four Legs Good. Weatherbys, which registers names, told me Four Legs Good was available and did not fall foul of any of their caveats – for example, you may not call a horse Mike Hunt.

We visit her from time to time. She has grown and her stable lad thinks she has the makings of a winning racehorse ... if I am patient. Patience, while you are paying £1.50 an hour, is a much-appreciated quality in owners – and much appreciated by trainers. Those knowledgeable men want horses to run when they are cherry ripe to give of their best. Owners, on the whole, want horses to run soon and run often to provide opportunities for recouping expenditure, and also to enable them to flash owners' badges as they pass the queue at the members' entrance.

As I write, Four Legs Good has two canters a day, eats up, sleeps and is uncomplicated – which I take to be trainer-speak for 'she has not so far savaged me or members of my immediate family.'

After doing three or four bits of work next month, she will run for real over six furlongs on some nice, even track – which rules out Brighton and Chester. Perhaps Haydock six Sundays from today if you believe in bloodlines; her 70 per cent owner once rode a winner at Haydock.

NOT A GOOD RESULT FROM FOUR LEGS II
11 JUNE 2000

THE COST OF sending a child to boarding school is about the same as keeping a horse in training, though children have the edge in that they are cheaper to shoe and to send by train – off-peak, at half-price.

I paid for my five children's education and cannot recall a single occasion when I telephoned a headmaster to ask how young Freud was doing, how he/she measured up to the other children, whether he/she ate up or was his/her coat shiny. And here I am, back on the phone to my trainer, Giles Bravery.

Clement (as I know he is busy, I decline small talk of the 'How is your dear wife?' variety and move smoothly to the issue): 'How is she doing?' (meaning our filly Four Legs Good).

Giles: 'She is doing well, ran upsides another filly on the gallops and settled to it nicely. She's in really good order.'

Clement: 'Did she overtake the other filly?'

Giles: 'She wasn't meant to overtake the other filly; she moved nicely upsides and the lass who rode her, who is French, says, "She is vair vair nice."'

Clement: 'Was she giving the other filly a lot of weight?'

The trainer was silent; this does not appear to be a subject for discussion.

'When can we expect her first race?', I ask.

'If all goes well,' says Giles with the assurance of a man for whom all things go brilliantly, 'a few days either side of July 10.'

I suggest bringing over a jockey from the United States. Giles thinks Michael Hills if he is available. And we talk about the Derby dinner, to which neither of us may go again. How can one have a really good time wearing black bow ties and in the absence of women?

Weatherbys, who are the kindest, most efficient and helpful people you could encounter, sent me a genealogical chart of Four Legs Good that goes back seven generations. I notice a minor blip: one of her great-great-great-great-grandfathers is also one of her great-great-great-grandfathers. Noel Coward – and if not him, it should have been – said that the only things he found unacceptable were incest and folk dancing. Coward was not a racing man.

Bravery has some dozen two-year-olds in his care, and the first of these ran at Catterick on Friday. This seemed a good reason for ringing him again. 'Giles, Clement. Your Siptitz Heights in the first at Catterick this afternoon. How does she compare with Four Legs Good?'

'Siptitz Heights is more forward.'

'How does she compare with the other two-year-olds?'

'Siptitz is forwarder.'

'Isn't the race you picked rather hot, I mean each of the four other runners has winning form?'

'And more weight. Torgau won that race for me last year and logistically Siptitz Heights is ready to run, wasn't ready last Tuesday and needs an outing before she goes for the Queen Mary at Royal Ascot.'

Now, was that a tip or was that a tip?

On Thursday, the probable SP on Teletext was 16-1 outsider of five. Friday's *Racing Post* put her in at 12-1. If she won and I had no financial interest, would that not be exactly what racehorse owning should not be about? My filly stands in her box, chattering away, as horses do, costing a fortune each hour, and here I have privileged information about one of her friends. A week's training fees on the nose settles four months' accounts; another week's divided by four gets computer straight forecasts Siptitz to come second to the field, which makes more sense than each-way.

As I have an 11am appointment on Friday I cannot travel north. A tax-paid-on monkey is invested at my local betting shop.

My wife has a name for these 'investments'. Losses, she calls them.

HOPE TRIUMPHS IN ERIC'S EXPERIENCE
18 JUNE 2000

OWNING A RACEHORSE is not a full-time occupation. I have spent the last week sitting beneath my lemon tree in Portugal (dry that starting tear, I have a villa that goes with the tree), eating modestly in order to be able to fit into my Ascot clothes, and watching Euro 2000 football on television – I backed Portugal v. the Czech Republic at 250-1 to be the finalists.

My involvement in racing was confined to the Racing Channel, whose sound I can get, though not the pictures.

Ownership of a racehorse, then, is not a full-time calling, but paying the bills for feeding and shoeing and exercising the brute affords no let-up. The just-shy-of-four-figure bill for my 70 per cent of Four Legs Good thuds monthly on the doormat and is returned with a cheque the next day. This makes me a good owner.

I also ring my trainer Giles Bravery – though not quite as often as I did before he made bullish sounds about a filly who failed to notice that the starting stalls had opened – which probably makes me a less than entirely desirable owner.

But while Four Legs Good is still unraced, the whole world is at her four white feet – admittedly, not the upcoming Royal Ascot, but prestigious two-year-old events occur in summer and autumn at York, Ascot, Haydock, Sandown – not to mention around the world.

Before she has had a gallop in earnest, this is the optimum time for an owner. Four Legs Good's value could now be higher than it will ever be again.

In her box in Hamilton Road, Newmarket, she has struck up a warm and trusting relationship with her lad, who speaks highly of her. Okay, he would, wouldn't he? However, her lad is no callow youth, but a man of honour, massive experience and an impeccable CV.

Eric Campbell was born in 1930, left school at 14, was apprenticed to Tom Hall and, after his indenture had been transferred to Sam Hall, led up Miraculous Atom, who won the Ebor when he was 21 (Eric, not the horse). He rode, among others, Miserable Monk, who broke the two-mile hurdle track record at Manchester, which he holds to this day and will retain for ever.

Eric married the sister of a fellow stable lad in Middleham and, of his three children, the daughter is Bravery's secretary, one son trained and the other rode.

Dad, despite having broken most things down his right side and had his thumb bitten off by a horse, and despite having two broken ribs where a colt leaned on him, rides out every day and does Four Legs Good.

Eric race-rode until he was 40, was head man to Ryan Jarvis – in the days of Long Roll and Miss Petard – then to Robert Williams for ten years, which included caring for Mister Majestic, who won the Middle Park Stakes.

Eric retired at 65 and hasn't stopped working since. 'Working on the basis of not getting bored,' is how he puts it.

At his home, in a Rous Memorial cottage in Newmarket's Old Station Road, there are pictures of Eric riding winners, his son Ross riding winners, his son Ian training winners ... And this splendid, dedicated man, who broke in and rides out my filly, says: 'There is every indication she will be successful.' That will do me.

I still have about five weeks of dreams of the very highest order, to which an owner is entitled until his horse appears in public and proves otherwise.

By way of consolation I cheer myself by the fact that if things go less than totally brilliantly, I will save substantial money by not having to supplement her for the One Thousand Guineas.

FOUR LEGS GOOD? FOUR LEGS GREAT!

25 JUNE 2000

THE FILLY IS well; the trainer is well ... I met him at Ascot on Gold Cup day and he wore a top hat that put mine to shame. On the subject of counting blessings, I am extra well, in exceptionally good shape. More about that later.

This series is about a man and his horse. Since last Sunday's report, the filly has eaten five square meals a day, walked to, and done a couple of canters on, the Limekilns, throughout which time the owner's bank balance has diminished by £1.50 an hour night and day, rain and shine.

The fantasy 'I've got what might be the very best two-year-old filly in East Anglia' has not much longer to go. Barring a setback, within a couple of weeks (say £500-£600 in training fees from now) Four Legs Good will be put into a horsebox, travel to a distant battlefield, be led around the parade ring, get shoved into a starting stall, run faster than she has ever run before in her life and cease to be a dream.

She will become a racehorse with a rating; a dream translated into a tangible statistic with a 'p' or 'P', but please not a 'squiggle', in Timeform.

One reads in racing columns that 'the horse has been laid out' for this or that event, so I telephoned the trainer: was there perhaps some contest for unraced fillies with four white feet and a blaze down their noses that we would be foolish not to go for? There was not.

What happens is that horses do their thing until, one day, the trainer decides the brute is ready.

How can you tell? Experience. One nods. Until such time as a race is run, an owner has nothing to go on but the trainer's form and the success rate of his next of kin. Trainer Bravery's first two-year-old runner finished about halfway down the field in the Queen Mary, which is respectable. 'That filly,' said the trainer, 'will win next time,' which is meaningful.

Be My Guest, Four Legs Good's sire, is only having an average season, which is meaningless. There is talent in the family, which is why she cost so much as a yearling. With hindsight, breeding can prove anything you want it to prove; if you could tell in advance, horseracing would lose much of its magic.

Owning a horse is not just about preening yourself in the parade ring at 2.35pm at Brighton on a Thursday. It is an ongoing situation. Owning gives you a cachet, permits you to pontificate and bore people, gets you listened to, causes folk to ask your advice ... all for no better reason than that you pay someone else to train. As a consequence, you seek the companionship of men and women who will recognise this fact, and where better to witness that than on the track?

I spent last week among the fashionable, behatted citizenry, where I am a member of the very wonderful Royal Ascot Racing Club, which entitles one to unlimited champagne, snacks, soft meringues with Cornish cream and Sovereign strawberries – also sandwiches which have not yet risen to great heights.

Royal Tuesday yielded one winner, five losers and a conversation with a woman who had backed a horse which paid £51 for a £1 win. 'Why did you pick that one?', I asked. She said it had a star against it in her newspaper. The star denoted that the animal was running with its tongue tied down.

On Wednesday, I decided to indulge in a Lucky 15 – four selections backed singly, in six doubles, four trebles and an accumulator, and blow me down with a hermaphrodite's codpiece if they did not all win. Every last one of them. One, two, three, four at odds of 5-2, 5-1, 7-1 and 10-1.

I left the course having acquired the price of a slightly shop-soiled Bentley turbo, enough money to buy a peerage from a minor political party or influence the result of three Test matches.

That afternoon, I had sat down to a cucumber sandwich wondering how long the good life might last. At 5.36 I was floating.

On Thursday, having had another successful afternoon, I stood in the Tote queue behind a man trying to negotiate a bet using a luncheon voucher.

This took so long that when my turn came, the race was off – which saved me a week's training fees. I would like to recommend being an owner to all my readers.

ALL WE NEED NOW IS TO FIND A JOCKEY
2 JULY 2000

WE ARE IN business. Trainer Bravery has decided that Four Legs Good, who worked extra well under Michael Hills on the Newmarket gallops on Friday, will be ready to run at the end of next week and the team is set to go to Nottingham on Saturday 15 July to cheer her on in the 3.50, the European Breeders' Fund Family Day Maiden Fillies' Stakes, Class D, over six furlongs.

As she has not previously raced, comes from a yard that has yet to have a two-year-old winner this season, and boasts a pedigree that makes you nod rather than stretch your eyes in wonderment, I expect her starting price to be generous.

I have kept pretty quiet about her, though last month I did put her first outing into a patent with Portugal for Euro 2000 and a dog at Monmore that got badly checked at the fourth bend. Thus there is no reason for bookmakers to believe that she is a hot-pot, a talking horse or even 'off'.

Finding a jockey is going to be a bit of a problem. On that same Saturday afternoon there are four other Flat meetings – Ascot, Chester, Salisbury and York – at three of which is a Listed race.

While the winner of our chosen race at Colwick Park picks up a prize a little north of £3,000, importing a jockey might not be economically justifiable, for I read that Jerry Bailey's air fare last month was close to twice the prize-money for which we will be competing. Nor am I persuaded that Bailey would ride Nottingham any better than he rode Ascot and, to be fair, there's also the likelihood that he may be unwilling to come over for the one ride.

The trainer thinks it could be a mistake to put up an apprentice; it will probably be a case of putting up whoever is available.

As other owners have two-year-old fillies and might well consider the EBF Family Day Maiden to be just what their little darlings need, there's also the chance that the race will be oversubscribed and Four Legs Good will get balloted out.

For trainer Bravery to choose that event is little short of brilliant. You could hear the man's mind working from a distance of 60 miles – wherever a two-year-old finishes over six furlongs, you would have to recognise that the distance was a furlong too short for her, or a furlong too long.

Then the track – this is so egregiously central a racecourse that, until the filly runs south, west, north or east of Nottingham, the result of her first outing is meaningless (unless she wins).

On the subject of the going, running her on hard, firm, soft or heavy is out of the question, and you wouldn't want to introduce a filly on a track that is good to soft, nor good to firm – which leaves good. Statistically, fewer horses win on good going than any other state of the ground. While this is caused by the fact that good going attracts more runners than other conditions, you cannot argue with statistics. McCririck would back me fervently there.

To run on a five-meeting afternoon means we probably won't be able to book Hills. When the pilot situation has been taken into consideration, it could be argued that we are lucky to be able to get a run at all – and there is still the introduction of blinkers, visor, tongue-strap and earplugs to add to the equation.

Let us keep in mind the good news – Hills was impressed, trainer Bravery is enthusiastic and Celine, the French girl who rides Four Legs Good when Eric doesn't, says she is 'vair nice' and Celine is not just any old stable girl. When Celine returns home, she is going to the Sorbonne to read economics.

IS FOUR LEGS TOO NICE FOR HER OWN GOOD?
9 JULY 2000

I HAVE PREVIOUSLY given notice to readers that Four Legs Good's public introduction to the trade for which she was bred was to take place at Nottingham next Saturday, at 3.50pm, in a two-year-old maiden fillies' event over six furlongs.

While the projected prize-money to the winner is around three-eighths of this year's training bills to date, each win achieved by a well-bred female equine increases her value both as a racehorse and broodmare.

Our syndicate, consisting of Andy, Charlie, Giles and myself, made plans to treat the occasion with the seriousness it deserved.

The outing was to commence with luncheon in the racecourse restaurant, where we were considering iced, minted pea-soup with ham croutons; crown of lamb in a herb crust, parisienne potatoes, spinach with butter and nutmeg, Stilton cheese, walnut bread; wine to be discussed.

However, working on the gallops last Sunday morning, Four Legs Good lightly grazed her near-side front knee.

Around the land, teenagers – the human equivalents of equine two-year-olds – lightly graze their knees all the time and are told to shut up, not make a fuss and think of all the children dying in Kosovo. In extreme cases, they are given a dab of iodine and a plaster.

It is worth remembering here that to us a knee is 50 per cent of what we have in the knee department, whereas for a horse it is but 25 per cent of the total knee count. So what happens?

A veterinarian is summoned, probably at time and a half for the Sabbath, and the knee is examined, the joint injected, bandages applied and further visits arranged.

In the opinion of trainer Giles Bravery, this will set the filly back three or four days (say £140 in training bills) and we are looking at giving Nottingham the elbow and considering Kempton's evening meeting on 19 July, when there is a similar race.

I like Kempton. In the members' restaurant the excellent Page Nine – his lapel badge spells his name Paganini – runs a tight ship, is a master of his profession and generous with it.

In the course of conversation last Sunday, the trainer mentions that he has two runners – one at Yarmouth, the other at Epsom – on Wednesday evening, both with live chances of success.

As the Epsom brute is available at 16-1, I go for him, which might be what caused Mr William Hill to reduce the price to 12-1, then 10s.

The horse, Kinan, wins – in fact, both Bravery runners win and when I ring the man to thank him, he tells me that my filly's knee is all better and that Saturday at Nottingham now looks on again.

He adds – and, after giving me the excellent and lucrative advice about his winners, there is no need for flannelling – that our filly is one of the nicest, best-behaved, most co-operative horses in the yard.

I wonder whether this is good news – in most branches of competitive life, impeccable conduct is eclipsed by charismatic villainy.

If Four Legs Good is Delia Smith, should we not be frightened of taking on Gordon Ramsay?

No-one says Mike Tyson is 'nice'. Look at his record. And while Tim Henman is well behaved and co-operative, look at his.

I have no desire to put ideas into the heads of the good folk at Revida Place, Hamilton Road, Newmarket, but if I got to hear that the filly had savaged the farrier, kicked in the walls of her box and dumped her work-rider on the gallops, it would cheer me.

Who wants Anna Kournikova, when Venus Williams is around?

My next dispatch will reach you from the battlefront.

THREE LEGS FINE, ONE ON THE MEND
16 JULY 2000

I LIED AND I am sorry. Last Sunday I promised that today's dispatch would come hotfoot from the racetrack where Four Legs Good was to pulverise a field of maiden fillies in the 3.50 at Nottingham. This was to be the week that was. Not now it is not.

It was possibly my fault in calling her Four Legs Good when she would more appropriately answer to the name of Three Legs Fine One Leg Slightly Dodgy. The graze on her knee is better, but not all better. Were it my knee, it would not stop me from any activity whatsoever; I could trot along to the pub or the betting shop without inconvenience, but then, were it me, you wouldn't mortgage the house and use the proceeds to back me to outperform the opposition.

So, while the filly gets better (the owners poorer, the trainer fatter), you, the reader, will have to wait for news of substance and make do with rhetoric.

On Tuesday morning, while I still expected the Sunday run, I drove to Newmarket to watch her work on the gallops. Owners do this to make them feel they are not standing idly by; stable staff feel they're working for a human being rather than a voice at the far end of their trainer's mobile telephone; and it persuades the trainer's wife to go to Tesco to buy streaky smoked, rindless bacon for morning butties to which punctual settlers of training bills are traditionally entitled.

There were eight horses who went out for second lot, our filly among them. She was ridden by Eric, her lad who occupies the saddle like one poured into it. The horses went round and round in front of Chateau Bravery, and when we had finished our morning meal we emerged. My host approached the head lad and said: 'Golf Club.'

I was impressed; £30-plus a day had always seemed quite a lot for training a horse, but when this includes golf it becomes something of a bargain.

I got that wrong. The Newmarket Golf Club, situated on the road to Six Mile Bottom, merely provides access to a ten-furlong strip of turf and another of sand. It is for galloping – golf does not come into it.

Bravery's second lot appeared. Riders were given instructions by the trainer, they cantered off to the far end of my sightline and, after a while, came back at speed – two by two. It was noticeable that the galloping companion of Four Legs Good was not as fast or as handsome or as balanced as our filly. But then if I were a trainer I would make damn sure that this was so. 'That's a pretty useful animal,' I said to Giles, pointing to the other horse, hoping he'd agree.

We talked of his runner in Thursday's Bunbury Cup and he said he hoped Kinan was good enough. As his strike-rate is over 20 per cent winners to runners, with nearly 50 per cent placed horses, I told him of my confidence in his getting it right and we discussed the irresponsibility of providing a track in which one side is much faster than the other. We also spoke of the importance of owners; if Kayf Tara had been mine instead of the Sheikh's, I would still be waiting for the Ascot Gold Cup. We agreed to speak later in the week, and we did.

Four Legs Good has had another injection, she is really well and the swelling has gone down. But in ten days' time – say £350 from now – she will be absolutely terrific, raring to go and in peak condition, unless something else happens. You will get to hear about it. Remember, whatever happens to the filly you read it here first. In truth no-one else knows about her, which is why we expect her to go off at a generous price.

KEEN TO GET GOING,
BUT THE GOING GETS TOUGH

23 JULY 2000

IN AN ALLEGORY on the tribulations of a small owner, there comes a time when the waffling has to stop. In respect of Four Legs Good, the time is near.

The filly was bought with care last October, broken and sat upon, and trained with expertise. Around Easter news filtered from Newmarket that she was going to be a racehorse – which is what we had in mind. For our part, monthly bills now exceeding £8,000 for this year were paid promptly, as is the duty of equine proprietors.

She did not run in May because she was still growing, then stayed in her box for a few days because she had a sniffle. Next, a grazed knee kept her housebound, and when that cleared up, the medication she was given had been a bit too recent to be sure it would not show up in a random sample.

The trainer has phoned a friend, asked the audience and indulged in 50-50, so the time for her initial contest cannot be held back much longer, even though a new snag has arisen – the going. 'You wouldn't want her to run on firm ground, get jarred up, give herself a leg, make her feel racing isn't any fun?' What we now need is rain, and I have made a note to that effect in my day book.

I ask how she compares with other two-year-olds in the Bravery yard, and am told that they're all different types.

Is Four Legs Good faster than Siptitz Heights? (She is the Giles Bravery filly who ran decently in the Queen Mary and subsequently won a maiden.) The trainer opined that our filly might, at this moment, not be as good as Siptitz, but he could be wrong. He does not work them together. What is certain about Four Legs Good is that she will give her all; she really does try, which is why he doesn't want to run her on unsuitable going, doesn't want to sour her sweet nature.

So she's ready to run?

She is indeed ready to run, but needs rain (have I said that before?). The filly is entered to run at Ascot on Friday, Thirsk and Nottingham on Saturday. Should you feel that three races in 24 hours is a fiercer introduction to the game than is consistent with good husbandry, the three entries are to see what the opposition is. She will run in one of the contests, or, of course, in none if something else goes awry.

Are entries very expensive? I inquire. 'Quite expensive, they always cost more than you expect.'

So I ask how the other horses in my trainer's stable are progressing, and he says: 'About a dozen of them are entered to run in the next week.'

Which will win?

'It would be quite nice if some of them won,' says my man, but it seems discourteous to press him for names and times. We talk briefly about cricket, which he plays with enthusiasm.

Everything is now going according to plan; I just hope that conditions such as 'thoroughpin', 'bog spavin' and 'nailbind' will not feature in next week's telephone conversations.

EIGHTH OUT OF EIGHT AIN'T GOOD
30 JULY 2000

WHEN VOLUME ONE of the Four Legs Good story, provisionally entitled *The Early Years*, is published, readers will discover that after being purchased for 25,000 guineas and ringing up training bills of £9,800, she ran her first race at Ascot at 2.15pm on Friday 28 July 2000, in the Capel Cure Sharp Maiden Stakes for fillies over six furlongs.

She finished eighth in this opening race on the card, but if you were to say 'eighth isn't bad in a prestigious £12,000-added race at Britain's best racecourse', you would, on reflection, have to modify that assessment. While eighth can be a satisfactory position to occupy, this ceases to be the case when there are but seven other contestants.

In truth, eighth out of eight is less than excellent. Eighth out of eight, also known as 'last', is something of a disappointment, even when the 20½ lengths that separated her from the impressive winner Regal Rose – now favourite for the One Thousand Guineas – could have been reduced to 18½ lengths had the owners listed on the racecard as 'Sir Clement Freud and Partners' not specifically instructed the jockey to let the filly enjoy her debutante outing.

When it comes to excuses, trainer Giles Bravery said we wanted going that was good and it was on the firm side thereof – but I fear this is akin to blaming the colour of one's boxing shorts when fighting Mike Tyson in the ring.

Four Legs Good ran against horses that were too fast for her. She has learnt how to go into starting stalls, but is less sure about how to come out, seemed thrown by the noise of their opening and lost a length and a half at the start. She then raced nicely for four furlongs at the back of the field, before weakening visibly.

After the race, jockey Jason Tate said: 'She is green and needs to strengthen and will appreciate an extra furlong.'

He thought she would make into a nice filly if perhaps unlikely to perform in the exalted company of the horses that had preceded her to the finishing post. Good jockey, makes sense in his report and is a nice man with it.

Trainer Bravery said that she blew very hard after the race. He would strengthen the filly for another £950-£1,200 ('three to four weeks' is how he put it) and then find her a race in which she might excel.

The *Racing Post* – whose summary is written by hard men, for whose future in the diplomatic corps one would weep – opined that Cloudy (sixth) should have her sights lowered and added: 'Four Legs Good gave little cause for short-term optimism.'

What an astonishingly unhelpful assessment that is. Were it not for short-term optimism, I doubt you would have more than a handful of runners in any stakes or conditions race.

It is harder for me than most to give an unbiased report of how racecourses treat owners. At Ascot I am a boxholder, a member of the Royal Ascot Racing Club and have a press badge. Consequently, the additional cardboard disc made little difference.

I had received a letter telling me of an Owners' Club where there was food and drink. It did not mention that this had to be paid for, and my partner Andy and I had a plate of salmon and one of lobster – the latter having left refrigeration with such reluctance that it tasted of little except its long, cold sojourn.

The service was kind, but the potted shrimps needed toast and the little buggers in their plastic cartons were topped by a shiny glow which may once have been the seal of butter, which it deserves. The Owners' Club does not accept credit cards.

The pre-parade ring was socially desirable, with famous and titled trainers, chain-smoking trainers, trainers on the up, and one whom I would back to win the all-comers freestyle dancing competition at the Hammersmith Palais.

In the paddock, I recognised my jockey instantly by the fact that he was wearing my colours. We urged him to let Four Legs Good enjoy her introduction to the sport for which she was bred and, naturally, should Her Majesty's horse Canopy be within a length or so at the end, to let it go by.

All eight horses cantered nicely to the start. The dreaded announcement of who had been judged 'best turned out' made no mention of Four Legs Good's name, glory be.

When it was over we drank a quiet glass of champagne and wondered why Richard Quinn, who had been offered the ride, had turned it down.

As I was on my way to watch the third race, a large man of certain age came up to me and said. 'You've got a horse running this afternoon – shall I back it?'

I replied. 'Absolutely not.' He looked at me with surprise and admiration, and said: 'You're an honest man – you tell it how it is. I salute you.'

The compliment did not make me feel a whole lot better.

The message yesterday that Four Legs Good had had a decent journey home, had eaten up and was becoming less green, as befits a horse that is brown and has four white socks, was pleasing.

GRIPPED BY DOUBTS AND SEARCHING FOR ANSWERS

6 AUGUST 2000

AFTER TEN MONTHS of being a racehorse owner with proprietorial dreams, I have now had a week as an owner with doubts. What is for sure is that had we not purchased Four Legs Good, we would be about £40,000 better off. What is in the melting pot is the rosiness of the future.

I had a friend who prided himself on the fact that his gelding once contested a race won by Arkle. His brute fell at the first but 'We took on Arkle, not a lot of owners can say that,' was his recurring boast.

Well, our filly took on Regal Rose – who is now fancied to win the One Thousand Guineas – and finishing last behind that star of the future could be significant. Some horses that finished similar distances behind Shergar were considered distinctly useful.

I bought Timeform in case they had observed something I had missed in FLG's performance at Ascot. 'On the burly side, scratched to post, having missed the break was always behind,' was the extent of their summary. I had noticed that too. In addition, she blew like Thomas the Tank Engine after the race.

Is that my fault, or that of the horse, or that of the trainer?

When your daughter gets a poor report do you blame her, the teachers, or yourself for begetting the child and sending her to that school?

I looked for analogies.

In greyhound racing you are sold a dog and if it fails to return sufficiently fast qualifying times, it gets shot. 'Just like that,' as Tommy Cooper used to say.

In pigeon racing you buy a homing pigeon, enter it in a race, it fails to return. No problem.

Cock fights. If your fighting cock comes second, it tends to be what Hitler called 'the final solution'.

To own a horse who disappointed on her initial outing is a situation open to many interpretations. 'It wasn't her day,' is the favourite, but I fear it is simplistic, for both her trainer and her lad said in the parade ring that she was extra-well.

'She was outclassed,' makes sense, but Giles Bravery has a high strike-rate, is no fool and would surely not enter a filly for a race in which she stood absolutely no chance.

A month ago I asked Giles how he rated her; his reply was: 'I have two-year-olds who are faster and ones who are slower.'

Both Michael Hills and Micky Fenton rode her on the gallops and pronounced her to be a nice filly, who 'could win first time out', but they would say that.

In common with all owners who attempt to find reasons for performances whether high or low – and ours was low – 'she missed the break' is the one I like best.

If you have no experience of competition and find yourself on foreign soil, two lengths behind seven other horses, a smart filly just might think to herself: 'As no-one expects me to win – look at my odds of 33-1 – I'd do as well having an easy today; then next time I run I'll start at 50s and my nice owners will have what I understand they call "a right touch", and then in a few weeks' time I'll run over seven furlongs and they won't go like the clappers and I shan't miss the break and it will be at some comfortable, undemanding track.'

I have tried to believe that. Deep down I think she came last because she has insufficient speed to compete at a high level. Goodness, I do hope I am wrong.

FOR ONCE, LET'S HOPE
FOR RAIN ON THE PLAIN

13 AUGUST 2000

FOUR LEGS GOOD has had £500 of rest and a couple of good gallops. After another £350 of training fees, Mr Bravery says she will be absolutely ready for her second outing.

What we have learned, partly because Sheikh Mo did not ring with an offer to 'Godolphin' the filly, but mostly because she finished last in a classy maiden, is that she would not currently feature in a list of the 200 top two-year-olds in the land.

What trainer Bravery tells me, with confidence, is that she would want going that was softer than good; we are looking at a seven-furlong event at Salisbury on Thursday and, as a consequence, I no longer switch off the television when the ghastlies come on flashing their teeth and waving their arms at the weather chart.

Provided mid-August rainfall bears some relationship to that of July, we shall be there.

By 'we', I mean us owners. The trainer is likely to be living it up at Deauville. When it comes to buzz, Deauville consistently has the beating of the Wiltshire cathedral city, but that is especially the case just now.

Salisbury racecourse, a brisk one-and-a-bit hours' walk from the station, is not my favourite track. On previous visits, I have found the natives less than friendly, the facilities ordinary, the viewing poor and the officials too official for my liking. Four Legs Good will be unbothered by these considerations – stabling is known to be comfortable. The track also has a seven-furlong straight with a finish which is uphill – it will find out anything that thinks it can make every post a winning one (this is my second least favourite sentence in the commentator's armoury, just behind 'they are not hanging about').

If you are a small owner, and your horse is trained by someone of similar size, you tend to keep an eye on the other occupants of the yard. Last Wednesday, a Bravery gelding, whom my filly is no worse than on the gallops, ran at Brighton, and I arose early to await the phone call instructing me on the proportion of the Freud millions that should be staked.

At 8.15am, just when I reckoned Giles B. would be back from first lot, the trainer did not ring. He did not ring again after second lot. I cancelled lunch so that I would be there when he telephoned from the course – the gelding was due to run at 2.40 – and when he did not ring, I watched the maiden auction stakes on the Racing Channel without taking a pecuniary interest.

Carnot, the brute in question, opened at 10s, drifted to 20s, was returned 16s, won. I felt mildly peeved. Giles said I should not be. He told me nothing, but he had told Carnot's owners he did not expect him to figure in the finish.

What is for sure is that my man is a trainer of quality, with a very respectable strike-rate.

To return to my filly, there is little doubt about the benefit of backing her by ever-increasing sums until she wins. If I knew whether the benefit would be mine or my bookmaker's, I would do just that.

In the meantime, I have a separate interest in the Winterton Classified Stakes at Yarmouth on Wednesday. On my last few visits to the Norfolk track, I could not find anyone who sold mushy peas, which was just about the only reason for patronising this most pedestrian of seaside racecourses. By 3.25 on Wednesday afternoon, I might have changed my mind.

CONTRASTING WORKOUTS AND A TARGET MISSED

20 AUGUST 2000

RACEHORSE OWNERSHIP IS not a full-time occupation, though owners do their utmost to try to make it appear so. My day job had demanded attendance on Thursday at a noon board meeting in London and when I cancelled this, the natives began to mutter. 'Bloody Freud, bloody horses, rhubarb rhubarb, if it's not one thing then it's another,' were the words I could distinguish.

One would think these people would be thrilled at the prospect of Four Legs Good having an opportunity to reveal her true form in the Class E maiden over seven furlongs at Salisbury. One thought wrong – moan, whinge, carp was all I got.

Then Four Legs Good did a piece of work on Tuesday, and my trainer, Giles Bravery, hastened to impart the news: 'She worked poorly. Something to do with being a filly. Won't run her at Salisbury anyway, because the advance going is good to firm and she needs give.'

'It might rain.'

'It might not,' says Giles, mentioning that the weatherwoman had advised leaving umbrellas at home.

I had an idea. 'Do you remember before Ascot you said she had worked brilliantly and then she ran crap – finished the length of a Curtly Ambrose run-up behind the winner?

'Maybe if she works badly on the gallops, it means that she'll run a blinder on the track,' I suggest.

Giles advises us to give her a week and think rain. I ask whether we still have to pay £1.50 an hour.

Yes please, says Giles.

What did the entry at Salisbury cost? The trainer thinks: 'About £30, but your Weatherbys account will tell all.' I reconvened the board meeting.

On Friday, Giles phoned with the news that FLG had done a fine bit of work on the gallops, demolishing the filly who had outperformed her three days earlier.

'Perhaps the other filly is coming down with something?'

'Not at all. Yours had an off-day, but now she's fine and all we need is some rain and a race and I have Michael Hills standing by.'

On Wednesday I went to Yarmouth, and would like to recommend the down-at-heel Norfolk resort to all my masochist readers.

The London train arrived in Norwich at 12.43. They let the Norwich to Yarmouth train leave at 12.41. An hour to wait.

I took a taxi, and got into a three-mile traffic jam outside town which made the taxi only a medium-good idea. However, at Yarmouth, behind the station, I did find a fish restaurant of genuine quality.

Being a raceday, it was patronised by trainers from each of whom the waiter solicited tips, which he generously passed on to other trainers sitting at adjacent tables.

On the gastro front, the lobsters are handsome, while the skate, plaice, monkfish and John Dory are resplendent with freshness and they did me a bowl of mushy peas, served with mint sauce. After the meal there were rich, heavy, black, bitter, walnut chocolate nuggets to take your mind off the bill. You should go nowhere else.

I foolishly failed to heed my own advice and went to the races. I lost, but the gelding I had come to back had really good excuses for finishing out of the frame. He ran a race into which optimists could read much – the event was run in a fast time, he got knocked about a bit, and was running on at the end.

As no-one was watching, a few more races for him to get the hang of it and come down the handicap and run in blinkers and go a bit further, maybe jump hurdles, and I could clean up.

My wife, an innocent woman, asks whether I might not clean up even more comprehensively were I to abandon horse ownership and take up solitaire.

I changed the subject to quality of life. How much of that do you get on a solitaire board?

Next Sunday I shall give a tip.

SIX SECONDS TO CHANGE THE TURF
27 AUGUST 2000

THERE WAS THIS song with the chorus, 'I dug 16 tons and what do I get? / Another day older and deeper in debt.' It's a bit like that with Four Legs Good and me. Since last Sunday, £300 has gone on training fees and £100 on entries, and I stand around getting older and poorer as I switch channels in search of a weather forecast that predicts rain – a commodity trainer Giles Bravery feels to be essential to the filly's optimum performance.

I empathise with divers waiting for the pool to be filled with water – hungry for action, frustrated. Next week, with the rain gods perhaps getting the upper hand over their cousins who take retainers from seaside resorts, Chepstow tomorrow, Salisbury on Thursday and Haydock on Friday are all venues staging suitable maiden events – events which, failing rain, will be slightly more valuable by virtue of our entry contribution.

If the powers of racing are genuinely concerned about the financial plight of owners, introducing a token entry fee in respect of horses who need a particular going, don't get it and therefore don't run, should be considered. I wonder how much BHB revenue is provided by wishy-washy, advance weather forecasts that persuade trainers to make multiple entries?

I spent the early part of the week at the Edinburgh Festival, where I was greatly taken by a stand-up comic who declared that he had neither time nor affection for people who took drugs, and when a few saintly folk applauded this statement he added, 'like policemen and customs officers.'

Reports from Newmarket about the filly's form are positive and encouraging. Of the upcoming options I favour Haydock; it's handy to get to – especially if you live in Newton-le-Willows (which I don't), it's a handsome track that tends to ride soft, and if you are a winning owner they look after you no end.

Let me move smoothly to last Wednesday's Gimcrack Stakes, worth £72,500 to the winning owner. He or she is then invited to make the speech at the prestigious Gimcrack dinner, where the subject matter is traditionally the good of the sport and how racing could be improved.

Bannister, a good-looking Inchinor colt who won by a short head, is owned by the 230-member Royal Ascot Racing Club. As I am one of their number, the colt's victory not only yields me a week's training fee for FLG, which is helpful, but also – if there is any justice in the world – gets me one 230th of a 25-minute address. Six seconds is not a long time, especially if you speak as slowly as I do, but perhaps I could squeeze into that narrow time slot a few suggestions to benefit racegoers.

In other major sports – cricket, football, tennis and coursing, you know who is in charge by the clothes they wear – white coats and Panama hats; short-trousered suit with a whistle in the gob; purple and green Wimbledon blazer; pink coat carrying two flags riding a horse (Waterloo Cup).

Yet stewards and clerks of the course wear suits and hats and ties like the rest of us, though usually better-cut and more expensive. This must stop. We have to know who to blame (also who to praise if praise is due). I favour the garb of football referees; many stewards have perfectly adequate knees.

Another thought, should one of the other 229 members give me their six seconds?

When your horse wins a race, no matter where it takes place, the brute goes up in value. You collect prize-money after having had a disproportionately massive bet to make you richer, and then someone presents you with a silver goblet. Your cup of happiness brimmeth over.

You can afford to indulge in champagne. While all around you lick their wounds, the racecourse officials invite you to take wine and make a fuss of you and present you with a video of the race.

This is a mark of the politically unacceptable (to me) philosophy of making the rich richer, giving to those who already have.

How about treating the connections of the beaten horses, or perhaps those of a horse who finished fourth in a 15-runner handicap?

FOUR LEGS GOODBYE ... BUT FIRST, THE ANALYSIS
3 SEPTEMBER 2000

SHE DID NOT come last, as she had last time. We now know that in this green and pleasant land there are three two-year-old horses who run less quickly than Four Legs Good.

On such slender statistics do owners plan the realisation of their dreams – standing in the winner's enclosure, having their photographs taken, shaking hands with people they do not know, and expressing gratitude for the commemorative cut-glass vase, chatting to Miriam Francome of the Racing Channel about future plans, before sipping the champagne generously offered to winning owners by racecourse management.

I wish this 14th and last episode in the trials and tribulations of a man and his horse could have ended on a happier note – which we so nearly achieved, would have achieved, had the deluge which caused racing at Haydock to be abandoned after the third race occurred 90 minutes earlier. But you can't have everything.

To the great British racing public, the Vale of Lune Median Auction Maiden Stakes (Class E) over one mile, value to winner £3,066, may have been of limited interest. To the owners of the Be My Guest filly – Sir Clement Freud and Partners – it was the culmination of 35 days (£1,200) awaiting an apposite contest over a stretch of ground in excess of the minimum distance on going that was good to soft.

Haydock, nestling in low, lush Lancashire (now called Merseyside) land beneath the massive traffic jams of the M6, was our selected venue. The team arrived, and consumed Peruvian asparagus spears with lemon hollandaise, followed by ham hocks, then summer pudding in Harry's Bistro on the second floor of the excellent main building. Near our table was a television screen, which at one point carried the message: 'If you would like to become a racecourse owner, contact the BHB.' I would like York and Ascot; Mr Savill will be hearing from me very soon.

At length, it was time to make our way to the parade ring. Four Legs Good looked a picture and after a couple of circuits the jockeys arrived. Just as I had instantly recognised my filly, mostly from the fact that she wore a number cloth marked 12, so did I pick out Mr Seb Sanders, who was attired in my colours. Sanders, who had no such handy guide, joined the wrong gaggle of owner/trainer until he was plucked away by Giles Bravery. My man took him a few paces away for instructions. The bookmakers made her a firm 25-1 shot, with not a 33-1 in sight, but the filly did not know that. She was drawn eight, which at Haydock is not wonderful but no deterrent to a horse of quality.

The *Racing Post*, describing her performance, summed it up in a sentence: Four Legs Good moved poorly to post and, as at Ascot, looked little out of the ordinary. Had I written the analysis, it would have been comprehensive.

There would have been mention of her glowing coat, her kindly disposition, the professional way she entered the starting stalls, the alacrity with which she emerged, the uninspired ride she was given, the fact that too much use was made of her and that, unlike at Ascot, she was in the hunt for all of five and a half furlongs and then tired – or perhaps does not yet possess the stamina for a mile which is a long way for a filly that has some growing in front of her.

Yes, I was disappointed. No, I was not very surprised, for the trainer had not made me feel that she had reached her peak. (He wouldn't, would he? Not at £1.50 an hour in training fees.) But now that she has beaten other horses, it is simply a case of giving her a fortnight to get over this exertion, one more race to achieve a handicap mark, and then go out there and see if we cannot find those three horses we beat with few horses that they just might have beaten and wait for a six-furlong race on good to soft, after which it could all be downhill.

What we know is that we have an honest and consistent filly: initially beaten 20 lengths by what may be the best two-year-old filly seen so far, now 13 lengths by what trainer Michael Jarvis considers his best juvenile. All is not lost. When I got home, I found a £50 note I had entirely forgotten about in an inside jacket pocket. The very latest news is that FLG travelled back well, ate up and walked around, showing not a sign of the stiffness that inconveniences her owner.

Four Legs Good ran twice more in 2000, finishing seventh of 17 at Warwick and ninth of 13 at Musselburgh, and three times in 2001: 11th of 20 runners at Yarmouth, 15th of 17 at Beverley, and 19th of 19 at Lingfield Park. Thus she finished her racing career as she had started it: last.

*

A fate far worse than finishing last was awaiting Freud's horse Orpen Wide, to whom he wrote a letter in November 2004.

A LETTER TO ORPEN WIDE
3 NOVEMBER 2004

DEAR ORPEN WIDE,
I have not previously written to a horse – it is something sane people don't do – but I am out of the country, will not have been

able to watch you run unplaced at Catterick yesterday and feel that you deserve an explanation for what is likely to happen to you at the weekend.

Let me begin at the beginning: I own half of you. An agreeable man called Michael who trains horses in Market Rasen telephoned me when you were in a breeze-up sale last year and asked whether I would be interested in purchasing a very well-built, nicely bred (he referred to your parents) yearling who, to his experienced eye, was a goodish thing for the Arc de Triomphe in 2005-06. He did not want to be drawn on which year, and of course it could be both.

We agreed an amount above which we would not bid and the way you ran along those few wet Doncaster furlongs enabled us to purchase you for what is known in the trade as a 'sensible price'. The fact that your father was a first-year stallion was also of help.

I would like to be able to say that during the course of the year I became fond of you; it would be a lie. To me, one horse looks pretty much like another and I mostly recognise you by the number on your saddlecloth or the person who leads you around the ring. Of course, when the jockey gets a leg-up, I recognise you immediately because your pilot is wearing my black and orange colours.

For the record, I am the one with a beard who strokes your nose before a race, tips your groom and tells your jockey to come back safely.

I expect that, to you, most humans look alike. Should this be untrue, the slightly smaller man with a beard is my friend Andy; he owns the half of you which is not mine.

The relationship between a racehorse and its proprietor is customarily some way from being close, but thanks to Michael, your trainer (he is the one with the white hair and ever-present wife) I get to hear about your training, your stamina and your proneness to getting tired; also the fact that you, unlike Andy and Michael and me, are still growing. 'Looks like an effing elephant,' said a man standing near us in the pre-parade ring at Leicester last month.

Let us not dwell on your first outing – the one where you cantered down to the start and limped around until the vet agreed that you might be lame ... whereafter you cantered back and everybody lost 5p in the pound on their winning bets.

You returned to Lincolnshire and the vet said you weren't well; three months later you went back to the races and finished last, quite a long way last. Which is why we were surprised when you finished third at 100-1 over six furlongs in a classy race, then third again in a less classy race and absolutely nowhere in the race after that.

A fortnight ago, over six furlongs, in an event in which you opened at 9-1 and were backed down to 4-1 second favourite, you led to the five-furlong post and finished an honourable second. (Do not feel badly about this; the money that shortened your price was not mine; it was what they call 'clever money'.)

The thing is – and this is the purpose of my letter – Michael told me that at Windsor you saw a filly and got excited, used up your energy on sexual fantasies instead of preserving it to make a forward movement as the winning post approached.

And Michael thinks that we should have that problem seen to.

If it were I whose thoughts strayed to the detriment of my competitiveness, I would be sent to a shrink; I would probably get a discount because my paternal grandfather invented the racket, but there are very few equine psychoanalysts and hardly any couches strong enough to accommodate a horse the size of an elephant. So you won't commence a lifetime of expensive treatment of dubious efficacy.

What we are going to do is to cut off your balls.

'Unfair', do I hear you say?

Well, in a word, yes.

I remember having a passionate affection for a girl called Patsy, who squeezed my hand under the table during lunch, whereafter I finished second from last in the school sports under-14s' sack race.

Retrospectively, I would have been beside myself with rage had they castrated me as a consequence, for though a virgin, I had read about, heard about and nearly seen things that looked as if what the Spanish call *cojones* were an important, even essential, part of male equipment.

By next Sunday, then, you will have a significant pain in the region of your genitalia and I shall get a bill from the vet. Were there a European Court of Equine Justice, you could take me to it and very likely win substantial damages, but the present order is two legs good, four legs bad.

As it is, next year when you run over your preferred distance on going that is good or softer than good, it will be as a 3-y-o b g.

The 'g' stands for gelding. I tell myself that no-one misses what they have not enjoyed, which makes me feel better, and come 2005 I shall find a little race somewhere and back you to win me bundles of dosh. If you are a vengeful brute and want to get your own back, you'll finish out of the money.

Yours respectfully Clement (Sir)

Orpen Wide showed that he was clearly not a vengeful brute in his first race with his new status.

'OWNER OF THE YEAR' HAS COME THAT LITTLE BIT CLOSER NOW
19 DECEMBER 2004

LAST WEDNESDAY I ended my column by pointing out that my horse Orpen Wide was running in the 2pm at Southwell the following day, and that if he won, I would be surprised.

He won. I was surprised.

Partly surprised because last month we had him gelded and he showed no hard feelings.

Also surprised because his previous run, as a colt, had been abysmal and this was his first try over the distance, on the surface, under that jockey and he was badly drawn.

'Why didn't I tell people he would win?', asks a friend.

Because I didn't know.

'Why didn't you just shut up?'

Because I'd written about him a few weeks previously (when he was a him before he became an it) and silence on the matter would have caused readers to think I knew something, when it has been clear to most people that I don't know a lot.

I don't even know who backed him on Thursday at Southwell in to 5-1 from 8s, while the favourite drifted. I had only a modest – for me – bet when I noticed on my return from the parade ring that his odds were shortening.

He did look magnificent; he has stopped growing, filled out, his coat shone. Overall, he reminded me of a poem of my youth:

Uncle George and Auntie Mabel,
Fainted at the breakfast table.
Children let this be a warning,
Never do it in the morning.

Uncle George is much improved since he's had his balls removed.

Brian Reilly did give Orpen Wide a brilliant ride. Also, his trainer Michael Chapman had brought him to Southwell three days earlier to give him a feel for the Fibresand. Long may they all live.

One reads much in the front parts of newspapers about the National Health Service spurred on by the Government who want to make our lives better. I have news for them.

Owning a horse who wins unexpectedly, who causes you to be paid a few hundred pounds in readies by a scowling bookmaker, having racegoers congratulate you and wish you well, and being entertained by the 'greeters' of Arena with champagne and a choice of presents from a gift cabinet, beats happy pills or any medicine I've had to date.

In just under 59 seconds my world became filled with contentment to the tune of my mobile phone buzzing with favourable texts. (For the record, I chose the engraved brandy glasses and my wife said: 'Pity about the inscription, we'll now have to keep them.')

Then, because Mr Reilly had ridden so very well, I backed him to win the next race, with real money, and made the angry bookmaker angrier still.

What is great about racing is that even winning a Class E nursery on the all-weather is a terrific incentive to dream ... which is what the sport is all about.

The Stewards' Cup, Ayr Gold Cup, Royal Hunt Cup – perhaps when Royal Ascot is at Pontefract – are all on the agenda. Owner of the Year has come that little bit closer now and, although I've waited in vain for a telephone call from the big man in Dubai, making me an offer I could not resist for my good winner, that surely is now only a matter of time.

What next? His weight is likely to go up and we shall look for a little race somewhere and, as I wrote last Wednesday before my minute of joy, I shall be surprised if he wins – though not that surprised.

Orpen Wide followed up the Southwell victory with two wins in January 2005. Then came a nine-race losing sequence, before a win at Newmarket's July Course in June 2005 caused Freud to ruminate about jockeyship:

JOCKEYS ARE LIKE AIRLINES
22 JUNE 2005

I OWN A horse, he likes to make all and has not been allowed to do that for his last five races; he reacts positively to being hit on the bum with a whip – and hasn't been encouraged in this way for half a dozen rides. He has raced unsuccessfully over six, seven and eight furlongs and been ridden by different jockeys who listened to their instructions – 'Jump out and hit him like hell until he passes the finishing line' – and largely ignored them. In turn they made their way back to the unsaddling area, a country mile from the winner's enclosure, to say that he needed further, acted on different going, required a visor, cheekpieces, a left-handed track, an uphill finish, and to be allowed to go into the starting stalls last.

Jockeys are like airlines: flight after flight you come home and say to the little woman, 'I am never going to fly that sodding airline again, not ever,' and then there comes a time when you've run out of airlines. I accept that if your trainer retains Mr Fallon, Mr Kinane or Mr Holland, this problem will not arise. But the estimable Michael Chapman, who trains at trendy Market Rasen, has to get whoever is available.

Brian Reilly twice rode Orpen Wide when he won for me three times on the trot on the all-weather. I rate Mr Reilly very highly, but had been unable to obtain his services since those halcyon January days, and used jockeys whose main attractions was that they had other rides at the meeting and could make the weight.

As for following instructions, rather than hit the horse, one jock, coming to the two-furlong post, rubbed his neck and gave him a Liquorice Allsort.

On Friday, I got Reilly. On Friday, Orpen Wide was drawn in stall 11, was his usual bouncy self in the parade ring, was going over his distance – front-runners like five-furlong events – and he had, as we say in the trade, 'been laid out for the race.' By this I mean we had a job finding an event for which a brute rated 68 could get a run against horses of the same age and this was one of six contests to qualify. Our sole imponderable was the form of the other 14 runners.

In the betting ring, Orpen Wide hovered between 14s and 16s (I got 16s). Mr Reilly jumped him out nicely, did not start hitting him until the four-furlong post and was still using his whip as he passed the finishing post marginally ahead of the field. Why didn't I tell you? Lord, as they say in Scotland, I didna ken.

Freud later sold his share in Orpen Wide to previous co-owner Andy Wright, for whom he continued to win. By late May 2009 the horse had run in no fewer than 122 races, winning 19 – ten on the Flat, six over hurdles and three steeplechases – and earning prize-money in excess of £138,000.

*

In his dispatches about Four Legs Good, Freud mentioned his membership of 'the very wonderful Royal Ascot Racing Club', but he considered the management of the RARC distinctly less than wonderful in its handling of the members' 'ownership' of 2005 Derby winner Motivator. His observation that the Club 'has done for syndicates what the Boston Strangler did for door-to-door salesmen' was just one of the memorable phrases he deployed while waging his ultimately unsuccessful campaign.

Late in May 2005, soon after Motivator's emphatic victory in the Dante Stakes at York had propelled him to warm favouritism for the Derby, the RARC's most disgruntled member set out his stall:

THE MOTIVATOR CONUNDRUM: I GOTTA HORSE – OR HAVE I?
25 MAY 2005

SHOULD A TELEVISION company be looking for a successor to *The Apprentice*, like a grown-up version which might be called *The Executive*, I have a good idea for the opening programme: instead of involving the sale of wine or art or the negotiations of advertising, contestants will deal with the following scenario and see if they can equal the performance of the Ascot Authority.

You have many of the 230 members of your Royal Ascot Racing Club coming to lunch. They will be in high good humour because the club owns the Derby favourite and the owners think they will share the prize-money, also most of the dosh when the horse is sold or stands at stud. Your job is to tell them they are not getting it, not as much as they think, not if you can help it ... and keep them happy.

I doubt too many contestants would have come up with an agenda that resulted in the following day's *Racing Post* headline: 'No dissent at AGM for Motivator members' (note that the *Post* is independent and only the previous day referred to Motivator *owners*). Someone deserves considerable praise.

Let us move smoothly to real life. I am a member of the RARC. Sadly, I was not at the annual meeting that 'enthusiastically endorsed rules that would deny any financial windfall from the success of Derby favourite Motivator' because I am in a clinic in Austria.

But I did get phone calls from bemused friends who are members, and to say they were content would be a lie; bewildered, more like. Let me state that none of us joined the club to make money. RARC is a wonderful facility; well-run, good value for the high fees we pay and the racing information from our racing manager is exemplary – and a bonus. I believe even bonuses should be fair and out in the open.

Were I chairman of the racing club I would not have called my AGM to compete with the Cup Final, at a track holding the third (in importance and prize-money) meeting of the day, but I would have sponsored a race wherever it took place.

After a traditional moment's silence for members who had fallen off the perch and a brief prayer for those close to descent, I would have moved to item one: Motivator. I would have congratulated the racing manager, whom we never blamed during the barren years, for his foresight in buying us the Derby favourite, and explained the following:

- What share of the prize-money each member will receive;
- What proportion of sale price and/or stud fee would go where;
- Confirmed that as owning a few horses was part of the advertised joy of joining and belonging to the excellent club, we will keep Motivator in training as a four-year-old.

Those three questions require answers.

Apparently the event that took place at Lingfield Park on Saturday was carefully and handsomely organised with an orchestrated standing ovation for the arrival of the racing manager, the Honourable Harry Herbert.

There was also, from the information I gleaned, a request for members not to talk to the press (why on earth not?) and the conclusion that if big M. wins at Epsom, we the owners – anyway, we the people who thought we were the owners – might (why the subjunctive?) not have to pay membership fees for 2006/07... 'The committee having decided this to be preferable to distributing cash on which members would probably have to pay income tax.'

I don't believe that. It all seems to raise more questions than it answers.

In a nutshell, who owns the effing horse? If we members are not getting the winnings in cash or kind and the horse loses, will we have to pay the club the £3 million or whatever? Is that in the small print?

Mr Darling, one of the two elected committee members of the club, said: 'Owning the favourite for the Derby in whatever capacity is high-octane stuff.'

As an owner, well, as someone who thought he was an owner, I want to know the precise capacity; I find it hard to believe that I am alone among the membership eager to watch the Blue Riband of the turf with specific knowledge of what is in it for me.

A couple of months ago Delia Smith, standing on the pitch at Carrow Road at half-time, shouted to her supporters: 'Let's be having you!' I think she meant, 'Let's be hearing you', which is my plea.

I wonder whether we might all have missed something – the humanitarian question: What does Motivator think? This suggestion is one that will greatly please the animal rights lobby.

As none of us depends on the money involved and most of us enjoy gambling, the whole business of who gets which part of what could be amicably resolved by using the 'Here, Boy!' option that operates in some US states' legislatures.

It is intended to decide ownership of pets, as in who gets the cocker spaniel when all else has been resolved in a contested divorce: the dog is placed in the centre of a room and covered with a blanket by an arbitrator appointed by the court. At a signal, the blanket is removed and husband and wife – at different ends of the room – do their utmost to persuade Fido to show a preference for one or the other.

In Motivator's case this could be done on the Thursday before Derby Day at Windsor Castle – or, if Her Majesty is concerned about starting a 'Here Boy' trend, at the register office or Windsor racecourse. On one side, representing the authority, will be the Duke of Devonshire, the Honourable Harry and the Brigadier who is chief executive officer. On the other, the members/owners waiting to know if it will be beneficial ownership or reflected glory.

The event would be sold to television, the fee shared between them and us as a gesture of goodwill. Pictures of the event, signed by all participants, would become as valuable as World Cup footballs signed by both teams ... then we could have other meetings to decide on the division of the spoils.

This story is going to run: I do hope our horse will, also. Please don't tell anyone in the RARC that you have read this.

*

As is testified by the likes of Weareagrandmother and Digup St Edmunds, Clement Freud approached the naming of his horses with characteristic wit and ingenuity.

GOOD HORSES DESERVE GOOD NAMES
27 JULY 2005

FOR SOME MONTHS now, since the death of His Holiness Pope John Paul II, I have been that rarity among racing people – the owner of a name without a horse.

I had watched the lying in state in St Peter's Square and heard the praying thousands murmuring, caught the murmurs: they were saying 'Santo Subito, Santo Subito, Santo Subito ...', which is Vatican-speak for 'make him a saint now.'

There is, and this might just be apocryphal, a story of the Wise Men following the bright star on their way to Bethlehem. One stubbed his toe painfully on a protruding rock and exclaimed, 'Jesus Christ!', at which another said: 'That's a good name for the child.'

I thought Santo Subito was a terrific name for a horse, but here's the rub: it is, rightly, a difficult, expensive and time-consuming job to change the name of a horse, so I registered Santo Subito with Weatherbys as a name and determined to find an unnamed brute worthy of that attractive appellation – a yearling or a store.

We move smoothly to Doncaster bloodstock sales in late May. Lot 141 is a bay gelding born on 23 March 2001, by Presenting out of a mare whose dam had three winners including Mighty Mogul; whose second dam bred six winners, among them Miller Hill, who won the Supreme Novices' Hurdle at Cheltenham.

'The gelding is unbroken but well handled,' it stated on the auctioneers' song sheet. And the gelding looked like an athlete: a nice big barrel of a scopey body mounted on four properly formed legs. He was good-looking, had an intelligent head, and as the groom led him around he bounced, as high-jumpers bounce when they approach the bar.

Well, yes, he cost a bit more than I expected, the way horses do, and it was in guineas and there was VAT and a dope test to be paid for as well as the journey back to the establishment of the excellent, underrated trainer Robert Stronge.

I briefly considered syndicating him, but the Royal Ascot Racing Club, since Motivator, has done for syndicates what the Boston Strangler did for door-to-door salesmen, so I invited two of my friends to join me in shared ownership.

While continuing to be well handled, Santo Subito has now

been mounted and has shown all the qualities you could ask of a horse: individuality, obedience with a touch of quirkiness, a swagger and a coat that shines like a prize conker. We shall give him ten weeks and then agonise over introducing him to a life of trying to outrun other Thoroughbreds via a bumper or a novice hurdle – over a proper distance. The Grand National in the year we host the Olympics would be our ultimate aim.

Santo Subito. Good name – would not look out of place written in gold letters on a mahogany board listing big-race winners.

I have always felt naming horses to be important. When I was an MP I called a horse I found in Paul Kelleway's yard Grunty Fen – an area in my constituency. He won for me at Taunton at 33-1 and I tried to call another two-year-old Pidley Fen – an adjacent hamlet – but Weatherbys objected. They did agree to my naming a horse Prickwillow, a village to the south of Ely.

My late friend Chris Brasher, Olympic gold medallist, founder of the London Marathon and wayward godfather to my eldest son, took up racing in middle age and was wondrously successful. His horses won frequently, including a hugely valuable race at Redcar; it was he who told me that his trainer had a 'store' who showed promise and of whom he thought a lot. He was not very expensive and I bought him and called him Digup St Edmunds to cheer up the people of Bury St Edmunds, a dullish town on the far side of the county in which I live.

Chris's trainer said he didn't like the name, that good horses deserve good names ... so after one poorish run for the disgruntled Mr Egerton I gave the horse to Venetia Williams, and she trained him to win races and give us much pleasure.

My first expensive two-year-old purchase was in 1965. I called the colt Overseas Buyer. Chancellor James Callaghan had just introduced legislation terminating tax concessions on business entertainment with the exception of taking out overseas buyers; it had been my intention to claim racecourse attendance as 'investigating overseas buyers' market', losing bets as 'supporting overseas buyer' and trips to foreign racetracks as 'pursuing overseas buyers'.

Alas, the horse was utterly, totally useless, moving steadily downhill from the comparative luxury of Toby Balding's yard at Fyfield to end up behind a shed in a field belonging to trainer Tim Finch in Norfolk. He finally packed it in with his curriculum vitae reading 000P00PP0.

I bought and named Weareagrandmother, when Mrs Thatcher made that modest remark at the birth of her son Mark's first child, and Nagnagnag, who was beaten a short head in a Group Two at Saint-Cloud. As he had led most of the way I could not understand why the commentator made no mention of the horse; in the winner's enclosure it was explained to me that in French the word Nagnagnag was unpronounceable.

There is a school of thought that believes you should try to sneak obscene names past the vigilant authorities at Weatherbys. I have never seen the point. An owner should be able to look his horse in the eye, man to man, and address him by a decent name – and neither Up Uranus nor Below Jobs qualifies.

*

Another of the joys of ownership is the memento, the remembrance of wins past ...

AN OWNER'S LOT IS SOMETIMES NOT WORTH THE CANDLE(STICK)

10 AUGUST 2005

SINCE MY LAST communication, I have acquired a box: it is black, made of superior quality cardboard with silver edging, measures about ten inches by eight inches by four inches, and if I were a member of the Mafia I would contemplate emigration, for such boxes contain the severed heads of animals and are sent to folk as a warning that they are on the not-wanted list.

My box was too heavy to contain the head of a dog, too small for the head of a horse and quite the wrong shape for a snake; also I have no Cosa Nostra affiliations, having visited Sicily but once, when I was guest lecturer on a Saga cruise ship where the only evening entertainment was my talk or bingo. I came a distant second, third if you bore in mind most passengers' propensity to spending the evening hours getting quietly legless in the bar.

Let me ask and answer a few questions: why would I have such a box?

It was a gift from a man in a suit at Worcester racecourse, presented after my Marathea won the 2.20 amateur riders' handicap hurdle over three miles.

Why did I not back the horse or tell my readers?

Because I thought the extra five furlongs of the race might not suit her, that she liked good to soft going and here it was good to firm, and that she tended to hang right and Worcester is a left-handed course.

Why did she start favourite?

Because other people, those who don't pay Marathea's training bills, did not know what I knew.

When the contest and the presentation were over I was invited to the stewards' room, congratulated, given a glass of champagne and a video of the race. This is such a very conservative way to go about life: rewarding someone who needs no reward, offering free drink to him who has just won the wherewithal to purchase his own.

Margaret Thatcher, the architect of this philosophy, never denied that under her administration, in which the poor became poorer, the rich did become richer. Might the Jockey Club consider reversing this agenda by rewarding the owners of worthy losers instead; it is they – not those wallowing in hugs, kisses, felicitations, bundles of £50 notes and the knowledge of having enhanced the value of a broodmare – who have need thereof.

Oh yes – the box: 'Thank you very much, it is just what I always wanted,' I told the man in the suit, and when I had undone the gold ribbon and removed the lid, there nestling in black, silk-like cloth were two heavy cut-glass candlesticks such as you send to the cleaning lady's daughter on her wedding day.

I am not complaining – but at Wolverhampton they give you a choice of gifts, at least one of which is a glass or a bottle. I wonder whether most winning owners of minor events would not prefer a subscription made in their name to the Injured Jockeys' Fund – keeping the money in racing, giving something back.

A nice man came up to me on the train, just managed not to tell me he had thought I was dead, and came out with 'What are you doing these days?' A sure sign that he had last seen me on *Blankety Blank* in the 1960s.

I told him that I had recently gone to a cinema to see *Charlie and the Chocolate Factory*, a very joyous film which people would be foolish to miss, also watched a televised debate from the Welsh Parliament that I got by mistake: was aiming for a repeat of *Bullseye* and pressed the wrong button.

Welsh Parliament was dire. A woman called Jones (Cons.) read a speech in which it became reasonably clear that she was unsure about ID cards, there were pros and cons. After this a woman called Essex (Lib. Dem.) suggested that it was absolutely right for people to have opinions.

I cannot believe that viewing figures reached three figures and thought of all the attractive programmes the channel might have broadcast; if hell-bent on a Welsh format, greyhound racing from Merthyr Tydfil, wall-to-wall coverage of last year's successful rugby internationals, even the shipping forecast spoken over a map of the Welsh coastline would have been compulsive by comparison. The shipping forecast is one of my favourite programmes.

I then remembered why I was on the train and told the man

that I owned racehorses. 'Is that difficult?', he asked.

I thought about this: look at the *Racing Post* with care and quite frequently they announce the jockey of the week, trainer of the month, stable groom of the season, horse, farrier, vet, stalls handler and ambulance driver of whatever period.

Owners, I believe, only get a mention at the annual Derby awards, and the prize tends to go to the Aga Khan rather than the owner of an all-aged seller at Yarmouth. I wonder what one has to do to be recognised as an outstanding owner if one has very few horses who don't often win.

If rewards came for being accessible and talking to the press, I surely qualify; should it be a sartorial award, I would start wearing a hat and a tie in the parade ring, perhaps they could tell me. Turning up is important; I once suggested that prize-money be withheld from absentee owners unless they could provide medical certificates. That did not catch on.

On the whole, your best bet – after making a fuss of the trainer and embracing the jockey – is smiling at officials, tipping the groom, complimenting the groundsman, sending a crate of Guinness to the stalls handlers, thanking the judge and writing to the *Post* in praise of the overall excellence of the racecourse. Then you too just might get two cut-glass candlesticks.

If you would like mine, send me one really good reason why; remember, you will need to have your own candles and matches to get the best use out of them.

The following week's Clement Freud column reported that there had been a healthy response to his invitation: 'Four people who had both candles and matches applied: three who had backed Marathea when I had tipped her to win at Perth and flown over Nina Carberry for the steering job (she came second) and felt the candlesticks would be compensation for their loss. I received a very long letter from a man whose friend was groom to a horse I had with Fulke Johnson Houghton in the 1960s and a couple from dedicated fans – one so that he could illuminate the fading, yellowing picture of me that stood on his mantelpiece. On careful consideration the silver-edged cardboard box is going to Roy Simpson of Bournemouth, who wrote to say that his cleaning lady's daughter is getting married. In a spirit of helpfulness, I'm getting the candlesticks engraved: "In recognition of your mum's fine work on the Hoover."'

*

Eau Good won twice in the Freud colours – on one occasion beating the Queen's runner into second place at Windsor – but all good things come to an end ...

AU REVOIR EAU GOOD – IT WAS ... INTERESTING

30 AUGUST 2008

HILAIRE BELLOC, IN one of his *Cautionary Verses*, wrote of the nicest child he ever knew, one Charles Augustus Fortescue: 'When eating bread he made no crumbs, / He was extremely fond of sums / To which however he preferred, / The parsing of a Latin word.' Belloc goes on to say that 'as for finding mutton-fat / Unappetising, far from that, / He often at his father's board / Would beg them of his own accord / To give him, if they didn't mind, / The greasiest morsels they could find.'

All went well for him. In later life he married Fifi, only child of a recently created peer, 'to show what everybody might / Become by simply doing right'.

It had always been my ambition to emulate that fine example, though my early life manifested none of the impeccable traits of young Mr Fortescue. I disliked Latin verbs, was and am anti-grease, married the middle daughter of an impoverished

schoolmaster, never seemed to do 'right'. I blame my
preoccupation with gambling and horses.

In 2006, some 50 years into owning racehorses – purchases
usually recommended by trainers whom I had met at functions
and liked, sat next to on trains or planes and found agreeable, or
admired for consistently doing better with their Thoroughbreds
than expected – I decided on a new plan: consult the man who
had engineered the purchase of Motivator for the Royal Ascot
Racing Club and commission him to buy me a prospective Derby
winner. I told him to bear in mind that as I would actually prefer
to have success at Cheltenham than Epsom, get me a Derby
winner who will go on to victory in the Champion Hurdle after
picking up the Triumph.

And in God's good time, I ended up with a colt by Cadeaux
Genereux at a cost, by the time he reached his trainer-to-be in
North Yorkshire, of about £40,000. He would have cost more but
for some minimal disfigurement. My initial reluctance to own a
cripple was nullified by a distinguished veterinarian's opinion that
his condition was of no hindrance to racing, especially as this
horse had been selected by Her Majesty's racing manager – a good
man who knows what he is doing. I wanted to call him Eau Good.
Weatherbys explained that there was a horse called Oh Good and
declined the name in case of mix-ups. When I found that Oh Good
was an elderly broodmare, I asked them to reconsider my
application. They did. Eau Good it was.

Early reports from Middleham were encouraging: handsome
horse, worked well on the gallops, will be ready to run soon, then
not quite that soon, then next Thursday at Haydock Park. Came
second. Would have learned a lot from that first run. He had two
more runs, one at Ayr, the other at York and was placed at short
prices each time, the short prices not wholly unconnected with
my investments. His rating went up into the low 80s, around my
age, though the losses I had sustained backing him to win made
me feel older.

After his third non-win, which nearly wiped me out, I moved him to a trainer in East Anglia who charged less than half the last man's training fees. He won a little race at Wolverhampton – not that there are big races to be won at Wolverhampton.

I fell out with the trainer, sent him to one in the West Country whom I admired. He charged rather more, but was very complimentary about Eau Good and won a race with him at Windsor, in which he beat a horse owned by the Queen – not too often does the combined age of the proprietors of the Exacta come in at 163 – and netted me the returns on £300 each-way at 28-1. He was now three years old and I was told that he jumped brilliantly, naturally: roll on high-class juvenile hurdles, watch out Cheltenham. In the autumn of that year we ran him over hurdles at Kempton and Folkestone. Nothing, or to put it another way, pulled up in one contest, tailed off in the next.

It was basically lack of success as well as failure in communication with trainer No. 3 that persuaded me to send him elsewhere. For the £20,000 a year one pays to train, shoe, vet, enter and transport a racehorse, I want to be able to contact his minder when I feel like it. I understand there are yards which inform patrons that telephone calls will be welcome once a week, but these are yards of important, successful, Group-winning trainers who would frighten the hell out of owners like me who are looking for quality early-morning bacon sandwiches on the gallops and dream of plotting a Bank Holiday coup at Huntingdon when no-one is looking. Back he went to East Anglia.

Eau Good's last public appearance was at Windsor a couple of months ago. Darryll Holland was up at my request. He cantered to the start, crab-like.

When they reached the starting stalls Holland told the vet he was unhappy about Eau Good's mobility and they withdrew him 'not under starter's orders', a humiliating occurrence and one unlikely to enhance his value, should I ever wish to dispose of him. The trainer explained that Eau Good was not a good mover but he had told the jockey that regardless of what it looked and felt like, once out of the stalls he would run like a stag.

The jockey denied being told that, and opined that it felt as if the horse had broken his back.

So I sent Eau Good to a friend who is a trainer and asked him to give me an opinion concerning his future as a racehorse. The report was disappointing. He had this severe injury to his front foot, I surely knew that? I did not.

He had a sore back, was deeply unhappy and bit anyone who came near him. I had not known that either.

Was I aware of the fact that he was a wind-sucking, weaving brute? That was another thing I had not been told ...

What shall we do with him?

I had intended asking him what he suggested, but it was surely time I began making my own decisions. Sell him, I said.

We move smoothly to Ascot last Tuesday. There was no racing on Tuesday at Ascot, do I hear you say? Right, say I.

There was a sale. Lot 41: well-bred gelding by Cadeaux Genereux, property of a gentleman, winner of two races and £12,000 in prize-money. Only 21 races on the clock, do I hear 5,000 guineas? Silence. After a while there was a bid at 500 guineas, whereafter the price rose slowly in 50-guinea jumps to 950 guineas, at which the hammer fell; went to a good home in the Midlands to go eventing. Eau Revoir ... unless Weatherbys decree that the name has gone.

So I almost did right. After expenses there is enough from the sale for a celebration dinner for one at Nando's: a corn on the cob for starters, half a chicken with chips and coleslaw and a cake made of puff pastry filled with vanilla-flavoured custard whose Portuguese name escapes me, and probably wouldn't mean much to you either. It is almost exactly what people with diabetes should avoid. Like owning racehorses.

3

THE JOCKEY

❛ I learned to stick my bum in the air and lower my shoulders, something you seldom see mounted constables do ❜

Clement Freud first rode in a race at Naas, County Kildare, in 1967. Five years later, on 19 September 1972, he rode Tsarzen in an amateurs' event at Leicester as part of his preparation for the match race against his friend Sir Hugh Fraser at Haydock Park 11 days later.

Peter O'Sullevan – fabled commentator, close friend of a man he described as 'the bearded cavalier', and a punter fearless enough to stake £700 to win £400 in the Haydock match – reported Freud's Leicester ride in the Daily Express: *'The physical effort of riding in the style of a jockey has to be experienced to be appreciated. And it is no reflection on Mr Freud's enthusiasm and clearly budding talent that, following the contest, he was temporarily rendered speechless for possibly the first time in his adult life.'*

This is Clement Freud's most complete account of his riding career, first published in his 2001 autobiography Freud Ego.

IN WHICH I RECALL MY SHORT CAREER AS A THIN MAN

I WAS WORKING for the *Sun*, long before it shrank in size and depicted parts of girls one does not see in Marylebone High Street. One day I wrote about an amateur rider (who claimed 7lb) and warned readers to be wary of supporting his mounts as he tended to carry overweight. 'What a disgrace to burden your horse with a stone more than the handicapper has allotted it; there should be a law against it,' I opined.

Some time later the sports editor said, 'You've got a horse. Why don't you ride him? Save money on jockeys and it'll make a good piece.' I explained that (a) I didn't ride, had not done so since pre-puberty, and (b) though Charles II competed in the Newmarket Town Plate at 14st 4lb, people of my build were not now accommodated by the *Racing Calendar*.

'Lose weight and learn to ride,' he said.

I lost 30lb. Having sat next to Jimmy Lindley on a flight to Washington for the International race, I rang him and asked whether he might give me race-riding lessons. He agreed. The following Tuesday and again on the Thursday he came to the stable where I had horses. I rode round and round a field and he kept shouting, 'Stop looking like a fucking policeman.' I learned to stick my bum in the air and lower my shoulders, something you seldom see mounted constables do.

I asked my trainer if he would recommend me as a jockey, and he wrote a note that stated: 'C. Freud is not much worse than some of the amateurs riding today.' I sent the note with my application to ride to the secretary to the stewards of the Irish

Turf Club; by return I received a note asking me to present myself for inspection at 11am the following Friday.

I flew to Dublin, made my way to the Merrion Square office and was called into a room in which half a dozen elderly men sat behind a table. They stared at me for a while, one of them remarking that I looked rather better on television – an observation to which I have still not found a good answer. It was the senior steward, Major Victor McCalmont, who kicked off proceedings.

'How long have you been riding, Mr Freud?' he asked amiably.

I was able to tell him exactly: 'I started on Tuesday of last week – early on, around 7.30am.'

He looked perplexed, had a quick whisper with his colleagues and came up with Question No. 2: 'Have you done any speed work?'

I assured him that it had nearly all been speed work: I would get on a horse and the horse galloped away. I added that if the stewards thought I was the sort of swine who pulled his horse to prevent it from winning, they could rest easy.

There was a longish pause before one of the men said, 'Give him a licence – what harm can he do?'

I was told that I could ride in amateur races and was warned not to make a nuisance of myself ringing owners and trainers at all hours asking for rides. I promised not to.

A dear man called Jo Hehir, who was a patron of my trainer, offered me a ride on his horse Saxon King on the last Saturday of the month.

'I am afraid I am unlikely to be much use as a jockey,' I told him.

'The horse is not much use either, so you'll get on fine together,' said Mr Hehir and poured us each a large glass of Bushmills.

I lost more weight, rode out two lots a day for whoever would have me, and read *The Theory and Practice of Flat Race Riding* by John Hislop. This is an invaluable volume, containing much excellent advice and some dubious statements such as 'Settle a horse on the gallops by sitting quietly with a long rein.' The first time I tried this, it took me a mile and three-quarters to pull the brute to a trot. There is an interesting paragraph dealing with starters. 'Jockeys who consistently refer to starters as ham-fisted deaf-mutes are unlikely to get the best breaks when the field is sent on its way. Also, some starters have an aversion to jocks shouting "Not yet, sir!" at them.'

I started my riding career in a bumper at Naas. 'What if the horse bolts on the way to the start?', I asked the trainer.

'Aim him at the other horses; they are gregarious beasts,' he said.

It all went swimmingly. Adrenalin flowed, I started well, and my bottom never touched the saddle. Coming into the home turn on the first circuit, Mr J. R. Cox, the best and reputedly most expensive amateur jockey in the British Isles, rode up beside me and asked me whether I was enjoying it. He took hold of my horse's head and pushed him into the lead, so that I was first passing the stands.

I hadn't realised that jockeys could hear the commentary and the shouts of the punters and the bookmakers. I was so taken with this that I forgot to steer, until I heard a man shout: 'Open the gates, he's coming in!'

Saxon King and I tired after 12 furlongs: I had been afraid that I would not be able to pull up after the finish: not a bit of it. Two miles of fierce galloping had both of us ready to call it an afternoon. I walked him to the enclosure, got off and found I was too weak to remove the saddle to weigh in, which is not essential when you finish 15th.

I rode a few more times in Ireland and at Leicester and Bath. Why did they dope-test the horse, I wondered, when it was I who was up to the gills with amphetamines and diuretics in order to make under 12st, which God had never intended as my weight? I was not always finishing 15th. One year I had a 50 per cent strike-rate; regrettably the amateur riders' table required a minimum of five wins and I had only won once, so my name did not figure.

My greatest race was an affair which started in June 1972, when I ran my five-year-old horse Winter Fair in the Hugh Fraser Amateur Riders' Stakes at Hamilton Park – to which the Scottish industrialist had contributed £1,000 in prize-money. In the parade ring prior to the event, modestly attired in Fraser tartan silks, stood the generous sponsor and I, recalling the halcyon days of yore, flung a metaphorical glove into the mud of Hamilton Park (the going was described as soft) and challenged the second baronet to a race.

'Done,' he said, pronouncing the word as men do north of the border.

'A thousand pounds a side?', I asked.

'A thousand pounds it is,' said he.

'Mile and a half ... classic distance?'

He nodded.

'Shall we say 12st 7lb?'

We shook hands.

I returned my hand in the general direction of my 14st frame and told Toby Balding, my trainer, what I had done. He received the information with limited amusement.

For the record my horse, ridden by that peerless rider Mr Philip Mitchell, won the race. And some yards beyond the finishing post Sir Hugh, who was in penultimate position, dismounted from his steed in what is regarded as an unorthodox manner, i.e. sideways, at considerable speed, picking himself gingerly from the turf and moving crabwise towards the weighing room, while an honest lad was dispatched to reclaim the horse. I mention this not in the spirit of what the Teuts call *Schadenfreude*, which means joy at someone else's misfortunes, but to put paid to vile rumours that I had waited till Sir Hugh had fallen from his horse before issuing my challenge.

The announcement of the match, carried quietly in a number of minority publications, caused a clutch of clerks of courses to inquire whether we might, perchance, care to hold the contest at their tracks; and in the fullness of time we settled on Haydock Park, 30 September. The choice was made for a number of good reasons: Haydock was roughly equidistant between London and Glasgow – my home and his; the 30 September programme featured a ladies' race, so that the pure academic seriousness of the occasion was already impaired; there had never before been a 'match' at Haydock, but when racing started there at the end of the 18th century the first event was for horses carrying 14st 4lb, proving that the terrain was suitable for feats of weight-carrying.

Moreover, late September would afford my horse the chance to frolic in a field for a month – something my trainer termed 'letting it down' and I considered a rare extravagance at 20 guineas a week – before he would be 'wound up' with the match in mind. For Sir Hugh, it meant a summer holiday and time to look round for a better horse. 'You're nay goin' to hold me to riding that animal?', he asked.

I shook my head in sorrow. We agreed that, whatever horse he bought, we would take the official Timeform ratings for the respective mounts, burden the better nag with 12st 7lb and let the lesser animal carry the lesser weight according to handicap.

There remained for me a number of small problems – like riding at 12st 7lb entails weighing around 11st 13lb, the remaining poundage being taken up by saddle, stirrups, boots, breeches, shirt, girths and other attributes without which equestrian propriety would be offended. Thus, around 30lb of C. Freud would have to go.

Mid-August saw me firmly inside the 14st barrier. Admittedly, 45 days in which to lose 28lb presented a steeper graph than did the original 36lb in four months, but I was playing Real Tennis at Lord's, walking, swimming and having odd games of golf, cricket and tennis.

By 15 August, in Hampshire Winter Fair had finished a month of road work and was doing some fastish ten-furlong spins on the gallops. In London I embarked on the Grapefruit Diet, an amazing method by which you eat up to 12 fried eggs and 12 slices of bacon for breakfast, lace your coffee with cream and provided you precede every meal with half a fresh grapefruit, you lose 10lb in ten days. There were a number of don'ts like no other fruit, no starches, no corn oil or margarine, no sugar, no sweet wines – simply as much fat and protein as you can gobble, with half upon half of catalytic grapefruit.

It seemed to me that such a diet should be taken seriously, away from the temptation of thin toast cunningly slipped beneath your caviar, so I accepted an invitation to stay on a Chinese junk in Majorca, took with me the diet sheet and explained to my hostess that it was in a grand cause: when I won Sir Hugh's £1,000 I would buy her something lovely at Harrods. She told me she did not remember ever seeing a grapefruit on Majorca, though in fairness she had not really looked. Together we looked. We scoured the fruit shops and greengrocers, supermarkets and harbour warehouses of the island and after each bout of shops we sat down and had a glass of wine and planned our next move. In six days I put on 5lb in weight and on the last day I lost 4lb; returning to London I preceded each meal with half a grapefruit, did exactly as I was told and, after five days, where the blurb promised that there would be a sudden 5lb weight loss, the scales flickered to show a decrease of 1½lb – 24lb to lose in 32 days.

I lost 1lb in four days. I was alone in London while my family was summering in Suffolk, and, with amphetamine pills prescribed by a doctor who advised against them but said that they would do no lasting harm, I lost my appetite and gained uncommon energy. So I spent days jumping up and down, playing Real Tennis wearing a polythene vest between two jerseys over a sweatshirt, and managed to drink sufficiently small quantities of white wine to make the weight loss realistic.

Down to 12st 12lb, I booked myself into Grayshott Hall Health Hydro in Hampshire, where the osteopath put me on the scales and said, 'We'll feed you a bit – 12st 12lb is on the thin side for you.'

'Hot water,' I said hungrily, 'with an occasional grape.'

He wished me luck.

My timetable was wake up at 5.30am and drive to Toby Balding. Ride at 7am and then again at 9am; then drive back to Grayshott. Gravitate between sauna and massage parlour and sitz-bath and gymnasium (where there was a static bicycle) until 3pm collapse. Watch television and go to sleep as soon after 11pm as was consistent with the foul taste of hunger and dehydration on my palate. I left Grayshott weighing 12st 5lb; used a belt to support my trousers and took up residence with my trainer, whose wife decided to go to Scotland – swearing that the journey had nothing to do with my arrival.

Sir Hugh and I met at the beginning of September. I gave him several large whiskies, and we sent in our joint challenges to the Keeper of Matchbook at Weatherbys in Portman Square. As there have already been eight 'matches' since the war, the man cannot afford to sleep for more than 364½ days in the year. We also gave a small press conference in the discotheque of the Playboy Club, to which we invited racing correspondents and Diary editors.

After the first case of champagne we announced the match, and answered questions which were of the what do you weigh/who will win variety until a man asked Sir Hugh (whose properties had that week been valued at £125 million) what he would do with the money if he won.

'Give it to the Injured Jockeys' Fund,' said the knight.

'How about you?' asked the journalist.

'Keep it,' I said, giving my colleagues of the Press the first quotable quote.

'On reflection,' I added, 'and bearing in mind the champagne I have dispensed, together with the fried prawns, devilled chicken livers and barbecued spare ribs, I would prefer you not to mention this in your papers.'

They smiled the way I used to smile.

On Tuesday 19 September, weighing 12st 1lb, I had a preliminary outing; a well-behaved racehorse, Tsarzen by name, the property of Mr Robert Marmor, was entered in an amateur 1¼ mile race at Leicester and I was permitted to ride. The weight it was allocated was 11st 7lb and, in view of having ridden fewer than five winners under any recognised rule of racing, I was to claim a further 5lb. After a morning of fierce squash following a day of no food or drink, I had the sort of tongue which any respectable doctor would have advised me not to put back in my mouth. Notwithstanding, in the words of the great P. O'Sullevan, 'Freud put up the equivalent overweight of 22 one-pound tins of dogfood' – a statement that hurt my pride, even while it delighted my masters who produced those fine canine products which permitted me to appear on television.

The race helped me greatly. I got into the swing of jockeys' changing-room talk, learnt a number of four-letter words the existence of which I had only suspected and gleaned from the valet that you put nylon tights on your legs, dust these with talcum, whereafter you can slide your riding boots on and off with a minimum of strain. I also came to grips with goggles, found that the chinstrap of a crash helmet fitted over my beard in such a way that I looked like every other clean shaven jockey and I had my first experience of starting stalls. Tsarzen and I were led into one labelled 7, the door slammed behind us and the honest horse moved so that my leg was squashed against one side. Having watched dressage in the Olympics I tried a few ploys to make him move six inches to the left, like beating him fiercely with my whip, also pushing him with all my weight; Tsarzen remained comfortably where he was.

In the stall next to me, the man said he could not remember a jockey ever leaving a leg or part thereof in the stall; nevertheless I decided to take my imprisoned leg from the horse's side and place it forward near its mouth. So there I sat. Right leg in horse's mouth. Left hanging down. Both hands on the reins, which were doubled over the withers while my two thumbs gripped the mane as per instructions. The theory here is that a horse might jump out of the gate with such celerity that, unless you hold on to it, only one of you completes the course.

I wondered about shouting, 'Just a minute, sir!', decided against it and saw the white flag go up, after which the stalls opened with a rare crack. We emerged, and by the time I had got my right foot back by the horse's side we were lying comfortably in 14th place, the other 13 runners kicking lavish clumps of mud into my face. Leicester is a right-handed course and one races far from the close scrutiny of the crowd until reaching the four-furlong straight; I rode a stirring finish, during which I passed a number of horses who were by then going backwards and came in eighth. The next day's *Sporting Life* noted that 'Tsarzen dwelt [official word for starting slowly with jockey's foot in horse's mouth] and made some late progress.'

As a result of the race my confidence was immeasurably strengthened; also I went out to dinner and put on 8lb in weight.

Two days later, riding Winter Fair for the first time, the horse bolted with me at the end of the gallops. Not unduly worried, I steered him down a seven-furlong straight; he had already worked a mile and a quarter, which had exhausted me and must have tired him, but I found that the harder I pulled the horse, the faster he went.

At the end of the gallop was a high hedge trimmed with barbed wire – and as Winter Fair was making straight for it there seemed little else to do but haul fiercely at the right rein with such strength as remained. This made the horse turn, fall and slide into the barbed wire, in which his legs became desperately entangled. I did what I could to ease the situation and finally he picked out, disentangled himself at the cost of a fair amount of flesh and blood and cantered away. I removed myself as best I could, and by the time the horse was caught it was clear to those assembled that

I had broken some ribs, bruised an elbow and was lame in my right ankle.

An hour later the vet came. Winter Fair had been cleaned up magnificently with iodine that blended into the deep chestnut of his skin; when I asked the vet what were the chances of his racing on Saturday week, he opined that they seemed a damned sight better than mine.

In the afternoon I went to Ascot to do a television interview about the forthcoming match and heard (a) that a lady called Jean Cooper was a smashing physio when it came to ribs, ankles and elbows; (b) that Hugh Fraser had sprained an ankle. News of my adversary's ankle was exaggerated, but I owe a great deal to Miss Cooper. Having ascertained that my sixth rib was broken in two places, she got me into a sound if in-pain state; and on the following Monday evening I drove up north to ride the Haydock course.

Two things happened on that Monday night. I was caught speeding on the M6. Park Ward Continentals with their hoods up have a notoriously small rear window, and what I diagnosed as a white jeep behind me turned out – at 92 miles an hour – to be a police Range Rover. Later, at the Midland Hotel, Manchester, I pushed myself out of the bath and with an audible crack such healing as my rib had achieved went by the board. I spent a night of acute pain and at 6am drove to Haydock like the hunchback of Notre Dame.

The course over which the match was to be held is left-handed – an oval of just over a mile and a half so that our start was in front of the stands, 60 yards beyond the finishing post. I walked the course with the groundsman, who explained that you stuck to the rails until you got to the BREW TEN advertisement hoarding, then made for the chestnut tree on the far side of the back straight, going to the inner by the mile starting gate and keeping there round the home turn, whereafter you made your best way home down the five-furlong straight.

At 9am George Owen, a kindly northern trainer, arrived with his stable jockey and a mare upon which I was to ride round. After some difficulty mounting I found that a walk and a gallop were bearable speeds for my strapped ribs, so we walked to the start and galloped round the course. My plan was for the other horse to take the lead while I came at him in the home straight, riding a fantastic finish to win by a neck.

In fact Mr R. Crank, George Owen's jockey, went so slowly that my mare zoomed past him and in the home straight he surged past me and there was no way I could get back on terms. In desperation, and remembering Winter Fair's reaction to being hard pulled and ordered to stop, I took a firm tug at the bridle and shouted 'Whoa.' Mr Owen's mare slowed obediently, so that I lost five lengths and experienced great pain in my ribs. However, I had learnt the right way to steer a horse round Haydock, got a feeling for the speed one would go in a two-horse race and thought that if I could ride within 12 hours of re-breaking a rib I would be absolutely fine in four days' time, especially if I took care not to get out of baths quickly.

Meanwhile, news from Winter Fair was that he was making a great recovery. His initial stiffness had gone and, according to his trainer, he was fit to jump out of his multi-punctured skin. On Thursday, 28 September I drove to Newmarket, where Toby was witnessing the sales and we spent an hour discussing tactics.

On form, I had the better horse – though the enemy had an advantage of 10lb in weight. Winter Fair had won over 1½ miles on the Flat; Star Award, Sir Hugh's three-year-old, had won a couple of races over a mile, come fourth over ten furlongs carrying 8½st – so there was no reason to believe that he would rocket down the final straight with an extra 50lb on his back.

The danger would be that if I went too slowly the three-year-old might do me for finishing speed and, if I raced off at breakneck speed and my horse blew up, Sir Hugh might just be able to bide his time and come in with a late run. The bookmakers had made my horse favourite at 1-2. If we were both experienced jockeys, mine would win and there seemed no reason why, as we were both thoroughly inexperienced jockeys, the result should be significantly different, except 'racing is a funny game'.

I drove back to London, and by the time I left for Manchester on Friday evening I had recorded four deathless episodes of *Just A Minute* and gone to a wine tasting at which I spat out more wine than any taster has ever before expectorated. I had also spent a fair amount of time rereading *The Theory and Practice of Flat Race Riding*.

After dinner with the Baldings and my elder daughter in the French restaurant at the Midland, two friends and I went to a club called the Cossack. Basically, this seemed to work in the following way: you stood outside and rang the bell and in God's good time the manager, with a half-smoked cigar wedged between his teeth, unbolted and unlocked the door. The opening was narrow, and the only way of getting past him was to take the active end of his cigar in your mouth and perform a quick pirouette. 'Clem,' he shouted, 'great to see you. Got a cough? Never mind.' I introduced my friends, he blew smoke in their faces and pushed us forward. The place was dark and full: men were square and middle-aged; girls young and acquisitive. If I understood correctly, the scene was that you danced with whom you liked – with the exception of the middle-aged square men – and if you had any proposal to put to your partner, the sum of £5 paid to the management gave you the right to go outside, get your face slapped and come back. But I probably got it wrong.

A waitress called Marie blew gently into my ear and I ordered two bottles of champagne. Two girls came with the champagne and left with the empties. And Cigar Face kept bringing along people to whom he introduced me as Clem – all of whom promised to back me the next day.

Back at the hotel I took two Mandrax pills, one Tuinal, two laxatives, an iron pill and a salt tablet, and asked for an 8am call. I woke at 5.30am, then again at 6.46am, when I took the two diuretic tablets that Toby had acquired for me. Before the Leicester race I had taken one and it had been almost entirely ineffective. With two, the yield was as follows: 7.35am, 15 fluid ounces; 7.58, ten; 8.16, nine; 8.39, ten; 8.58, three; 9.15, two.

In view of the previous night's dinner and champagne I decided to while away an hour in a sauna and found one, open 24 hours a day, which gave me five shillings' discount for being a member of Equity. I tried to get a further discount as a member of the National Union of Journalists, but discounts, like contemporary prison sentences, seem to run concurrently rather than cumulatively. The sauna had a door which was so stiff that I was as apprehensive about getting locked in as I was about damaging my ribs trying to get out; 45 minutes at 100 degrees resulted in a loss of 2lb. The scales registered 11st 9½lb; short of amputating a limb, which would not significantly have helped my equestrian thrust, I had done what I could.

At 11am Toby and Caroline Balding and I drove to Haydock Park and as we approached the owners' and trainers' car park my wife and three younger children landed on the course in a Piper Aztec plane. Then I heaved my bag containing saddle, boots, breeches etc. into the weighing room and walked the course with my trainer, 'Emma, Dominic and Matthew in attendance', as they say in Court Circulars.

We noticed that the going, officially described as 'hard', was well covered with odd patches in the back straight where the previous day's racing had left a wide path of hoofprints; these could only be avoided by going far into the centre of the track, or by sticking so close to the rail that the chances of your left leg remaining attached to your body would have been poor. Walking the home turn there was all of 300 yards in which one changed from south-east to north-west, but riding it at 35 miles an hour one would be likely to be carried off the rails – in which case, Haydock specialists said, you are better making straight for the finishing line than going back to the rails.

We returned to the stands at noon, I gave Julian Wilson of the BBC a quick one minute of voice to be put over the television coverage of my horse being led out on to the course prior to the race at 1.15pm and, with time galloping on, I made for the weighing room. Halfway down the near-side wall is an aperture that leads to the jockeys' changing room and as I made to go in I was stopped. The man explained that the changing room was for jockeys only. He knew who I was – 'Goodness, yes, wife's a great fan of yours ... but not in here you don't come.'

'He's riding,' said a man behind me.

'He doesn't come in here,' said the man.

'He's Clement Freud,' said the valet from within, waving my riding boots.

'I know that,' said the clerk of the scales.

The man finally withdrew, I was reunited with my riding gear and received valeting of an incredibly high order: the man in question steadily held trouser legs or jacket sleeves at the angle at which they most appropriately slid over the limb in question.

It was now 12.40, 35 minutes to go. I was dressed: bandages, tights, breeches, boots, silk blouse, stock, crash helmet, saddle cloth, saddle, breast plate, surcingle, number cloth – got on the scales and weighed 12st 2½lb, 4½lb less than I need have weighed. I could have had two roast grouse, bread sauce, breadcrumbs, game chips and a magnum of Chateau Palmer 1955 ...

They gave me a leather belt with slots for lead weights and fed lead into it until the pointer hovered on 175lb. Then, on reflection, I asked them to take out a weight and had a cup of tea. Toby and I went into the trainers' luncheon room and as my tea arrived Toby asked whether I had had my salt tablet that day. I said no.

'Very important, salt,' said my trainer. 'When you are dehydrated, it stops you getting cramp.'

'I am dehydrated,' I said.

He got a teaspoon, filled it with salt and I swallowed it, washing the stuff down with tea and feeling as sick as I have ever felt.

Had there been a bookmaker around, my odds might well have lengthened to 4-6; instead they contracted to 4-9 with Fraser at 6-4 against, though I learnt later that such support as the tycoon had came less from the people with faith in him or in tycoonery than from those confident that 6-4 against represented fair value when it came to a real live gourmet remaining on a moving horse for 12 furlongs.

The fact that I have not yet mentioned my adversary on this great day is due neither to egocentricity nor forgetfulness, for Sir Hugh Fraser had failed to show. Even my idea that he was being barred from entering the course by some further representative from Rent-a-moron turned out to be false when it was learnt that he had flown over the course at noon but his pilot had refused to land because of cross-winds. He was diverted to Liverpool and Sir Hugh was currently gnashing his teeth in a taxi somewhere along the M6.

If what had passed to date was comedy, the next 20 minutes belonged to high farce. Here was Haydock racecourse on a glorious September afternoon with 17,000 people in attendance. Also, a television audience estimated at eight million. Over in the paddock two horses walked quietly around the ring, watched by humanity ten deep. Outside the weighing room, and lining the route to the paddock, was a crowd that would not have disgraced Newmarket on Guineas day. In the weighing room I sat and waited, as did the clerk of the course, the stewards, the stipendiaries, the starter, the course commentator, and the valet deputed to help the absent Fraser arms into the waiting tartan sleeves.

Officially, lips were sealed – with the odds against the Jockey Club ever giving their consent to another televised match lengthening minute by minute. Unofficially, I was approached by all manner of men with all kinds of helpful suggestions. Would I, for instance, care to claim the race, issue another challenge and race at the end of racing, like after the last race? I said no. Would I mind waiting a little longer – like till Sir Hugh arrived? I said that would be a very good idea.

It was 1.10pm. On the television set in the weighing room, the BBC commentator was explaining that there could well be a delay and over now to the baths at Aberafon for some wrestling ... and at 1.17pm there was a stirring in the multitudes and a buzzing and a cheering – and Sir Hugh arrived, wreathed in smoke, cigarettes protruding from every orifice. The air was thick with Celtic apologia: 'Hoots, och the noo, sorry, ye ken I've wrecked it all ..'

'We waited,' I said. 'Get changed.'

Jackets, shirts and pants flew, boots were kicked off and in the course of three minutes Sir Hugh was clothed and weighed and lit another cigarette and threw it away. Escorted by two policemen we walked into the paddock amidst many a cry of 'Hurrah,' 'Yippee,' 'At last,' and the inevitable 'Where's your dog?' The stewards stood in hollow square; Winter Fair's connections, consisting of Jill and my children and the Baldings, occupied pride of place; some way distant stood Sir Hugh's trainer and a factotum who looked as if he had come straight from Harrods, where, I seem to recall, you can get absolutely anything.

With our arrival and the stewards beaming with relief, there was one further delay. Star Award, having been taken away to be tacked up with the saddle with which his owner-rider had weighed himself, took a few minutes to return to the paddock, so that Winter Fair completed his 47th circuit alone. Sir Hugh lit a quick cigarette, but after that it was not unlike when they brought the good news from Ghent to Aix. We sprang to the stirrups, were led out. The starter omitted to have a roll call but did explain that he would raise his flag and drop it – which he did, almost immediately, around which time I galloped, Hugh galloped and the relieved crowd, noticing in passing that it was 1.29pm, shouted 'God speed,' 'Cor, look at them,' also 'Where's your dog?'

Having been drawn outside my opponent, I made for the rails ahead of him and steered, as planned, on the rails, across the course by the BREW TEN sign and back again to the mile gate, round the far turn into the straight, which carried me wide and into the home straight with the crowd cheering and the commentator, whom I heard very clearly, saying that I was in the lead – which I realised – and that Fraser was second, which he, too, must have observed. In that order did we pass the finishing post, the official distance 2½ lengths and such fears as I had about being unable to pull up and have to compete in a ladies' race (which was due to start at 1.45pm) were quickly dispelled. The horse behaved immaculately. As for my weight, it was 11st 8½lb stripped at 1pm on Saturday, 30 September.

Around 2am that night I went to bed, a 12st 12lb ex-jockey. It was the drink that did it: when you are thoroughly dehydrated, a pint of lemonade can put on 7lb; as for a magnum of Chateau Petrus ...

Some time ago I went to a Hall of Fame celebration in New York where the greats of basketball were nominated for lifetime achievement. A man of 70 made an acceptance speech, during which he said, 'The older we get, the better we were.' On reflection, some 30 years on, I don't think I was much good in the saddle, but I did have fun.

A silver-framed picture of me riding Winter Fair to victory at Haydock stands on my desk. As it was taken sideways on I have to explain to people that it was I who was riding – though really you can tell because I look a bit like a policeman.

4

THE JOURNALIST

❛ I had a lined A4 pad, drew in vertical lines to create boxes, and put one word into each until the 400 boxes were filled ❜

LIFE IN THE LAND OF
THE FOURTH ESTATE
20 OCTOBER 1999

'DEAR SIR, I enclose a short story; am thinking of embarking on a literary career and would like to start with a rejection slip from you ...'

This was a letter from C. Freud to the editor of the *New Yorker*, then the most prestigious magazine in the world. I was 24, living and working in Cannes, drinking also. I got jaundice, was told to go away, not come back until I was cured and stayed with an aunt-figure in St Tropez, where I wrote this story about a ploughman and a professor. The *New Yorker* published it.

Journalistically, that was it for eight years. I had opened a London nightclub and one of my members, who was Assistant Sports Editor of the *Observer*, telephoned one Friday evening and said: 'John Arlott is ill; can you do a football report from Portsmouth tomorrow afternoon? 400 words. Deadline 15 minutes after the final whistle. You get five guineas and expenses.'

I said, 'Wow', rang a journalist I knew and asked about the mechanics of transmitting copy. I travelled to Portsmouth on a cheap-day return, having ascertained the price of a first-class ticket for my expenses, went to the United Services Club, found it closed and telephoned the Asst. Sports Editor.

'Nothing going on here.'

'Where are you?'

'United Services Club, Portsmouth.'

'Not that football, you oaf; go to Fratton Park.'

I took a cab to Fratton and, when the game was over, found a telephone box, put through a reverse charge call to Fleet Street 0202, asked for 'Copy', and dictated: 'Portsmouth 2 Huddersfield Town 0. This was a minimalist game played in the oyster-light of a damp Hampshire afternoon and from my hard seat in the cramped press-box, from which I could see little, I heard enough to be able to report that the home team took both points. A pipe-smoking old chap in the front row said the first goal was scored by Dickinson after 31 minutes, a bald man sitting to his left thought it was more like Froggat after 32.'

I had a lined A4 pad, drew in vertical lines to create boxes, and put one word into each until the 400 boxes were filled. The next day I spoke to the Asst. Sports Editor and asked what he had thought.

He told me he had thought very little of it. 'You might like to know,' he said, sounding grim, 'that you are probably the only man in sports journalism ever to get a byline on his first piece.'

'What's a byline?'

'"By Clement Freud" ... like it said over your bloody match report; it was so crass we couldn't put "by our football correspondent".'

A month later he telephoned to tell me that the paper had had quite a few phone calls saying that if the *Observer* must waste space on sports reporting, the way Freud wrote about the game at Portsmouth was best. 'Can you do Bolton Wanderers on Saturday?'

For the next eight years, until I was appointed chief sports columnist for the pre-Murdoch *Sun* and got nominated for Sports Writer of 1964, I did reports on football, cricket, racing. And I learned a lot. On the whole, editors don't read what you write. What is crucial to success is writing to a length and getting the copy in on time.

Every now and again I would write something of which I was proud and ring my editor to ask whether he liked it. 'Yes it was good.'

'Did you read it?'

'Don't have to read your copy, I trust you.'

As sports columnist for this exciting new paper, I was sent around the world; to Olympics, World Cups and, perhaps most memorably, Madison Square Garden for Muhammad Ali's first defence of his world heavyweight title.

The *Sun*'s London office had done an admirable job, got me a ringside seat and a telephone. I sat within hand-shaking distance of the great American sports writers of the day: Red Smith, A. J. Liebling, George Plimpton, Norman Mailer ... and when my copy-time came I picked up the phone, dialled the switchboard, asked for copy, leaned back and said: 'Clement Freud, Madison Square Garden.'

'Who?', asked the copytaker.

'Freud,' said I, rather quietly, because people were listening.

'Spell it,' said the copytaker.

I spelt it, was then asked to spell my first name, daring people around me to smile. They cracked up.

Friends say how lucky I am, being paid to write about a subject I love. I agree, but it is not quite like that. As a sports journalist, you may be where you want to be, but everything you see has to be translated from vision to words. You are working all the time. They shout 'goal' or 'come on, my son' and have a good time. You have to note who did what, when and how.

As a species, sports journalists are reluctantly welcomed by venues. While they don't pay to come in (boo), they bring in spectators (hurrah) but have to be fed, even if it is only tea and a stale cake (boo), and are prone to write beastly things about events (boo). But without them, venues would be in dead trouble, so on the whole – 'hurrah'.

At racecourses, journalists are considered a necessary evil, though there are exceptions. Writing for a trade paper like the *Racing Post* is different but I wonder whether clerks of courses realise how reluctant are sports editors of other national newspapers to devote so much of their precious space to details of six Saturday meetings and what a disaster it would be for the tracks if this were not done.

Horseracing has its idea of the function of journalists: to wait quietly until a race is run, then ask intelligent questions about the horses' future engagements and occasionally write enthusiastic articles about horses and courses, also hagiographies of trainers and jockeys. You can criticise the going, but not the groundsmen or the officials who misled trainers about the turf.

And yet people, perhaps especially racing people, do like to see their names and pictures in the paper, and treat journalists as others treat psychotherapists: tell them everything, finishing up with, 'But don't print that.'

And they are clannish. I did a series on 'Breakfast with the Trainers', started with Henry Cecil and mentioned in my article that he had not offered my photographer a cup of coffee or a slice of toast while we were eating and my man was snapping away for some hour and a half. Cecil now looks into the middle distance when he sees me and the next three trainers who had agreed to be interviewed, cancelled.

Someone wrote that racing journalists who don't bet on horses should be ignored. I think that is sensible: the most readable writers are those activated to work by bookmakers' bills. I have tried very hard to achieve a ratio between the bets I make and the income I receive for writing about racing. The answer to my wife's, 'Did you have a good day?' is now only rarely, 'Wrote a good piece but lost six times the fee.'

*

The 1998 series 'Freud's Breakfast with the Trainers' covered early mornings at the yards of Henry Cecil, Lynda Ramsden, William

Muir, Jenny Pitman, Paul Webber, Charlie Mann, Martin Pipe ... and Venetia Williams.

SIMPLY TOO BUSY TO EAT

13 NOVEMBER 1998

AFTER RIDING OUT third lot, Venetia Williams sat at the rectangular wooden table in the kitchen of her house near Ross-on-Wye and said: 'In Hereford, breakfasts hardly happen.' I had been warned. When I telephoned to ask if I might come to share her morning meal, she said I was welcome in principle. In practice, she did not eat breakfast, she had no time for it.

Venetia gets up, feeds the horses, rides out two or three lots, works in the office, then goes to the races. She tries to have a glass of fruit juice and a bowl of cereal on the hoof. If owners come, they are pointed towards the kettle and the microwave.

No egg, bacon, sausage, tomato or mushrooms to which I have become accustomed? Just chocolate biscuits – Hobnobs.

Chocolate plays a pretty important part in the daily life of the establishment of Miss V. Williams, racehorse trainer of Kings Caple, Herefordshire. The top righthand drawer of the dresser is full of it. Venetia, who carries not an ounce of excess weight, especially loves Galaxy bars and worries about getting fat. Shirley Vickery, her secretary and an ex-champion lady rider, needs chocolate as a lush needs liquor, but has to ride at 9st 7lb the next day. Martin Bellamy, who is in charge of owners, will not refuse chocolate either.

Aramstone House is situated above the lush water-meadows adjoining the River Wye, a sensible dwelling on the Williams family farm (sugar beet and potatoes) near the Williams stud (half a dozen broodmares). Venetia's father has been heard to describe his *modus vivendi* with the addendum, 'Oh yes, and my daughter trains one or two jumpers.'

The actual number is 60, with a winner-to-runner ratio that would make Nicholson choke on his Pipe ... and vice versa.

By common consent, V. Williams is a genius in her field. I ask if there is a secret. 'What do you do that others don't?'

I should have known the answer. She doesn't have breakfast. She doesn't stop for lunch, either, and she doesn't have a dog.

Is food important?

Halfway through saying 'No' she decides that food is important, in that she very much enjoys eating the food she likes.

'Do you cook?' She cooks ... thanks to the deep freeze, the microwave and Marks and Spencer. 'St Michael and I have a very close relationship.'

I ask how she entertains owners. 'There is a very fine hostelry in the nearby village – The Cottage of Content, with flagstones, flowers and good food.'

In her kitchen there is an electric cooker passive with disuse, a switched-off Aga (November), a microwave and seven disparate chairs surrounding the kitchen table. We eat sensational croissants, with hand-churned, Normandy creamery unsalted butter, and a fine bitter orange marmalade from a hand-inscribed jar – I had brought these with me from London.

A large electric coffee percolator stands on a sideboard; we drink coffee which would get about five and a half out of ten. Venetia considers a peppermint Aero from the chocolate drawer and decides against it. Photographer Edward Whitaker sets up photographs and is met by an uncomfortable, tense apprehensive face which relapses into calm assurance after the shutter has clicked.

One has seen Venetia Williams lookalikes all around middle-class society, at art galleries, first nights, charity balls and dinner parties. The difference between them and the trainer is that they eat, drink, smoke, chatter and flirt while Venetia works, makes plans, agonises about feeding, exercising and campaigning Thoroughbreds who have upwards of 240 legs requiring her care, attention and expertise.

For the first 18 years, she was like her contemporaries – primary

school in the West Country, then Down House, near Newbury, where
she played hockey to the touchline-crowd's chants of 'up-down'.
('Clare Balding was head girl before my time.')

Then it was on to secretarial college in Oxford, and when her
friends became chalet girls, or got jobs in art galleries or on fashion
magazines, she spent three years with Gavin Pritchard-Gordon as a
stable lass, before spending time in California and Australia. She also
spent six years as assistant to John Edwards, who trained a mile up
the road from the Williams land, and six months each with Martin
Pipe and Barry Hills.

Then she set up shop with a couple of NH horses. The rest is
history.

Her first runner on the Flat won a Group Three. An inspector from
the Jockey Club came to examine her stables for suitability as a Flat
racehorse establishment, and suggested she buy three starting stalls.

Venetia explained she had only two Flat horses.

Before embarking on further expensive installations, she has
plans to build an equine swimming pool and have a games room –
'everyone should have one.'

It is lunchtime. The choice is bread rolls and chocolate at home,
or a trip to The Cottage of Content. I choose the latter. She drives a
ten-year-old BMW 325 like a rocket. Stopping by a ten-acre field, she
climbs over a gate and lays her hands in turn on six horses. Then we
are off.

In the pub we order home-baked pork pies with chips and
vegetables. She drinks fizzy Lucozade, leaves most of the meat and
reluctantly eats some strawberry and sloe-gin ice cream, and we talk
about marriage.

No-one has asked her since she was 21. It would have to be a man
she could respect. Her friends Philip and Sarah Hobbs have the
perfect partnership: he comes home from the races, they go to bed,
he tells her all that is troubling him and turns over and goes to sleep.
She remains awake all night worrying about his problems. I think
Venetia aspires to the Philip role.

I can sense that she wants to be back in her yard, arranging things, booking Norman Williamson (or Shane Kelly if Norman is unavailable), reading the *Racing Post* and Saturday's edition of the *Daily Telegraph* – the only general newspaper she takes ('Good paper for bedding down horses').

With Venetia, everything comes back to horses.

*

The 1999 series 'Behind Enemy Lines' examined life on the bookmakers' side of the great divide between punters and layers, and was prefaced by a crisp summary of Freud's view of the bookmaking profession:

THE HUMAN RACE, to which so many of my readers belong, tends to rate bookmakers as socially unacceptable – 'gents' rather than gentlemen. By and large, the profession is unloved: if not uncouth certainly less than wholly couth, sartorially second division, seldom encountered at good dinner parties.

It is right that one does not become close friends with these men. The high-octane joy of winning is too precious to be tainted with empathy or compassion for the enemy.

But anger at the niggardly odds is as misplaced as feeling aggrieved at the high asking price of tomatoes at Harrods. As we go to press, betting, like buying vegetables in Knightsbridge department stores, remains optional.

Among his interviewees was the larger-than-life figure of Gary Wiltshire:

FUTURE FAR FROM ROSY

5 MAY 1999

FATHER AND MOTHER were in flowers, so were grandfather and grandmother before that. It was the Wiltshire family business.

They stood in Leather Lane market in Holborn in central London and Gary – who not only went to Highbury Grove School but was caned by Rhodes Boyson himself (for gambling) – had his own flower shop in Gray's Inn Road in his twenties. 'It was opposite the old *Sunday Times* building, till the anti-Murdoch pickets smashed it up,' he recalls.

Gary had always been favourite to become the first Wiltshire to abandon the rose for the ring. The lad who had played in goal for London District Boys, who had trials for Leyton Orient and Arsenal, started clerking at point-to-points. His upwardly mobile family moved to Enfield, where he did not know anyone. He got lonely, put on weight and became arguably the biggest bookmaker in the land, tipping the scales at 23 stone-plus. He married, had children, and separated.

In an average spring week, Wiltshire stands every afternoon at a racecourse, usually on the rails. He tries hard not to miss any Midland point-to-points, and does four evenings at Milton Keynes and Oxford dogs. His one shop is small, 'In Raunds near Kettering, takes practically "nothink"'. Raunds is an old leather industry town fallen on hard times.

He drives 85,000 miles a year in a Mercedes diesel; he changes car every four or five months but retains the number plate – MIODDS. He has homes in Norfolk and Worcestershire, five horses in training with Norma Macauley and Patrick Chamings, a partner called Su and a three-year-old son, Charlie. Proud of Charlie, is Gary; his face lights up when he talks of him.

Wiltshire is not the only bookmaker who suffered on Frankie's golden day at Ascot in September 1996, but his suffering was the stuff legends are made of. 'Got carried away with the atmosphere; went there with no intention of losing money, but thought laying 2-1 about a 10-1 shot was a good thing to do. I just never got out of it.'

He gazes into the middle distance where his six-figure losses went that afternoon, whence they will come back a few thousand at a time. 'But things aren't what they were, and racing [he means racing from the bookmaker's point of view] is in a bad way. All that buying and selling of racecourse pitches to people who haven't worked their way up means there are no percentages in it any more, no profit. The big boys can no longer shorten up. The way we're going, there'll be computerised starting prices; we already have to use computers to give tickets and all the bookies' boards have to look alike. Any day now they'll make us wear uniforms with peaked caps.'

He goes on: 'And another thing, the new Pitches Committee makes you decide where you're going to stand the day before the races. It takes the skill out of it. I used to sit down with a paper and decide at which track I'd do best. I went where I fancied. The ring is now like a factory floor. If it wasn't my way of life I'd turn it in.'

But it is his way of life. Could it be that in every athletic London florist there is a plump country bookmaker trying to get out? Probably not. Wiltshire is unique, in his size, his work-rate and in his love – not just of bookmaking but of the whole sport of racing, owning and breeding. He loves the country, too, and has gone off London.

There can't be many like the man who spends his life on racecourses and nominates Ludlow as his favourite track, who left Newmarket's Guineas meeting after the fifth race to go to a point-to-point to watch his 14-year-old ex-hurdler run in the members' race, and who stands at Milton Keynes dogs where he is now in his 18th year. He also spends much time dreaming of success for the foal of his mare Vado Via, who won him four races in eight days and was covered by Sure Blade.

Su went to a fortune teller who looked into her crystal ball and said: 'I can see a baby horse, you must keep it.'

So Gary kept the foal, had him gelded, sent him to Norma Macauley, and intends calling him Miodds.

Are you expanding?

The answer is in the affirmative. At last month's Wolverhampton auction he bought pitch No. 34 (out of 43) at Newmarket for £10,000. He got £5,000 of that back in winnings on the first day – that was before he left to go to the point-to-point, where he won £100.

He bought a Folkestone pitch for £5,500, lost £7,000 in bets there and sold it for £2,000. At Nottingham the result was almost identical; at Fakenham it was worse, and at Aintree, 'nothink'. But he paid £15,000 for Tatts pitch No. 72 at Cheltenham, 'right at the back of the jungle and it's worth every penny.'

We discuss racecourse food. He says: 'That's all gone, and Barry Cope's stuff has gone down also.' I look at 325 solid pounds of bookmaker and ask where he would go for dinner, anywhere in the land.

He says: 'The Bull's Head at Wootton Wawen – lovely food.' Just like that.

*

In 2001, another Freud series in the Racing Post *involved taking celebrities for a day at the races – including Harry Redknapp, then manager of West Ham United.*

SINKING FEELING FAILS TO GET HARRY DOWN AFTER WAITER SAVES THE DAY

8 FEBRUARY 2001

HARRY REDKNAPP'S GRANNY was a bookies' runner, so his racing pedigree goes back. Before he had learned to read, the old lady would put the racing page in front of him, give the lad a pin, and say: 'Pick out three, Harry.' He would do his bit, she would put on three tuppenny win doubles and a tuppenny each-way treble, and now and then – when the results came in – he got a particularly affectionate hug.

As bookmaking was then illegal, granny was taken away on a regular basis. Redknapp recalls coming home from school and seeing her leave in a Black Maria, from the rear window of which she shouted: 'Yer dinner's in the oven, Harry.' I said she sounded like a good woman. She was a good woman.

For the first 15 years of his life Harry supported his local team, West Ham. Then he signed for them, played for the juniors, had a long and distinguished career in the first team, went off to manage Bournemouth (he was manager there when they beat Manchester United in the FA Cup), and has been back in charge at Upton Park for more than seven years. He is the second-longest serving manager in the Premiership.

I invited him to come racing. He said: 'Yes please,' before I could suggest where or when and, as neither of us are much cop at geography, we decided on Fontwell Park, which we reckoned would not be too far from Poole where he lives. It took him two and a half hours; he parked where the attendant told him to – 'Over there, Harry, you'll be all right.'

When we left Harry was all right, but the car had sunk in the mud. There was no tractor and he had to charm a clutch of heavyweight passers-by to push his massive Mercedes on to dry land. He takes adversity like a man.

Harry loves racing, nothing better than a day at the track. It is important to him to be able to have the horses always in view. He likes the dogs as well.

At Fontwell Park the restaurant is a mock pavilion with windows overlooking some horseboxes, and with insufficient television screens to be able to eat and follow the action with enjoyment.

The restaurant door is stiff – it only opens from the outside if you turn the handle and kick the bottom of the frame, nor does it close properly unless you slam it very hard. If you fail in that, as most folk did, the door flies open, according us diners blasts of Siberian wind.

The food was acceptable, the spelling on the menu gets eight out of ten. We had smoked salmon, beef that was less tender than it might have been and, while I was out negotiating a bet, Harry ate a blackberry and apple tart.

How was it? He said: 'It was all right.' Coming from a man who enthuses about the smallest thing, that was bad news for the caterer.

Harry likes Barry Cope's seafood and fish, especially jellied eels. We promise to have jellied eels next time we go racing and salivate in unison.

Being enthusiastic, extrovert and gregarious has its drawbacks. Before each race strangers come up and ask him for autographs, give him tips and, where I would recommend they go forth and multiply, Harry is friendly, supportive and listens to all advice that comes his way – he even bets on a tip from our waiter, which has to be monumentally daft. (Depressingly, the tip won at decent odds.)

The Redknapp mobile rings incessantly – friends who know he is at Fontwell and offer advice, mates to discuss late-night drinks at Crockford's Casino in London, an agent trying to sell him an Icelandic midfielder, his daughter about her baby who has swallowed some Flash and been taken to hospital in an ambulance, screaming. (Later, when he hears that the child is well, he says: 'We might use her to mop the kitchen floor.')

He has bets with an Irishman at the next table, one who operates in Northern Cyprus. He phones his spread bet to an Index firm, buying lengths at Leicester and Fontwell. Whenever there is a close finish on the track or on the screen, he shouts: 'Come on one of you.'

Over coffee, Charlie Mann offers to sell him a £100,000 Sadler's Wells horse that is certain to win a bumper next weekend. He asks what I think. I think £100k is a lot of money. I would have asked how many people have been offered the horse and refused it. Harry is too nice to be objective, and he is saved by a phone call from a foreign football agent with a dodgy proposal.

After a while he goes off to have a bet in the ring. Everyone recognises him, smiles, calls him Harry. He fits comfortably into the racecourse environment. But it would be hard to imagine an environment into which he did not fit – were he to become an MP he would never lose his seat.

'What's a bad day's betting for you?', I ask.

'My usual is three £50 doubles and a £50 treble; losing £400 would be a bad day,' he says. I fear on that criterion our day was disastrous, only marginally helped by a Leicester chaser who won by a distance, and the waiter's selection. Redknapp is an instinctive rather than a canny bettor – he does not worry about odds, let alone getting fractions.

We have to leave straight after the last, give or take a dozen autographs and some phone calls, because Harry is on Sky TV in Isleworth at 7pm. Neither of us is too sure where Isleworth is, other than near London Airport.

After 25 minutes dislodging his car from the mud we follow signs to London. The car has an electronic system which requires the typing of a destination to advise the route. Harry is not absolutely sure how it works – he drives by instinct – and at 6.52pm, near Osterley, he impulsively takes a left into a housing estate. He reverses out skilfully and makes the broadcast with a couple of minutes to spare.

It would have been three minutes had he not signed an autograph on his way in.

*

The series 'Freud's Unsung Heroes' in 2002 featured 11 of the behind-the-scenes operators on whom horseracing depends: flagman, racecourse doctor, judge, course chef, stalls handler, handicapper, head groundsman, betting ring inspector, stable manager, clerk of the scales – and that hero of the jockeys' changing room, the valet …

MORE THAN JUST A CLEANER – A RIDER'S RIGHT-HAND MAN
1 AUGUST 2002

IAN LAWRENCE IS 35, an Essex boy from Witham. He began his working life breaking in horses for Clifford Percy and had a desire to be Harvey Smith. When he realised that rosettes didn't buy groceries he became a jump jockey, was apprenticed to Bob Champion, had his first ride at Worcester in a two-and-a-half-mile chase on a horse called Lismore.

I wait to hear how he won cleverly, by a neck, to the cheers of the populace. However, Lismore broke down, was pulled up. Ian's first win was for Andy Turnell at Windsor; in a career that spanned nearly a decade ('Brilliant career, I loved it') he rode 120 winners, then became a valet. After that he bought the valeting business from Richard Floyd, who was retiring. He does not want to tell me what he had paid for the business. 'You buy the goodwill; there's nothing else to sell,' he says. 'If a jock does not like the stable from which his valets come, he switches.'

What you do is start with apprentices. Reg Hollinshead trains brilliant apprentices and Ian valets them, hopes they will become professional jocks when they lose their claim. He gets £8.80 for the first ride of the day, a bit less from subsequent rides, and reckons it's not what you take in a day or in a week or month, it is the annual turnover that matters. He makes out.

Ian drives 50,000 miles a year in his people-carrier. Steve Drowne and Richard Quinn are probably his best customers, John Reid was his favourite one. Not all jocks use valets – Chris Rutter, for instance – and it's not a job in which you get good racing info.

'All my jocks try to win; I'd rather spend my money on living than giving it to Ladbrokes,' says Ian.

My dictionary maintains that a valet is 'a gentleman's gentleman; a servant who looks after his master's clothing, food and needs'. Ian, while referring to his job as 'a cleaner', is officially a valet.

I had asked where he would be on Thursday of last week. He looked at his diary and said: 'Sandown or Bath ... it depends.'

Depends on what?

'Decs,' he said, 'and where my jocks are.'

When will he know? 'Half past eleven on Wednesday.'

By noon on that day it transpired it was to be Bath and he offered to give me a lift to the course. Hacks go to the track with a laptop, stewards with their hearing aids, bookmakers take money and tic-tac men bring white gloves. (Come to think of it, I haven't seen a tic-tac man for a while – the species might be extinct.)

Ian's people-carrier has in the back a dozen jockeys' bags, each containing a saddle or two, whip, breeches, boots, tights, white vests and a helmet. To me, the bags look pretty similar. Ian knows exactly which belongs to whom, has washed and tumble-dried and polished the contents, as well as filling up his own bag with all the paraphernalia of his profession: talcum powder, Savlon, shoe polish, saddle soap, stain removers, goggle cream, weights, gloves, aspirins.

We drive up to the back door of the weighing room and he decants the bags, hangs up the saddles on appropriate pegs on the wall strictly in order of the jockeys' seniority. Gary Hind has pole position today, the peg to the right of the scales, though of course if He had been there, He would have had pole. He is Pat Eddery, king of the weighing room, everyone's hero. Dave Curry does Him.

David Mustow, 'Musty' to his friends, is the doyen of the weighing room, with an impressive string that includes Fallon,

Hughes and Fortune (and he remembers valeting me when I rode at Bath 28 years ago). Also in the business is Daniel Fortt, who rode Cogent to win the Hennessy in 1993. Daniel was apprenticed, as was Ian, to Andy Turnell. 'Great trainer of valets,' is the opinion among the weighing-room wags.

In country houses, gentlemen's gentlemen look after their own master. In racing, valets have their jockeys in respect of whom they receive fees, but everyone helps everyone else. The weighing room is abuzz with chatter and banter, comings and goings, shouts of 'Jockeys get ready for the next, thank you' from the doorman who is wholly ignored, and trainers arriving and leaving. Throughout this apparent chaos the valets put out the right clothes, saddles and boots for their clients, remind an apprentice he will have to shed a pound for the fifth, find the appropriate colours brought in by the travelling head lads and answer their jocks' mobile telephones.

'Hello, darling sweetheart,' says Ian, picking up Vince Slattery's. 'Vince is riding in the two o'clock at Bath, ring back at five past two ... though being Vince you'd better make it ten past.'

To one not used to life in a weighing room, the sight of a large wooden-floored, mini-gym peopled by short, thin men smoking cigarettes, mumbling into their mobiles and endlessly checking their weights on the scales is a memorable sight. Being stark bollock naked makes them all equal, despite major differences in equipment.

Before racing began, they gravitated from sauna to scales to tea room and back to their benches and mobiles. Once into the contest, the noise and the nudity abate somewhat. Jocks come and go, arriving wearing green and white, leaving in orange and black. The valets open bags, polish a boot, remove a stain, slip weights into a saddle, get cups of tea and chat about their skiing expedition to France last winter and plans for hunting with the Cotswold on Christmas Eve.

They also ring their girlfriends and their divorce lawyers. One common factor of the weighing room is marital problems not

unconnected with leaving home at sparrow's fart and not coming
back until evening racing is over.

A marriage-guidance counsellor, possibly paid for by selling
postcard-sized pics of naked jocks, would be a valuable addition
to the cast.

*

ON THE COUCH

2 DECEMBER 2004

I DECIDED TO go to Orpington to meet a tipster as I thought
this column could do with a little inside information on how to
make money – especially with Christmas coming up. I was last
in Orpington 40-odd years ago, when my political party won a
by-election and Harold Macmillan was so distraught he sacked
half his Cabinet. 'Sacked the wrong half,' said Jeremy Thorpe, our
leader. For good measure he asked the Prime Minister at
Question Time whether it was not a bit unusual to lay down his
friends for his life.

Mark Winstanley, the tipster I am meeting, is generally known
as 'Couch', a name gained for his preference for lying down when
all around him were up and about – doing things like kicking
footballs or running marathons. Couch is six foot four inches,
weighs upwards of 18 stone, is married to a wife from Thailand
and has two very young children, formally known as Number-
One-Son and Number-Two-Son.

He has telephones the way other people have mice; also television
screens and DVD players to permit him to watch Bangor, Fakenham,
Wetherby, Thurles and Lingfield at the same time.

Travelling from Charing Cross, I have given him my time of
arrival, thinking he might meet me. He does not; he doesn't
drive, took the driving test six times and failed each one.

Does his wife drive? She doesn't speak English. Does Couch

'In the paddock, I recognised my jockey instantly by the fact that he was wearing my colours.' Briefing Jason Tate before Four Legs Good's first race at Ascot, July 2000.

Naas, 1967: Clement
Freud's race-riding debut.
Left: in the paddock with
trainer Toby Balding;
above: last-minute
adjustments as he
introduces himself to
Saxon King; *right*: returning
to the weighing room.

The £1,000-a-side match against Sir Hugh Fraser, 30 September 1972. *This page*: on Toby Balding's scales and aboard Winter Fair on the gallops; leaving the paddock at Haydock Park. *Opposite*: Freud and Winter Fair come home clear of Fraser and Star Award.

Four Legs Good: *above*, with (left to right) Charlie Wilson (10 per cent),
trainer Giles Bravery (10 per cent), groom Eric Campbell, Clement Freud (70 per cent)
and Andy Wright (10 per cent); *below*, second from left, finishing eighth in her
first race, the Capel Cure Sharp Maiden Stakes at Ascot, 28 July 2000: 'While eighth
can be a satisfactory position to occupy, this ceases to be the case when there are
but seven other contestants.'

Above: 'What we are going to do is to cut off your balls' – following which Orpen Wide wins three in a row, culminating in the Littlewoods Bet Direct AW Jockeys' Championship Handicap at Wolverhampton, 14 January 2005, with Phillip Makin in the saddle.

Right: Freud with trainer Robert Stronge at a rainy Ascot on 2 November 2002, before his horse Star Protector won the United House Heating Novices' Hurdle.

Contrasting lunch styles: *above*, Freud on the railway bridge at Plumpton, 1965; *below*, Freud in his box at Ascot, 2004.

speak Thai? He does not. The ingredients of a perfect marriage.

A taxi drops me outside his house – neat, detached with a nice garden at the back. 'Worth over £300,000,' says the driver. I tell him to wait in case I have the wrong address, walk up the path, ring the bell, am greeted with a smile by a small Oriental woman and give a thumbs-up to the taxi man.

Couch is in his sitting room, on the telephone. He's saying: 'What price?' and there follows a pause and he then says: 'I'll give that a swerve.' He greets me warmly (I have known Couch since he was a footstool) and says: 'Woodrow's working.' Thinking he means the late chairman of the Tote, I inform Couch that Woodrow is dead. Couch is, not unusually for him, speaking in rhyming slang. Woodrow means diet. Wyatt – diet, get it? I got it. I have indeed lost a stone and a half in the last month.

We talk racing and he mentions that he has a greyhound running at Hove in an A2 hurdle race that night. 'Won't win, too high class. Keep an eye on her when she runs 695 metres. Her name is Mrs Couch.'

He sits on ante-post vouchers: Shamardal at 33-1 for the Two Thousand Guineas, Calling Brave for the King George at the same price and Beef Or Salmon at 14-1 for the Gold Cup. He bets via a friend who puts money on Betdaq, and he has a five-grand deposit. 'I don't owe anyone anything,' he says.

He writes for papers, sells tips via advertisements on racing channels that cost £36 a day and bring him in £1 of the £1.50 punters pay for their call.

There is a noise from behind the sofa and he gets up, comes back with sub-one-year-old Number-Two-Son, whom he nurses with skill – until his wife comes and takes him away to collect his brother from school. Couch likes appearing on TV. His language causes TV to rest him a lot.

He has one great fear: having to work – like his school-mates from Downham, near Catford dog track, who go out to earn £40 a day labouring. He talks, watches videos and racing programmes, admires John McCririck – 'He's irreplaceable' – and Jason Weaver – 'Best sense-talking jockey' – and is generous with his tips: phone rings, he tells them.

That day the tip was an odds-on Martin Pipe-trained novice hurdler. Couch says: 'If you don't tip winners, they stop ringing you, and I don't cheat – I don't give five odds-on favourites and one 100-1 shot, then claim average winning odds of 16-1.'

On the whole he works on form and watches races over and over on television. Sometimes he gets inside information and pays for it. We watch a race from Lingfield and he points to a horse who runs into third place, whose jockey is sitting absolutely still. 'Watch out for that one next time.'

I tell him of my part-ownership of Motivator. Couch says the horse is a serious player for the Derby if the going is soft.

Couch supports Chelsea; his dad was a steward at Stamford Bridge for about 30 years. He started betting aged eight – 'Mum and Dad don't gamble, but my grandfather took me to a betting shop and I put 10p on Gay Trip.'

The family went on holiday to Ramsgate and his sister rode in the Donkey Derby. Couch backed her at 6-4. She fell off – 'Haven't spoken to her since.'

After school he became a telephone engineer, had a year at Brixton College, was a trainee accountant, and after that got sacked from being a city messenger for spending too much time in the betting shop. He then worked for *Racing & Football Outlook*. 'Went there as a tipster, tipped everything Pipe trained, did that for five or six years, did my money learning my job.'

His biggest win was £6,000 on Snow Ridge at 5-1.

We talk of racecourses – 'Towcester is so steep I saw Ranulph Fiennes leave.' And on the subject of trainers, he likes Stan Moore, the only trainer called after a London Underground station. Annually he does the Breeders' Cup, then Las Vegas. He

plays blackjack and loves American football. He supports
Baltimore and Seattle.

It's time for us to go out to lunch. Do I like Italian? He rings for
a taxi, tells me it will be there in 25 minutes.

The Italian is closed, there's an Indian next door and he likes Indian
(his wife won't do Indian) and we get some really ordinary Indian
food. Couch drinks pints of Cobra beer and as our Madras curry
arrives, his mobile phone turns itself on, blasts out the commentary
on the race for which he has tipped the Pipe horse. It wins at 4-6.

Couch is 41 and intends to retire when he is 50 – before he
loses it. He will go to Thailand, buy a house, lie on the beach, get
drunk, find some illegal bookmakers, bring up his children and
probably start a business related to gambling.

I tell him Buddhas don't gamble. I am wrong. It is just that
they are not supposed to gamble.

He says: 'The wife plays cards every night with dozens of local
Thai friends.' Do they play for money? He looks at me in some
surprise: 'What else do you play for?'

He tips me a horse that nearly won the Hennessy and I forget
to tell him that we have something in common – couches were
the bedrock of my family's trade.

*

'Why is there no Racing Post *cookery correspondent?', asked Freud
in this piece, published just before Christmas 2004. But there was ...*

ALL THE INGREDIENTS
FOR A HAPPY CHRISTMAS
15 DECEMBER 2004

AS A TOKEN of seasonal goodwill it had crossed my mind to
commend to readers investment on a horse that would win at

long odds at Kempton, and suggest a double with a talented outsider for the Welsh National, one who has worked astonishingly well over the last few days, and still represents excellent value for money at the odds on offer.

And then it occurred to me that the *Racing Post* subscriber is already showered by a multiplicity of serious advice that can be gleaned from professionals of proven accomplishment; thus my contribution to readers would be akin to bringing yet another Christmas pudding to the feast. Yuletide exhilaration should be a matter of absolute enjoyment rather than open to discussion. So we'll write about food.

The trouble about Christmas turkey is that it ill-becomes a host to err on the side of meanness in the matter of the bird's weight; as a consequence there is much turkey meat left over from the festive dinner and do what you will – braise it, stew it, curry it or mince the meat to make turkey burgers – you are on a loser. Turkey sandwiches are dull (stuffing sandwiches have much going for them) and in truth, turkey meat on its second, third and subsequent appearances should play a minor rather than leading role in the gastro-event it graces.

Why is there no *Racing Post* cookery correspondent? Good question. Possibly something to do with the fact that betting is a more satisfactory form of gambling than cooking. There are also those who resent wasting time that could be spent studying form, on moving among the pots and pipkins and having to reach for reference books to make sense of words like blanch, sweat, seal, clarify and bard.

And many feel that £10 each-way on a 33-1 shot in a handicap provides more pleasure for your money than 600g of fillet steak. Next week, when the dread Lady F. and I go to Barbados – she for the climate, me for Garrison Savannah racecourse, where it is not unusual to witness major races won by horses of my sort of age who are tubed, fired, gelded, visored, tongue-strapped and fitted with earplugs – my *Racing Post* diary notes that three days have been set aside for race-track holidays. So, what will you do – apart from feeling apprehensive about the turkey days that lie ahead?

Go to the kitchen, say I, and produce delicacies of quality and longevity that will enhance the taste of the broad-breasted bronze turkey and its cousins: birds all, that had short uneventful lives spent in considerable discomfort for the express purpose of providing gastronomic pleasure.

Bread sauce is classic and English and frowned upon by the folk across the Channel who think they know it all, even though they use many of our culinary terms – like consommé, soufflé and hors d'oeuvres.

There are a number of things to remember when producing this sauce which is fashioned of bread, butter, milk, onion and cloves:

The acidity of onions tends to curdle milk.

Bread which has been boiled has nothing going for it.

Cloves, which are principally grown in Zanzibar and Madagascar (they only flourish near the sea) are the flowerbuds of tall evergreen trees, plucked when pink, and dried in the sun on mats. They give forth a great flavour but are no fun to chew.

What you do is peel an onion the size of a tangerine, chop it finely (or give it ten seconds in a blender) and simmer this over a low flame in a covered pan with a sherry glass of white wine or lager, 2oz butter and three cloves. After three minutes, add half a pint of milk (the acidity of the onions will have been taken up by the butter), bring to the boil and simmer gently for five more minutes. Turn off the flame, add soft white breadcrumbs (liquidise rindless slices of white bread) until you have the consistency of rice pudding.

Now fish out the cloves, add salt and pepper, stir well and store the sauce in a cool place until you have need of it. The best way to warm this is to add some cream and heat gently in a pan. If you are quite thin or unworried about extra weight, you can add a tablespoon of the fat from the roasting dish in which you have cooked the turkey.

For grown-ups you might make one of our other great British sauces, one which the French cannot pronounce and of which they are jealous. Cumberland sauce: a confection made of redcurrant jelly, ruby port and English mustard garnished with slivers of lemon zest. It is eaten cold or lukewarm and goes wonderfully well with boring white meat – like sliced breast of turkey. It is also brilliant with boiled ham.

Put into a pan the contents of a jar of redcurrant jelly and a rounded dessertspoon of made English mustard (Colman's powder plus milk) and whisk this over a low flame until blended.

Turn off flame and when contents of pan are no longer very hot, add half the redcurrant jelly jar of port. Mix, cool and add the zest – the outside layer of a lemon cut into thin strips and boiled for ten minutes in a minimum of water.

If the sauce is too strong, add more melted jelly. Too bland, more mustard. Too thin, add a little dissolved gelatine.

Too time consuming, buy Cumberland sauce at a supermarket … but it won't be the same and you can't claim ownership.

Please have a good Christmas and if my horse wins the 2.00 at Southwell tomorrow, I shall be surprised.

For the surprising outcome of that 2.00 at Southwell, see page 54 above. And a year later, on 21 December 2005, Freud's pre-Yuletide column contained further expert advice on Christmas cooking:

This year I shall be eating turkey; not just eating roast turkey for my Christmas lunch, but breathing in roasting turkey from when I get up on Sunday. The previous night I wrap my brute loosely in tin foil, having anointed it with well-seasoned, sizzling butter and put into its cavity some lemon halves and mixed herbs.

I let it cook overnight on gas mark hardly-anything-at-all, what is called a cool oven. The house is wondrously filled with forthcoming succulence. Turkeys are poorly designed – the legs needing a different cooking time from the breast – so I tie the bird with string to present a tight parcel and by mid-morning it will have given up a pint or more of glorious liquid, while the meat needs nothing sharper than a fork to be portioned and served with bread sauce and stuffing.

I cook my stuffing in its own vessel, rather than ignominiously sticking it into wherever it fits inside the bird. I use minced pork, minced bacon, onions, chestnuts, juniper berries, mustard, candied peel, stale bread and chilli pepper; the mixture is blended in a liquidiser with raw eggs and ruby port. I take a teaspoonful of the mixture, fried for two minutes each side in a pan over a low flame and taste before adjusting the seasoning: salt, tabasco and black treacle are all at hand. This then goes for an hour or two in an oven at gas mark two. Baking stuffing is not an exact science.

*

AN INSPECTOR CALLS: BREAKFAST AT WOLVERHAMPTON
19 JANUARY 2005

WHEN I WORKED in a hotel in the south of France, the managing director impressed on us staff the importance of recognising *Michelin Guide* inspectors and ensuring that all went well with their meals. Approval by Michelin was, still is, money in the bank.

I remember asking how I would know such a man, to be told that they tended to come on their own, have dandruff, order really inexpensive wine, make surreptitious notes on a pad, nick a menu and under-tip the waiter.

I never identified an inspector myself, but used the information to have better-than-I-should-have-had dinners by going to restaurants with a notebook in which I pretended to scribble ... and I stole menus to make them believe I was the genuine article. I also left very small gratuities.

When I decided that it might be of interest to 'inspect' stable staff facilities, I toyed with doing this anonymously, then realised that neither my age nor my weight made me appear a likely person to earn his living shovelling horse shit, driving a box or leading up in the parade ring.

As a consequence, the information you are about to read (if you read on) came to me anecdotally; what I gleaned was from conversations with stable staff, to whom I promised confidentiality. Hacks do not disclose their sources, unless of course the money is right.

Every racecourse is expected to accommodate and provide sustenance to grooms and box drivers, all of whom would aim to arrive several hours before the race in which their charges run; not infrequently do they travel in the evenings so that they and their horses can have a night's sleep before the big occasion.

They speak highly of the hospitality at Cheltenham, Sandown, Ascot and York.

Salisbury and Wincanton are deemed to be expensive: '50p for tea or coffee when it costs hardly any money at all to buy a teabag.'

Warwick is a dump, Bath is plain bad and when it comes to staying the night, Doncaster is grotty, Beverley and Catterick are worse (Catterick *the* worst). Carlisle puts grooms into a portable building and leaves them to it, while Cartmel provides a scout hut … not even with any scouts.

They speak enthusiastically of Kelso, where they are invited out to dinner, and Musselburgh radiates Scottish generosity, accommodating grooms at bed-and-breakfast places at the course's expense.

Epsom was bad, is going to get better; Towcester has improved and, when staff get to go to French tracks, B&Bs are so inexpensive they find one near a patisserie and achieve contentment at small cost.

Last Thursday, my excellent Orpen Wide won his third race on the trot since we had him gelded – making us wonder what to cut off next to keep him winning. He ran at Wolverhampton and I thought I would try to infiltrate the canteen, then decided it would be more courteous to ask the clerk of the course if he would mind my going there. 'Not at all, come and have breakfast with me,' said this good man.

Wolverhampton is an oddity of a racecourse; wide open spaces, minimal attendances for their all-weather afternoon meetings, no rails bookmakers, a Tote credit office where you have to go to the counter and shout 'Shop' to get attention and, on the track, a run-in which may be the shortest in the land.

Nevertheless, the prize-money is respectable, the natives are friendly, and when you own the winner they do all the right things: give you a piece of silverware, a bottle of champagne and a video of the race and then invite you upstairs where drinks are dispensed to winning owners as a right – rather than because they want to make a fuss of you.

The staff hostel is tucked away, not far from the weighing room. It is a chalet with half a dozen pleasant, clean, twin-bedded rooms. There are adequate ablution facilities for men and for women and in the caff below, £3 gets you egg, bacon, sausage and baked beans, tea or coffee and toast. They do a £5 steak-and-chip lunch, which is nicely produced. The chef/manager shifts 100-plus meals a day and, unlike the great restaurants of Europe, hardly anybody sits on their own, makes notes, nicks the menu (predominantly because there are no menus) and, for the record, you don't leave a tip.

We worry about stable staff, all of us – worry about their wellbeing, their pay, their hours. Now I am not saying this in order to get a bundle of mail telling me I don't know my arse from my elbow, but I am not sure that they all worry about their plight as much as we do. Staff do the job they do because they love it. If they cannot ride or train, they prefer to be with horses than away from them.

Just as I, when I became a Liberal Member of Parliament, did not expect high office (it's coming up to 90 years since Liberals held office) but simply preferred to be in the House of Commons rather than fill supermarket shelves and read the *Liberal News* in my lunch hour.

There are important things with which to be concerned in racing: the ratio between monies spent on buying, training and running a horse and the rewards that come back to owners via prize-money is about the most serious. In the United States, the average owner sees his annual investment returned, whereas in Britain, the money that comes out of racing is about 20 per cent of what the average owner puts in. Orpen Wide, a cheap horse at the breeze-up sale, has won thrice and been placed the same number of times in 11 outings. He has now just recouped.

*

IN THE LAND OF ELDERLY NUTTERS
16 FEBRUARY 2005

ONE NO LONGER sits next to people in Upper Class on Virgin Atlantic. Each passenger is an island and, on the island to my right, in a chair that is very much too big for him, sits a man reading the *Racing Post*. Our eyes meet. I thought he might recognise me from my photograph, which appears in the paper with monotonous regularity, but I am wrong.

When we are about halfway to Miami the man falls asleep and I observe him closely: his pixie face does not relax in his slumber, as do the faces of most sleeping people. His eyes are closed, his breathing regularly causing his chest to rise and fall, but he looks like a man with purpose, a man about to ask complicated questions or respond to an accusation, albeit with his eyes closed.

When he wakes and starts to look into the middle distance, I cross the aisle and introduce myself, explaining that I write for the paper he has been reading, was going to Gulfstream Park where I know he is riding and ask whether he would care to have dinner with me in Miami on Saturday or Sunday ... if eating food is something in which he indulges.

He tells me he reads the *Post* for the form pages not the features, that he enjoys eating and that dinner on Sunday will be fine. He owns a flat near the racecourse, but can't remember the phone number so he writes in capital letters on the back of a visa waiver form, 'USA MOBILE K FALLON' and an area code – 975 – followed by the seven-figure number.

He thinks that his ride in Saturday's big race has an excellent chance of winning, and I am chuffed by his reaction, for Fallon is famously wary of hacks, who have given him a hard time. We talk of Henry Cecil, for whom he has high regard, and I tell him I know it was not him who was rumoured to have been in Natalie Cecil's shower. He knows who it was – as do I.

Gulfstream Park, some 25 miles north of downtown Miami, is a mile dirt circuit on the outside of a tight turf track. The huge grandstand has been demolished and is being rebuilt to open next January – the workforce is at it night and day. Tented accommodation has been put up to cater for members of the Platinum Club, the Turf Club and the restaurants. Sadly, the finishing post remains where it was, in front of the building site, a furlong beyond the temporary canvas enclosure.

Racing in the States seems to attract nutters, unlike the sport in Britain and Ireland, which is frequented by gentlefolk. In view of the average age of folk in Florida – which is not far from deceased – Gulfstream is patronised by elderly nutters who contribute little to the atmosphere; in three days I hear only one winner being cheered. The racing is handsomely organised, the Tote works properly and, despite minimal attendances, the substantial off-course betting ensures decent pools.

The sun shines in southern Florida and jockeys like riding there, so Fallon has stiff competition.

Last Friday he had one ride, in the tenth race, and over the weekend he had only two a day. He is considered a turf rather than a dirt rider, and has a total tally of six wins from 50 rides. But they like him – jockeys, punters and officials all say he is good on the grass, and a nice, quiet man.

I ask him why he does not get more rides.

Probably has a lousy agent, is the reply, and there are too many jockeys chasing too few rides. Also, trainers put up jocks who ride three or four lots each morning for nothing.

On Saturday, our ex-champion jockey's big-race mount, Angela's Love, is 7-2. She leads from the start, but Fallon is outridden by Edgar Prado on Binya, the 5-2 favourite who surges past him half a furlong from the post. On Sunday, he picks up a spare ride and does brilliantly to come second at 12-1, then steers a fancied mount three horses wide around four bends before dropping out.

That morning, I ring Fallon to give him the name, address and phone number of the restaurant where I have a reservation for dinner, Palm's. However, the number he has given me on the plane is unobtainable. I ring the operator, and am told that there is no area code 975. I write him a note on my headed paper with the address and phone number of Palm's and put it in an envelope bearing the name of my hotel and have it delivered to the Gulfstream weighing room.

When I return after racing there is a message for me from Mr Fallon's American agent saying Kieren has received a letter about dinner, but knows nothing about it and doesn't know who it is from.

I ring the agent and explain.

When I get to the restaurant there is no Fallon, but the manager tells me there is a message from a jockey's agent.

I ask whether the agent said if the jockey was coming for dinner.

The manager says: 'That did not figure in the conversation, but I'll keep a look out for a jockey-sized customer.'

After a while, I order a small lobster. Palm's don't do small lobsters, they start at 4lb and go up to 7lb. Would I like a male or a female lobster? I have never been asked that question before, but got one about the size of my no-show guest with enough creamed spinach to last me forever, followed by a chocolate cake that measured a cubic foot and cost what I had won on the Pick 3 a couple of hours earlier.

On Monday afternoon, on my way to the airport, I stop at Gulfstream to watch Fallon ride Watershed Event in the 3.35. On the Morning Line the horse is 6-1, but is backed into 5-2 favourite and, when the field passes me a furlong from the winning post, Kieren is in fourth place making terrific progress.

There is a phot-finish, but he comes third. I catch my plane home, marginally wiser, but significantly poorer.

*

EXCLUSIVE: RACING NEEDS A ROONEY
19 JULY 2006

IT IS EVERY journalist's ambition to come up with a scoop: a story of arresting importance that is yours and yours only, that can be published under a banner headline marked 'exclusive'.

I once achieved a scoop. It was in 1964, I was on a bus that shuttled between the Olympic Village in Tokyo and the main stadia where athletics, swimming, boxing, etc. took place, and a young woman who was standing in front of me asked whether I would not give her my seat. She looked fit and well and was younger than me; I asked her why.

She said: 'Because I won a gold medal last night.' Any decent person would have congratulated her. As a journalist devoid of finer feelings I asked whether anyone else knew. No. It had been late at night; she was a fencer and the press people had all gone home.

So it was I who scooped the newspapers of Britain with the information that Gillian Sheen of London had won one of our very few golds (Mary Rand was another), and I got a 'well done' telegram from my editor.

I thought of this at the weekend when a Sunday paper's front page announced a World Exclusive: Wayne Rooney ... in his own words – I Can't Sleep Without Noise Of Hoover.

It is symbolic of my obsolescence as a hack that if I had gleaned this information, I would have been unaware of its import, let alone its value. As it is, I am probably in possession, unknowingly, of a string of World Exclusives: My Distinguished Younger Son Doesn't Eat Mushrooms. I wonder how many people knew that.

Do not snigger, as Frankie Howerd used to say, adding 'snigger ye not' to enhance the laugh. We all know that were the story about anyone but Wayne Rooney, the conditional insomnia would not have got a mention – unless perhaps Rooney is paid a retainer by Hoover, who are having a hard time of it with everyone buying Dysons.

Where I am getting to, and I admit it has taken a time to reach the destination, is that racing badly needs someone of comparable fame to the young Manchester United striker.

Frankie Dettori had it through sheer skill and niceness and riding seven winners in an afternoon at Ascot, but will have to do that again to make the front page with trivialities. Kieren Fallon is a name on many peoples' lips, mostly for the wrong reasons, but his exploits remain firmly on the sports or legal pages.

What we need for racing to make an impact is a new star, preferably female, who is stunning, photogenic, plays poker, comes from a titled family, has a disabled sister and drives fast cars. Ideally, she should be a jockey, but it would not harm her fame-to-be were she a stalls handler.

Until she makes an appearance, we just have to sit back and see the sport we love overshadowed from a publicity point of view by overpaid footballers and their underused Wags.

*

SALES OF ORGANIC BROCCOLI REMAIN STEADY

10 MAY 2008

STOKE CITY ARE back to playing football in the top division. There's not much point being an old journalist if you don't tell anyone, and write about how it was a couple of generations ago. In 1958, on a bridge over the River Trent, I picked up the telephone in a box, dialled 0 and asked for a transfer charge call to Fleet Street 0202.

'What is your name?'

I told the operator and when I got through, asked for the sports editor. 'I am near the Victoria Ground in Stoke and the match I was to report on is postponed due to a waterlogged pitch,' I told him.

'So?', said Michael Davie.

What shall I do?

'Write 450 words before five o'clock is what you do.'

So for my £6 match fee I wrote paragraphs of purple prose about the pride of the Potteries, the return from Blackpool of Stanley Matthews and the Bluebell line that ran special trains to Stoke for the home matches. I was dictating this to a copy-taker who interrupted me about halfway through to say: 'You haven't given me the effing score.'

'There is no effing score due to there being no effing match.'

'Go on with your crap then.'

Filing copy in olden days used to involve telephone operators, copy-takers, sub-editors and hot metal printers. No more, although sub-editors still decide how and what to put in and where to place headlines and straplines around articles. Worst-case scenario: a statement about sales of organic broccoli remaining steady appears under the headline SALES OF ORGANIC BROCCOLI REMAIN STEADY, a considerable disincentive to read on. One of my favoured headlines appeared over a story concerning the escaped inmate of an asylum who sexually assaulted two women in a launderette and ran off:

NUT SCREWS WASHERS AND BOLTS.

On 26 July 1992, Sunday racing in the UK was finally introduced at Doncaster. They did all that could be done to make this acceptable to everyone – except Julian Wilson, who was never going to be having any of it. Like a member of the Flat Earth Society, his views were constant and advertised: change was not an option.

It all went rather well, from the opening address by the Bishop of Doncaster to the results, which proved that failure to rest on the seventh day does not affect form. I was there, and wrote about the event in the *Sporting Life* the following morning to find my report headed: OH GOD OUR HELP IN WAGERS PAST.

5

THE RACEGOER

❛ And it came to pass that I was looking through my *Racing Post* diary, chanced to examine a map of Irish courses, saying: yes, hum, been there, rode there, got drunk there, drenched there, fleeced there ...❜

From the world's most exotic and glamorous racecourses to the most humble, Clement Freud was an avid racegoer, enthralled by the different personality and atmosphere of each track. A measure of the appeal which racecourses had for him is that in March 2009, the month before he died, he travelled to a remote corner of west Wales to witness at first hand progress on Ffos Las, the new racecourse under construction in Carmarthenshire. 'It is wet in Wales,' he reported, 'and in west Wales it is wetter.' While he did not live to see racing take place at Ffos Las, a visit to Roscommon in October 2004 provided a significant landmark.

IN PURSUIT OF A COLLECTOR'S ITEM
6 OCTOBER 2004

MY DICTIONARY DECLARES that a collector is one who seeks to acquire and set together examples of specimens such as books, minerals or mementos. My dictionary wraps up the whole English language in 1,984 pages, which is why there is no mention of philately, insectology, let alone the anoraks who stand at the end of Peterborough station platforms, checking engine numbers as they flash past.

I am a collector only in as much as I hesitate to throw away anything: I retain cricket scorecards from my youth – partly filled in and lightly stained with Tizer.

Plymouth Argyle programmes are there, dating back to the managerial days of Jack Tresadern, as are copies of Hansard and articles written for the late lamented *Punch*.

Were the definition of a collector more detailed, I doubt I would begin to qualify, for while I possess all these things, I would not know where they are. My filing system used to be a box marked Good and another Bad; my secretary had instructions to clear Bad every six months and keep Good until the box was full, prior to consigning it to an attic bulging with cardboard containers. The system was simple to execute, hard to decipher, for a bill would be in Bad until it was paid, when the receipt is filed in Good.

There were Plymouth programmes mostly in Bad and some of my horses' exploits never, ever made it into the Good box.

Let me return to collecting: I do not – not any more, not consciously – collect, but by the time a certain age is reached, the multiplicity of things done, places visited, events watched, makes me a collector of sorts. For instance, as a sometime politician, travel writer, sports correspondent and man whose hand shoots up in the air when the question is 'Who wants to go on a freebie?', I have visited every European country except Albania. Not deliberately, you understand, but when asked whether I had been to Iceland – yes, I watched Bobby Fischer play Boris Spassky in Reykjavik.

Finland? Covered a parliamentary election in Finland.

Wrote about football matches in Sweden and Denmark, drove in a rally in Norway, fought in the Army in Germany, visited my grandfather in Austria.

I have eaten and drunk for magazines in Romania and Bulgaria, made after-dinner speeches in Turkey, had a rich godmother in Greece and was once asked to design a national cuisine for Israel: did not work, because of the dietary laws.

Try as you will, you can't miss Belgium – although I have never seen the point of Belgians. I spent a holiday in Yugoslavia, skied in Switzerland, wrote about punctuality of trains in Luxembourg, cooked in a casino in Spain and had a villa in Portugal.

I have been racing in Poland, tried to find Robert Maxwell's millions in Liechtenstein and judged goulash in Hungary.

What has this got to do with the *Racing Post*, do I hear you ask? In a nutshell, it has to do with 'collecting' racecourses.

In press boxes from Newton Abbot to Perth, hacks speak of courses they have visited and those they have not. If you are a master of your trade, there is no good reason why you should ever have been to Leicester, Folkestone, Hamilton, Catterick, Beverley or Towcester. Minor journalists don't get to Ascot, York, Newmarket, Goodwood or Epsom. Welsh scribblers avoid Yarmouth and few Scots are sent to cover Brighton. Hardly anyone goes to Ludlow.

Some years ago, I realised that of the 60 courses in Britain, I had been to all but Cartmel. No earthly reason why I should go to Cartmel ... other than it was there and there was a column to write. So I went.

It transpired to have been similar to my eldest daughter's schooling. Each day she left home to go to school, but never seemed to get there. I had a letter about a parents' evening, went along, and they were hugely pleased to see me: watched me on television, listened to me on the radio, read me – what was I doing at the school? Had I a child who was thinking of going there?

I explained about my eldest daughter. Had she perhaps another name than Freud? No. It transpired that she took the bus in the direction of her school and then went to a café and worked part-time at Ladbrokes.

I set out for Cartmel one Saturday morning, changed at Crewe, went to Preston to be told that there were no stopping trains for Lancaster, best to go to Carlisle and get the branch line back to Barrow-in-Furness, then complete the loop to Grange-over-Sands, which was near the course, and that would get me in only ten minutes after the last race.

For many years I was a 59-racecourse man (counting Newmarket as two), although I have made up for that: been to Cartmel five times in the last four years.

There are 27 racecourses in Ireland. I have ridden at two, watched horses which Eddie Harty suggested I should buy at many others, covered festivals at Listowel, Galway and Punchestown. I have watched a five-year-old blinkered gelding win the Derby at Down Royal, never managed to be at Fairyhouse when the oyster bar was open and experienced one of my all-time embarrassing moments at the Curragh.

At the pre-race lunch party, a girl with a pen and a piece of paper came up to me and I shook my head. As she did not go away, I explained that I do not give autographs, ever. She moved away, came back a minute later, approaching me from the other side. 'I am sorry, I don't do autographs. Never have. Won't.'

She wouldn't take no for an answer, so I said it more slowly, more loudly, and she said: 'I am the waitress trying to take your order for lunch.'

And it came to pass that I was looking through my *Racing Post* diary, chanced to examine a map of Irish courses, saying: yes, hum, been there, rode there, got drunk there, drenched there, fleeced there ... until I got to Roscommon.

I have never been to Roscommon; have been to Laytown, which only has one meeting a year on the sands, at low tide; never to Roscommon.

The racecourse is situated one mile north of the town on the Castlebar Road. It is 85 miles from Dublin, 48 from Galway, 50 from Sligo and 20 miles from Athlone, the epicentre of the Emerald Isle.

My encyclopaedia informs that Roscommon is a county in the province of Connaught, covers 990 square miles and is bounded by the Shannon and the Suck. I hadn't known about the Suck.

There are hills in the north and east and the country has many lakes. Cattle, sheep and pigs are reared, oats and potatoes grown and there was a little coal. Roscommon is the county town and I learned from my diary that one of the eight annual days' racing was Monday 4 October.

I telephoned the clerk of the course, spoke to the manager, told him I was coming to take a look at his track ... might we meet?

He was entirely supportive.

'How will I find you?'

He explained that the place was not overlarge, he would find me. I set about planning my trip. Going to Ireland used to be an 'event'. You gave a farewell dinner party, looked out clothes suited to 'soft' weather, promised to bring back Barm Brack and Bewley tea and smoked wild salmon, also send postcards. No more.

Taxi to Victoria Station. Gatwick Express (late) to the airport. Stand in a queue at the Ryanair desk until 40 minutes before take-off time when the woman behind the counter said 'That's it' and left. The man in front of me blew his top. This, he said, was the last time he would fly sodding Ryanair.

I pointed out that he hadn't flown Ryanair, so he got angry with me, too. I telephoned the car hire people in Dublin to cancel my vehicle and rang the course manager to explain my inability to make it and apologised.

He said: 'That's all right. The course is waterlogged anyway.'

Undaunted, the following week Freud tried again.

FREUD'S FULL HOUSE AT ROSCOMMON
13 OCTOBER 2004

THE TRANSFORMATION WHEREBY Nearly-man became Been-everywhere-man took place on Monday. *Mastermind* contestants who select 'The Life and Times of Clement Freud' as their specialist subject would be wise to commit to memory the date: 11 October 2004. That's when Freud's visitation of all British Isles racecourses was completed.

Prior to this I had a nagging feeling which pertains among collectors who are an item short of fulfilment – that gods of chance who monitor human progress take pride in furnishing impediments. Only last week they prevented success by causing me to miss my plane and waterlogging the course for good measure. Some might have taken this as an omen and let matters stand, resting on the tally of 26 out of 27 Irish courses. Members of the Horserace Writers' and Photographers' Association are made of sterner stuff.

No longer does the question, 'Have you been to all Irish racecourses?' receive the answer, 'All except Roscommon.' 'Yes', is the elective reply. Yes, it was going to be; yes it now is.

Roscommon, the county town of that name, is similar to other Irish midland towns: a wide main street, car parking as its major industry, and I found a newly opened eaterie called the Comfy Coffee Cafe; it is painted pink on the outside and customers sit on sofas, which is actually a rotten position in which to drink cappuccino and consume a bacon sandwich.

None of the many local newsagents had copies of the *Racing Post* – 'We ran out early because of today's meeting here' – and several shop windows had notices proclaiming that the Coachman's Inn presented *Wallop the Cat* on Saturday ... last Saturday.

There appears to be a glut of Queens potatoes (€2.50 for a 10kg bag) and had I had a couple of million euros on me, I would have bought the Royal Hotel, which is a splendid, faded Edwardian edifice and could become a national treasure.

I found the usual goodly number of pubs and bookmakers, funeral parlours and Presents-From shops.

The races take place on a track outside town, between Knockcroghery and Ballymoe, and for the record they say that if you can see Mount Bellew from the top of the stand, it is going to rain; if you cannot, it is raining.

The crowd was sub-2,000: many farmers, hardly any women, no children, eight races and lots of runners. The first four events were on the Flat, then two chases, a hurdle and a bumper.

The course is an oval mile with a fierce uphill finish and the official racecard – €2.50 – provides the information that this is the 'Award Winning Racecourse of 2000'.

One wonders about the Award. I would consider nominating it for overall kindliness or perhaps for 'improvement' – it has apparently got much better than it was; I search for other categories: my first Hot Irish (whiskey, sugar and boiling water) would have put it in with a chance of 'Best Bar', but for my second glass they had forgotten to switch on the kettle.

The 'Gents' – a five-minute hike from the action – was adequate but not prize-winning. I had a cup of soup; it was of the 'Chef says you're right; it was dishwater and he is sorry' variety and I missed an oyster bar or indeed anything that smacked of regional excellence.

I hugely enjoy the atmosphere on Irish tracks: punters are knowledgeable, bookmakers innovative and even the tote out-performs ours in having a Quick Pick operating on all races, for every type of bet.

This is for punters who have left their pins at home: go to a tote window, ask for a €5 quick pick trio (the first three in any order) and the tote machine buzzes and spits out a ticket.

In the days when I had a wife, five children and Plymouth Argyle to support, my betting was, of necessity, modest – but even then I would await opportunities for maximum investment on races in which layers gave odds without the favourites.

In the fifth at Roscommon, a Grade 3 chase worth €40,000, Kahuna was 13-8, Always 100-30 and Old Flame ridden by Ruby Walsh 4-1.

A rent-a-goblin of a small bookmaker laid 5-4 Old Flame without the favourites and I placed a substantial bet in sterling, causing him to wipe the price off the board. Old Flame came second to Always.

I recouped my air fare and hotel bill but the man had the last laugh: he paid me in Bank of Ulster £20 notes.

Prize-money across the card is impressive – even the bumper was worth €8,500.

Having arrived in good time I read the form book and listened to the gossip and decided to keep my powder dry until race four – an apprentice handicap in which Catherine Gannon, the riding sensation of the moment, had a not-unfancied mount.

I backed her Cashmere King, trained by John Oxx, at 9-2 and then again at 5-1.

She was beaten a short head by a horse at the bottom of the handicap, one summed up on the racecard as 'Doesn't look any great threat on form shown so far' though it was backed down from double figures to 6-1.

Around this time, sipping my lukewarm Irish, the course manager invited me to present the prize after the next race and I accepted: stood in the winner's enclosure and at the right moment handed a big, heavy, cut-glass chamber-pot of a vase to a man I took to be the owner of the winner. Had he backed the horse?

He replied that he did not bet.

I shook my head in wonderment, let go of my side of the trophy and he exited towards the stables.

I didn't see him again until he reappeared in the winner's enclosure with the 7-1 shot who scooped the next race and then again with the 4-1 winner of the bumper. Not an owner, a trainer.

Noel Meade, a bit of a lightweight when it comes to small-talk with people who bet and hand over rich prizes, probably did not realise that I would have been interested in a bit of information, though in the seventh race his horse only came second.

So I drove back to Dublin airport passing many strange signposts, such as Caution Plant Crossing and looked in vain for a gooseberry bush or a rhododendron racing across the highway.

*

A SIMPLE DIET
WITH PLENTY OF CHIPS
2 SEPTEMBER 1998

NEWTON ABBOT IS a small Devonshire country town, once known for its brewing and pottery, now noted mainly for the profusion of plastic gnomes that adorn the gardens of its houses. It's also known for the railway station, at which passengers can leave the Penzance Express and meander to the coastal resorts of Torquay, Paignton, Brixham and Dartmouth; and for its racecourse – the southernmost, westernmost track in Britain where people go when it is not sunny enough to lie on the beach. Rumour has it that on racedays the course management look to the heavens and pray for cloud.

The track is a flat oval that could be run by a competent athlete in four minutes. The estuary of the river Teign is at one end; the Great Western trains – many of which ignore the place – rattle past the other. Newton Abbot races is not a place in respect of which one makes serious preparations; you get the impression the people go because it is there. Their dress-sense would make Armani weep. Children outnumber adults; beer and cider outsell wine; there is a restaurant and a carvery, and most racegoers eat chips.

The course is unremarkable; it nicely carries out its function of providing occasional entertainment, does this with simple honesty and does not interfere. I think it should.

It might have looked at the large William Hill betting shop near a bank of TV screens giving odds from around the land, but taking bets only at starting price.

A sufficiency of Tote windows are open for trade, each bearing the message that, with so many meetings today, the Tote will restrict itself to betting on home runners, i.e. those at Newton Abbot.

If there are gatemen they keep a low profile, which is how it should be. And when a horse wins, irrespective of whether it is the 'jolly' or a rag, the good people cheer.

For the first four races I went through the tactics of knowledgeable-racegoer-at-course-with-which-he-is-unfamiliar: back horses that come from stables with high strike-rates. Trainer Hobbs leads with 30 per cent winners-to-runners here. In the opener his Abfab was 25-1, got backed down to 14s. I went in. Abfab, to the best of my knowledge, is still running.

In the second, Hobbs's Pair Of Jacks started favourite and came second, so I played safe in the third and backed Martin Pipe's Palladium Boy. Another loser, though Pipe's won the fourth when I had been told by a man who bought a Cornish pasty at the table to which I had brought my cider that F. Jordan is the trainer who always goes for a touch here. My selection was beaten by Fill The Bill. 'Not one to rely on,' had been Timeform's verdict.

What I found uplifting was the large numbers who gathered around the parade ring and discussed the runners knowledgeably. Here were men and women determined to have a good time, to take every opportunity of participating fully in what went on. In the cafeteria before the first, I watched a man write out two pages of a complicated permutation involving some 20 horses, sit in deep thought as he calculated the stake, and then tell his long-suffering wife that it would cost £3.50.

On a wooden bench on the lawn – the course is generous in the provision of seating – I was joined by a 20-stone woman who had been to buy a cardboard dish of three sausages and a pile of chips beneath a comprehensive coating of HP Sauce. 'Blow the diet,' she said to no-one in particular and slapped one of her children who tried to help himself to a chip.

An announcement came over the Tannoy: someone owning a blue Renault has left three dogs locked in the car and they are very distressed. I do feel that, rather than pontificating on the use of the whip by a professional jockey, this is what the RSPCA should be doing.

After the third they paraded Cool Dawn in the ring. A voice sounding as if it had not previously ventured west of Berkshire extolled the virtues of the Gold Cup winner, and I wondered whether there might not be money in an equine lookalike service. I went to a party not long ago at which there was a dead ringer for Fergie, right down to the freckles. My host told me he had got her from Doppelganger of Houndsditch, £35-an-hour plus fares.

A similar quadruped exercise in which grey, would-be Desert Orchids are passed off to open garden fetes and speech days would generate cash flow, promote Brother Horse to new heights of popularity and do little harm. I ate a pork roll with crackling – good, but needed salt.

The fifth race was the Tom Holt and Reality Novices' Chase over three and a quarter miles, the most valuable event of the day with

£4,500 added to the stakes. Three runners. Crabapple Hill trained by David Nicholson and ridden by Richard Johnson opened 100-30 on, hardened to 1-4. The second favourite Fort Gale, mentioned by Timeform as jumping 'none too fluently', drifted from 11-4 to 7-2 and the best they could say about the outsider of the three, Lets Twist Again, was that he changed hands at Malvern Sales for 4,200 guineas. He was generally available at 8s.

People who go racing because it is a bit windy for the beach are not big on odds-on chances, and Lets Twist Again was the subject of some activity, starting at 6s. When he had surrendered the lead to the favourite, who had been niggled at from about halfway, Timmy Murphy started looking over his shoulder in search of Fort Gale (nowhere) and the writing was on the wall. Two out the favourite veered to the stands side, Lets Twist Again lived up to its name and crossed to the far rail, accelerated and won by seven lengths.

He would, said the know-alls. Outsider of three. They always do it.

For the record, the outsiders of three win very much less often than the favourite and not as often as the second favourite.

If the racecard gave times of trains leaving Newton Abbot station, perhaps published them where it now announces the fact that it reserves the right to refuse admission without assigning a reason for so doing, it would be helpful. Everything about the track is friendly, but geared more to folk who have gone AWOL from a tea dance than to serious racegoers.

*

CALM BEFORE THE STORM
9 SEPTEMBER 1998

THE YEAR WAS 1782. King George III, still fit and well, sat on the English throne, and there were southern racecourses at Abingdon, Ascot, Aylesbury, Basingstoke and Bedford – I am speaking alphabetically – when they started racing at Brighton.

The track was where it is today. It consists of a three-sided, irregular square over land that drains well and invariably provided going that was fast. The sea fret tended to obscure runners from spectators until the last few furlongs. As the jocks had to canter their horses down the track to the start, then gallop back, a winning Brighton horse needed to be relaxed. It needed to bounce off the turf and keep up with the pace – this is a hard track on which to come from behind – and have stamina for an uphill finish.

In the 18th century, Brighton, a moderately successful fishing town, was playground for the Prince Regent. Later it came to be a centre of medical quackery to which the rich and sick were sent to take the waters.

It achieved a few decades of fame as a suitable location for dirty weekends. (*Punch* cartoon of my youth: public school man and office girl at Victoria Station on a Monday morning. *She*: 'If there is any outcome to this weekend I don't know what I shall do; I think I'll kill myself.' *He*: 'Oh I say, that's frightfully decent of you.')

And the place is now blessed with more foreign students than anywhere in the land.

All the while the racecourse at Kemp Town continued to do its own thing, reaching notoriety in Graham Greene's *Brighton Rock* with the book and the film.

The post-war grandstand was built to take 16,000 people, a reminder of the sport's one-time popularity. Today's crowds hover either side of 2,000 and the average Brighton punter is elderly, makes his half-pint of beer last and gets his wife to pack the sandwiches. I have seldom seen so few children at a race meeting, though I did encounter a woman who used a pushchair containing a toddler as a battering ram.

If you want to go to a track that does not have a lot going for it, hurry to Brighton, for it will not stay that way long. Stan Clarke is the man who turned the remote and unfashionable

Uttoxeter from a galloping gaff track into a haven of
sophisticated entertainment and equestrian desirability, and
used to shake hands personally with most racegoers like Liberal
politicians outside supermarkets. He has bought the place and
there are major plans for development. Already the staff wear
uniforms, there seems to be more grass to ease the going, and
the stalls have been moved so that the draw no longer matters
as much as it did. While I was chatting with the manager about
this and that, his phone rang and he sanctioned free admission
for two people from the *Colchester Guardian*. (Directory
Enquiries, whom I phoned later, deny the existence of such a
paper, but it is a clear sign that the milk of human kindness
flows from above.)

The first September meeting took place under leaden skies. It
attracted a decent number of runners, providing favourite backers
with four results, and persuaded me that Mr R. Forristal claiming
5lb is an amateur rider of talent who is ignored at the backer's
peril.

I know nothing of the new chairman's improvement priorities
but I would urge him to look at the lift which is intended to
transport punters to the upper reaches of the grandstand. A
notice advises: 'In case of fire avoid lift.' I believe you would be
wise to avoid it even if neither you nor the lift are in a state of
combustion. The lift has no memory. It can be summoned only
when stationary. You have to keep pressing the call button as it
takes only one command at a time. If you want to go to the
ground floor from the basement and someone inside or out has
pressed 2, that is where you stop next. Then if someone in the
basement calls the lift before you inside press G, you return
whence you came.

The racecard, black and white with a green cover, costs £1; it
does not rate the runners, which is a pity, but it has a Form Focus.
A full-page advertisement gives details of a raceday package to the
St Leger – return fare, racecard, coach transfer and Members'

badge for £48. People in Brighton will be saddened to learn that the deal is from King's Cross, London.

How about a London–Brighton train timetable on the racecard? Connex run an Express from Victoria; a cheap-day return costs a tenner and the journey takes under an hour.

The jellied eels were excellent, the chilli vinegar was particularly fine. The food was rather ordinary and they had no draft beer in the terrace bar until after the third. You would think, having had nine days' respite since Brighton's last raceday, they would have been prepared.

There is a Ladbrokes betting shop, as untidy as any I have encountered, a sufficiency of Tote windows, and two dozen bookmakers, which is all one needs.

As you get used to the place and rehearse the peregrination of stand to Tote to gents to paddock to ring to bar, you recognise a genuine party spirit on the course. Not necessarily a party to which I would go, but camaraderie pervades. People nod to people they don't know – neutral nods meaning 'What are we doing here?' 'When will it stop raining?' 'About time we had a winner' 'It's all going to get better now the course is run by Stan Clarke.'

On the train home I read Einstein's definition of insanity: 'Endlessly repeating the same process, hoping for a different result.'

He could not, could he, have meant us who go to the races – reading the form, checking the advice of tipsters, assessing the going, the draw, the ability of the trainer and the jockey, the value offered by bookmaker and Tote before investing, watching, drowning sorrow and then doing it all over again half an hour later?

If he did mean that, we psychopaths should get together and form a club, were it not that there are enough associations of nutters in the sport we pursue.

*

THE 'TAXIS', BANGERS,
AND VERY LONG QUEUES
10 OCTOBER 2000

TO OBTAIN MAXIMUM enjoyment from an excursion to the Pardubicka, it is recommended that you learn some of the local language. Fluent command of Czech would be overdoing it, for much of what goes on is universally understood: see a sausage, point to it, offer its keeper a 50-crown note, accept change and plate containing the shining, bulgingly handsome 8oz banger which is ever-placed between a rounded tablespoon each of mustard and horseradish, without which it would not taste of much. 'Dobs' is Czech for 'good', a word widely, although not always wisely, used.

On Sunday afternoon my vocabulary was further enhanced by 'Pole Porti', meaning 'I bet the favourite to be beaten', and 'taxis', colloquial for Velki Taxisuf Prikop – the awesome fourth, and then again 11th, fence of the Velka Pardubicka, the four-and-a-quarter-mile race which may be uttered in the same breath as Aintree's Grand National and Maryland's Hunt Cup.

From the take-off side, taxis is no more than a massive fence, some five and a half feet high and about as wide.

Go round and look at the landing and there is room in the ditch for banqueting tables with chairs on both sides before the steep upward slope gives to the continuation of the track. A cross at one side is 'in memoriam', not of one of the many pilots who failed to make it, but of one who rode a dozen times and requested that his ashes be scattered there on his death.

The racecourse is in an Army encampment; it is not an oval track as we have come to expect but a large field, such as we use for gymkhanas, and on the far side there is a clump of trees behind which the horses disappear and then later come back into sight – probably, although not necessarily, with the same jockeys.

The run-in is a straight three furlongs in front of the stands which are large and ugly, more reminiscent of incarceration than entertainment.

On the non-track side of these buildings is a grade A car-boot site. Dozen upon dozen of stands dispensing inexpensive knick-knacks and clothes and pink sausages and equestrian pictures and brown sausages and beer and thin dark sausages and more beer and corn on the cob and skewers of pork and short fat sausages and more beer.

There are queues. Everywhere at every sales point at every tote window is a queue. Men and women from security firm Group 4, chain-smoking as if their lives depended on it, move on traders who have no licences.

All is good-natured, even the static queue outside the executive suite where I was seated, which contained people waiting to bet, to be paid, in need of lavatorial services or just wanting to get into one of the rooms beyond the totalisators and the WCs. All take it as part of life, in God's good time everyone will get there.

Betting in the Czech Republic is tote only, though there was an Irish layer; a loutish lad from Louth who introduced me to his boardman as Keith Floyd.

'What odds do you give?'

'Same as the tote; but you don't have to queue afterwards.'

The Czech 'Toto' could teach Peter Jones a thing or two: you can bet win, forecast and place on the first two, place on the first three, the first four and the first five.

While there is no indication of the size of the pools, it is perhaps worth reporting that when I put 300 crowns (there are 57 to the pound) on an outsider three minutes before the first race, its odds on the electronic screen contracted from 39-1 to 8-1.

The good people of this republic, possibly the worst-dressed assemblage in Europe, come to shout and eat and drink rather than to bet; 40p a first-four-place bet is about the norm in most races – odds of 1-10 being the customary return on investment.

Pardubice is 90 minutes drive east of Prague through flat, wet, heavy countryside dotted with tall factory chimneys. Flowers are rare. If you have land you grow pigs or chickens.

The eight-race meeting attracted a crowd of 10,000 who arrived in buses and Skodas and on bikes, smoked and ate and queued and drank and watched the action with some interest but hardly any passion.

There are 25 minutes between races, an hour between race seven and the big one. It is a magic hour of queuing, munching, slurping and, for us Britons trying to get the ever-polite tote operators to understand our bets, pretty hard work.

'Five hundred crowns on number 11 [the Len Lungo entry],' prompts the reply 'Write it down,' and the man leaves the queue to simmer while he fetches paper and pen.

We of the English contingent at the track stood for the anthem, cheered the parade, inspected the limply roast suckling pig that oversaw our buffet, wondered how so much froth could be generated in a glass containing so little beer.

Soon after the off we were saying 'Oh dear', for the Lungo horse and rider had parted company. 'Oh dear', although on the credit side we would not have to join a queue and these were now stretching as far as the eye could see.

Peruan, the favourite, had won as he had done last year and the year before and as each favourite had won the seven preceding events on Sunday.

And so we said goodbye to Pardubice, farewell to the roast pig on the buffet, ambled on to the track to stand and stare on the landing side of the Taxis, where I observed Chris Collins, who won the race in 1973, telling his wife and daughter how much mightier it had been way back when …

In the car park, guarded by a platoon of smoking Group 4 men, stood the sozzled winning jockey, beaming contentedness and surrounded by friends and family, using the impressive crystal trophy to drink red wine. A five-gallon plastic container of the stuff was handy for refills.

*

A FREUDIAN SLIP AND ILL FORTUNE IS NO RECIPE FOR SUCCESS
12 DECEMBER 2002

SUNDAY WAS THE day racegoers of Mauritius had awaited with keen anticipation: International Day, the Indian Ocean's answer to the Breeders' Cup. When I first flew into Pleisance Airport on Friday, my taxi driver was very full of it: 'Horses from around the world ... Africa, Australia, Ireland, and I will be there. I shall bet hundreds of rupees [45 to the pound sterling]. I shall look out for you.'

I asked what the crowd would be. He said: '50,000 – it is a big day.'

My driver was not entirely correct. The internationalism of the day was vested in the jockeys, rather than the horses that are annually sent to Mauritius 'to continue their racing careers.' And the crowd was about 30,000, most of whom looked like my friend who had driven me from the airport, and I missed him. I have to admit that if it was a big day for what the French call Ile de France, it was a very small one for me: a fierce hangover from the hotel's opening ceremony the previous night coupled with a knee twisted gyrating to Mr Bryan Ferry, gave me the appearance of Douglas Bader with a hernia imitating Oliver Reed.

Then there was my reluctance, in view of the 96-degree temperature, to wear formal clothing. Adorned with a white cloth emblem pinned on my shirt, an emblem such as one wears in memory of Aids victims, I was admitted everywhere and not welcomed as I might have been had I stood up straight, been sober or worn a suit. (I had thought 'lounge suit' on my invitation was a printing error.)

From a room marked 'secretariat' – where there was cold fizzy drink and bridge rolls containing dead ham – I was shunted via a number of watering holes to a presidential enclosure in which champagne flowed and white-suited waiters offered canapés with diverse toppings, from cured salmon to jellied octopus ink spiked with chopped mothballs. At one point, they brought miniature soup bowls of green melon juice.

Champ de Mars racecourse lies on the outskirts of Port Louis, the island's capital. It is as metropolitan a track as Chester, picturesque as Bangor, with the viewing facilities of Windsor, the crowds of Cartmel and officials who would put to shame for their co-operation those of any sporting venue I have attended.

Champ de Mars (the 'Mars' refers neither to the planet nor the month but has something to do with slavery) is claimed to be the second oldest racecourse in the world. Readers will recall that Britain took Mauritius from the French in 1810 (the French had taken it from the Dutch a century earlier) and not long after that, to earn the esteem of the French population who hated us, one Colonel Draper, backed by the governor Sir Robert Farquhar, held the first organised race meeting on June 25, 1812.

Today, the track is a flat, seven-furlong oval with two chutes; races are worth between £1,000 and (exceptionally) £2,000; £3 gets you into the enclosure and a 72-page magazine/racecard costs 65p.

There is music and fierce amplified noise wherever you go; in the centre of the track, what appears to the casual observer to be a mammoth car boot sale is the car park, picnic area, barbecue space, tote buildings, mobiles selling coconut and rum drinks and behind the enclosure, in a Tarmacadamed version of Longchamp, thousands of people mingle to no purpose one can discover. The race commentary is loud and incomprehensible, the words stumbling over each other, and when it is over, people turn to one another and ask who won.

For entertainment, troupes of musicians, dancers, jugglers and people who do interesting things with parrots all gather crowds; on the course itself, between races, there is a competition for dogs who fail to jump hurdles, crawl beneath nets or scramble through tunnels. They are cheered regardless.

The first race is for Mauritian apprentice jockeys. Irish Playboy, an eight-year-old ex-South African horse, wins and people cheer. The result comes up and people cheer again. People cheer everything, even in one race when there was not a single ticket for the Exacta with a huge carryover to the next race.

The parade of international jockeys was the highlight of the afternoon. We all cheer. They stand on a podium, are introduced one by one with the flag of their country fluttering behind them in the breeze: Dominique Boeuf and Thierry Thulliez, from France, wave as did General de Gaulle. Johnny Murtagh, from Ireland, accepts our hurrahs with both hands outstretched in the air. Jimmy Fortune gives the double-handed wave, Iovine and Demuro, from Italy, milk the applause like failed comedians, while Chris Munce and Corey Brown, from Australia, do bows in the manner of pantomime dames. Finally, Jeffrey Lloyd, born in England, apprenticed in South Africa and now the winningest jockey in Mauritius, gets three times the applause of his fellow riders which he meets with a double-handed wave.

It is an interesting concept, this race day: horses that are not entirely from the top drawer on a difficult, tight, hard oval track and a double handful of jocks unacquainted with the terrain who have all, in their own ballparks, achieved fame and fortune. I went for Fortune.

In the One and Only Le Touessrok Trophy over a mile, Jimmy F. was mounted on The Piper, a seven-year-old ex-South Africa whose form stood out: in five previous races, he had reared and lost two lengths, half-reared and lost one length, twice hung in badly and once checked 100 yards out when running well. Just the sort of horse an ex-British champion apprentice jockey who had ridden for the Ramsdens and Robert Sangster would know how to handle. The Piper neither reared nor half-reared at the start but came out last, was settled on the inside behind the field and if he overtook another horse, neither I nor the commentator noticed.

As a consequence the Indian Ocean Totalisator became many thousands better off. Luckily my bet was in rupees. Soon after that I left. People watching me were impressed with my overall consistency: a 13,000-mile round trip from England to back six consecutive losers.

'But then,' they said, 'you come for the sport, not the winning.' If they believe that, they believe anything. Gordon Ramsay is cooking dinner at the Touessrok, sorry, the One and Only Touessrok, tonight. I shall drown my sorrows, mostly to relieve the pain in my knee.

*

A PRIZE-WINNER'S TALE
14 MAY 2004

'WE NOW COME to the tipping competition,' said the man who looked like Brough Scott. 'The first prize is a luxury flight on Singapore Airlines to the Singapore Cup plus four nights at the many-starred Shangri La Hotel and it goes to' ... he waffled on a bit about the identity of the winner ... 'Clement Freud'.

Me. Me, what hardly ever wins anything and was actually quite looking forward to the second prize which was a seven-course dinner for two at Raymond Blanc's Manoir Aux Quatre Saisons in Oxfordshire.

The occasion was the Racing Post Chase luncheon at Kempton Park in February, and I had selected two winners and a third. Far be it for me to bite the hand that feeds me, but a competition in which a winning horse scores ten points; the second five and the third three – regardless of the starting price – dissuades one, anyway dissuades me, from going for value in the selections. I went for likelihood: chose horses likely to start at cramped odds.

The significant thing is that I won and Singapore beckons. There is the small matter of surviving 26 hours of air travel, but Singapore Airlines luxury class is not hard to endure and Brough Scott (the man who looked like him was in fact Mr Scott himself) has said that he looked forward to seeing me on the plane.

I have been to Singapore. It is small, about one and a half times the size of Rutland but densely populated (four million) and run with a firm touch, if that is not too mild an expression for an administration that dishes out custodial sentences to folk who leave chewed pieces of gum on the pavement. Mr Agnelli, the charismatic founder of the Fiat motor company, once said: 'In any successful business there must be an uneven number of directors and three is too many.' The Singapore President took that to heart; but then I am not going as a political commentator. I'm going as a prize-winner.

Now here is an odd thing: I have been racing for most of my life, lost two shillings on the Tote at Buckfastleigh before I reached the age of puberty and now have a bus pass celebrating its 15th birthday. I have gone racing as a punter, as a jockey, as a journalist and as a commentator. I've gone because I wanted to buy a horse out of a seller, claim one out of a claimer, gone because I was invited and as a host, even made my way to Thirsk and to Perth and to Cartmel because they were then the only British courses to which I had not been. I have never gone racing anywhere as a prize-winner.

I said thank you to Brough Scott when he announced my name at Kempton Park last February and I suppose I will be thanking people for the next four days: thank you for my flight, thank you for my hotel, thank you for the car to the track, for the chocolate on my hotel bed pillow and the complimentary shoeshine.

As a hack you embrace a lifestyle a shade grander than the editor expects you to lead; you keep the bills (and pick up bills other people have paid) to claim as expenses. As a guest, by virtue of winning a prize, you have no status, nor do you have duties other than to say thank you.

Did you enjoy the flight? It was great, thanks.

How was your hotel room? Terrific, thank you.

Pleased you came? Chuffed.

I look forward to 12 hours flying out and 14 hours flying back; to security, to queues, to having my nail scissors seized yet again because I left them in my sponge bag and they might have helped me to hold up the plane. It is going to be quite hard to eliminate from my mind that niggling feeling that but for the distance of a head in the third race at Kempton in February, I might have come second in the tipping competition and now be trundling along the M40 for half an hour before turning left to Great Milton and Raymond Blanc's seven courses. Shame on that fuddy-duddy thought.

As a journalist one had to do homework. As a prize-winner nothing is demanded so you bask in anticipation of a freebie, leave apposite messages on your home answer machine and watch the financial pages for the exchange rate of the Singapore dollar ... currently slightly more than three-to-the-pound sterling.

And while you luxuriate on Singapore Airlines' premium class, extra wide, particularly soft seat, you give a passing thought to the horses that are making their way from around the world, hardly getting any champagne, let alone lobster canapés; just water and oxygen and care and the hope of raising a few million dollars for their owners.

At York on Wednesday, a man asked whether I was going to Newbury at the weekend. I felt mildly superior. In Singapore, the weather is to be fair, the temperature 30 degrees Celsius and I expect I shall sit opposite the winning post in the new multi-

million-dollar grandstand. I wonder whether Ascot considered
Singapore as its 2005 venue for the royal meeting.

*Brough Scott, who led that prize-winning party, recalled how Freud
captivated them one morning with a poolside rendition of the Stanley
Holloway monologue* The Lion and Albert: *'In his white towelling
bathrobe and special hotel slippers there was, of course, no hesitation,
repetition or deviation ... As we all applauded, Clement dipped his
head to one side in the mock-modest, "it was nothing" gesture of the
infuriatingly clever boy at school. He had lived about seven lives
already and here, in the precious shade of an Equatorial morning,
there was nothing to do but shake our heads in wonder.' But there was
no time for poolside monologues on the day of the big race ...*

A SINGAPORE SMILE
IS A SHORT-LIVED THING

17 MAY 2004

IT IS HOT and you miss the bookmakers and the noise and resent
the tote which, at a flick of the illuminated board, reduces your |
9-1 selection to half those odds.

Singapore is where they work so hard not to upset anyone that
no-one seems able to produce the exuberance to which we are
accustomed when all goes well.

Here, a favourite wins and you wait in vain for cheers or cries of
'Come on, my beauty', though, if you look carefully, the odd
Singaporean bettor taps his pencil on the table at which he is
eating his noodles with a chopstick. (Did I mention that it was
hot?: 93 degrees Fahrenheit; and humid with it.)

Whoever wrote 'Maybe it's because I'm a Londoner that I love
London so' would have trouble ascribing lyrics to Singapore.

The island, apart from being hot, is well regulated and orderly,
punctual, sober and hardly criminal at all. Everyone is

scrupulously polite and they smile ... but, unlike the *Alice in Wonderland* Cheshire cat smile, which remained after the cat had gone, the Singapore smile is a short-lived thing.

What is important is efficiency: at the turf club this means collecting tickets and passes and locking and unlocking entrances, ensuring people go exactly where they are meant to go. In the huge, four-tiered stand that extends for two and a half furlongs, parties – like our *Racing Post* winners' party – have a buffet and a bar precisely suited to our standing. We had beer and wine, no spirits; fish and meat, no seafood, and on the dessert tables were half a dozen variations on the blancmange theme, no cheese.

Brough Scott, my host, who is a regular visitor here, found a location on a higher floor where we could buy brandy, which we quite needed after all those losers, and we passed a room replete with caviar and champagne. The double VSOP Hennessy cost £5, a third of the price charged in our hotel.

In my room at the Shangri La – a room which is, of course, impeccably clean, handsomely appointed and permanently serviced – I have a bowl of fruit: two oranges, one green and one red apple. On my first night I ate an orange, which was oval but for a slight bump, medium-juicy, neutral in taste. When I returned to my room after breakfast, the orange had been replaced with an exactly similar fruit, the way a damaged cricket ball is substituted by an umpire. I expect three or four hotel officials oversaw the matter.

Kranji racecourse has a meeting each Saturday. This year's prestigious Group 1 Singapore Airlines Cup was their first Sunday opening. The crowd was massive. The air-conditioned grandstand housed most, though there were a goodly number who stood trackside as, if you gamble the way all Chinese seem to gamble, this is the only place and the only time you can indulge. The local paper talks of the expected opening of a Singapore casino as the natives lose an estimated US$1.7 billion in the casinos of other nations. A local casino would clean up.

I know not how much the racecard costs, but it is an admirable 60-page publication replete with technical information, form and only two full-page advertisements – for the sponsors. (At Saturday's meeting, my racecard was equally serious, but did contain a few ads for 'clean and cosy massage by experienced and charming practitioners.')

While the racecard form is excellently, factually presented with the horse's position in the field at three points of the race and its weight in kilograms so that you can tell if it has been on the Atkins diet, the 'comments' are confined to a couple of dozen phrases: I understood 'crowded', 'bumped', 'checked', 'brushed', 'dipped', 'earned out', 'balked' and 'interfered'. 'Throat infection', 'resp. disease', 'stood', 'laid out' and 'tightened' (in respect of a horse who finished last) were less obvious.

The huge screen in the centre of the course was well managed showing an oriental version of *The Morning Line* before racing began, interesting remarks before, during and after races, and the President arriving, met by Singapore Airlines officials. Five people applauded. Four paper dragons from rent-a-dragon fluttered around him before he disappeared to a designated location where there was surely apposite hospitality.

And I backed a winner at 15-1; backed it partly because the jockey carried my racing colours, but also because the trainer was called Clements. The form column stated of a previous race: 'Queried.' Sounded good to me.

As we approached the big race, there was a very slightly audible murmur of anticipation and on the screen a Chinese Clare Balding asked a few people how they were feeling.

'Nice not to have people waving into the camera the way they do with "Big Mac", said one of our prize-winning party.

A German horse beat one from South Africa in the Group 1 race. No-one cried, 'Come on, my son!', and Brough Scott, who had told me that Imperial Dancer was a good thing despite the heat, which cannot but inconvenience a six-year-old entire, disappeared.

I, who don't go a bundle for 93 degrees Fahrenheit either, got a taxi back to my hotel for an £18 brandy and all-night sumo wrestling on television.

I look forward to an afternoon at Plumpton, which the inscrutable Singaporeans would probably find a disappointment.

*

GARRISON SAVANNAH – WHERE BILL MARSHALL IS NUMERO UNO
29 DECEMBER 2004

THE GOOD LORD caused the sun to shine from an azure sky. Fortunately there reside on this Caribbean island a sufficiency of neighbourhood gods to act as presidents, secretaries, stipendiaries and stewards, starters, timekeepers and judges to enable the last meeting of the Barbados Turf Club's season to take place.

It is the day of the Diamonds International Audemars Piquet Challenge Series and Sunset Reef Stakes Trophy – verily a name that slips from the tongue.

I was there, among the spectators, beneficiary of a deal which cost the equivalent of £65 and embraced pick-up from and return to my hotel some 20 miles from The Garrison; entry, a racecard, a seat in the air-conditioned Finishing Line restaurant and a six-course meal of impeccable quantity.

I have paid three times that sum for a seat and a meal in the Champions Gallery at Newmarket, had less fun and saw hardly anything.

I like 'deals'. One of my local pubs had a Christmas deal: food, drink and a kindly word £4.99. I availed myself of this, received a slice of meat pie and a glass of red wine and waited.

'What?', said the barman.

'Kindly word,' said I.

'Don't eat the meat pie.'

The racecard made interesting reading: 'Under the distinguished patronage of His Excellency, the Governor General Sir Clifford Husbands GCMG' – an honour of such magnitude that the letters are believed to stand for God Calls Me God.

It distances itself from the punctilious verbiage of our own rules of racing by announcing: 'The Barbados Turf Club will not hold itself responsible for any inaccuracy in the weights; ages and pedigrees have been added for the convenience of the public ... but are not guaranteed to be correct.'

There are explanatory pages for newcomers: under 'Positions at Finish' they include, as do we not, BO which stands for 'bolted at start'. Following the heading 'Equipment' the capital letter D fooled me. It stands for Nasal Dilator, while from the glossary of terminology I gleaned that a 'ridgling' is a male horse of any age with either one or two undescended testicles.

I ate coleslaw with a hot sauce, got a plate of many cooked meats and fishes and sauces and salads – and halfway through the meeting, behold the buffet was replete with iced custard tarts.

I searched the runners on the card and assessed the selections and history of the tipsters for something which in Damon Runyon-speak would 'spit in my eye'. I found it.

In race 5, the Happy Holidays Conditions Race over 7.8 furlongs worth just north of £1,000 to the winner, running from stall two was Senor Clemente – a three-year-old gelding with a lifetime record of one win and five places from 11 starts.

The horse was owned and trained by Mr W.C. Marshall DFC, SCM – the latter a local honour similar to an OBE. It was Bill Marshall, a well-known, red-haired, British jockey then trainer of whom I had not thought for a while.

He is big, numero uno in Barbados racing. As he had a box at Garrison Savannah, I went to see him to be greeted the way octogenarians greet one another – quietly. When I quiz him about the horse that virtually bore my name he said: 'Only got one eye but will probably win.'

I beamed. I drank a glass of his sound white wine, shook hands with his guests and removed myself. I had a tip straight from the trainer's mouth; what more does a punter need?

As the previous event had been won by a 15-1 shot trained by a trainer who did not figure in the league table, ridden by a jockey who similarly failed to feature in the standings, I knew that form would come into its own and went for the one-eyed grey who was bouncing around the tote indicator board between evens and 4-1 (there are no bookmakers).

We nearly had no race at all as the ambulance had gone to take a spectator to hospital and we had to await its return. What we did get were lots of announcements: mostly about drivers who had left their cars blocking other cars whose occupants had plans to attend a marriage or catch a plane at the airport.

Bill Marshall sat quietly by the parade ring in an automated pope mobile with Zimmer attachments: bright of mind though bent of body, he watched until the race was finally run and Senor Clemente, having cut out the pace, finished a distant sixth.

He seemed to take it better than I did, so I had a glass of rum and walked around downstairs where the noise was constant, the sipping of bottles and beakers of liquor uninterrupted and parents, mothers especially, sat among their animated children who shouted encouragement to friends, relatives, passers-by and horses – waving their limbs from their prams.

Sartorially too, it was an experience – especially in the millinery department where triple-tiered tea cosies of matching colours were the must-have garments of the occasion.

In race six I backed Kabul – Barbados's number one horse, seven wins from ten starts and the course record-holder at five and a half furlongs.

I backed him heavily to win and comprehensively to beat Peace Angel in a forecast. Peace Angel, Irish-bred by Goldmark, won.

Kabul, having played up at the start, did not come under orders and I got my money back after the tote computer had emulated recent race commentaries and gone down.

There was a longish wait before all was working again and we got a really interesting announcement – after the stuff about cars needing removal. 'The jockey of the second horse in the third race had, at the two-furlong post, been hit across his or possibly his horse's head by the winning jockey's whip and objected to the winner ... which objection had been overruled; on reassessing the objection the stewards had decided that the jockey of the runner-up should have his deposit returned ... and Mercedes number NM970 must really move to let the folk get to the airport.'

At a British racecourse we would have had appeals for lost children. Not in Barbados. They don't mislay children here. Children are precious.

＊

RACECOURSE FOOD: THE RENTAL CHARGE
12 JANUARY 2005

RACECOURSE FOOD IS a matter that deserves careful consideration. In ordinary establishments, they count on each place being occupied twice or more per session. At racecourses, punters book tables less to eat than to have a base from which to carry out operations and provide somewhere for the little woman to sit while we invest the housekeeping money in the betting ring. For us, food and drink is regarded as a rental charge.

Caterers have to pay substantial money to the racecourse for permission to trade on their premises, money they can only recoup by charging serious sums for food and drink. Therefore no-one is particularly happy, nor is the fare on offer always as good as it is at Sandown – where the head waiter is a jewel in the crown.

I asked a friend who had been to a West Country course to assess the meal he had eaten, to be told that 'if the soup had been as warm as the champagne, the champagne as old as the chicken, and the chicken as fat as the waitress, it would have been adequate.'

The best racecourse food I have had was at a country track in New Zealand, where a steward invited me to the officials' restaurant, warning me that it was not 'high-falutin' food such as you are used to'.

On a buffet were half a dozen freshly baked crusty loaves and a bread knife. A five-pound slab of golden dairy butter, a pot of mustard made with Colman's powder dissolved in cream, pacified with honey ... and in a huge vat of simmering broth swam three mammoth hams: these got lifted out of the liquor and could be carved to any thickness, in whatever quantity one had in mind, fat or lean. That was it, though there were bottles of local wine, which happened to be Cloudy Bay Sauvignon of the previous year.

Why don't we do that? I'll tell you: officials serving at a racecourse want to be able to say, 'They gave me a five-course lunch', and if a restaurant tried it, they could not recoup their outgoings, for one simply cannot charge £45 for ham sandwiches, though you can for boring soup, overcooked meat and veg, followed by trifle, cheese and biscuits, and an After Eight mint.

Is it all getting better then? It depends on how long you have been going racing and relied on the track to provide provender, rather than bringing it in the boot of your car.

Sixty years ago at Yarmouth, there was choice between sausage rolls and custard tarts in the tea room; apart from that, a fish and chip van was on hand to sell what St Paul in his letter to the Philippians called 'the piece of cod that passeth all understanding.' There were mushy peas; that has changed. Now there is a fish bar but you have to go into town for the peas.

*

PRIMED FOR UPSET AT SANTA ANITA

9 NOVEMBER 2005

DESPITE RUPERT BROOKE'S contention to the contrary, there are some corners of foreign fields that are forever foreign – and Oak Tree/Santa Anita, which is situated in a south Californian city named Arcadia, is one, even though they have a red-coated huntsman who regularly blows his bugle.

A search for a cathedral would be in vain, for every town and village in the United States calls itself a city.

Arcadia is what Americans call 'nice', which means middle-class, clean, tree-lined, dogless streets in which hardly anyone shoots anyone else.

The track hosts the California Cup, a valedictory weekend meeting that ends the 31-day season with a Sunday card in which eight of the 11 events are worth in excess of $100,000 and the ninth race on Sunday, the California Cup Classic Handicap run on dirt over a mile and one furlong, rewards those who return to the winner's enclosure with a quarter of a million.

I was there. The day was bright and sunny, the crowd about 20,000, sufficient to cause my waiter to tell me: 'Your Fisherman's Plate will take a while, there are six orders ahead of you.' When it came some five minutes later, I got deep fried squid served on a small mountain of rather good, thin, crispy chips. Long live fishermen, say I.

Racing starts at 11.15am and as my host and I arrived early, we found a nearby restaurant where the waitress, a failed anorexic weighing some 20 stone, brought us coffee, toast, cakes, waffles, omelettes, hash brown potatoes, a chocolate sundae and a diet coke for a tenner: the price of four copies of the *Daily Racing Form*, the cost of having the car valet-parked and tipping the man $5. Admission to the turf club is $20. US racing is affordable, but goodness, one does miss bookmakers.

To compensate for this, the operators who man the tote windows are fast, knowledgeable, accurate and never fail to wish you luck.

Most other staff are equally caring, telling you to 'have a good day', a phrase to which the late Sir Peter Ustinov used to reply: 'I'm afraid I have made other arrangements.' I had not. I should have.

At 10.45am, a woman came and stood at a microphone on a platform to sing the national anthem: not a great rendition, but as we had all stood up, we remained standing regardless, right through to the last of all the verses. There was even muted applause – I think for her courage.

The following day's *Daily Racing Form* is in the shops by lunchtime, so I had ample opportunity to hone up on the next day's action, acquaint myself with jockeys' and trainers' current success rates, assess the speed figures of the horses and read both the brief comments 'Back better than ever' for a horse that finished out of the frame in a race won by 'Comes here sharp'.

I also admired the race analysis, that retains the author's honour, whatever the result. None of our 'Others preferred'.

The paper has four in-house tipsters: Brad, Art, Scott and Michael; on Sunday, none of their nap selections made it.

Outside the track, you can buy tip-sheets at $3 a go; there is choice. I purchased Bob's Card – 'Over 100 years of experience and tradition. Established 1896'. There is a picture of Bob on the cover. He looks tired.

Neither his 'best bet' nor his 'value bet' succeeded, although in the 11-runner fifth race, a mile-and-a-half handicap on turf, his four selections were the first four home and a $24 superfecta would have netted you $1,300.

My favoured bet on US racecourses is the Pick 3, necessitating the selection of any three successive winners.

I picked three horses per race, making 27 bets in all, and the results, because this is a popular wager, are impressive, with massive dividends, way in excess of the multiplied odds treble.

I feel a bit like the golfer who hit four successive new balls into the lake and, as he unwrapped a fifth, his playing companion said: 'Why don't you use an old ball?' He was told: 'I've never had an old ball.'

Well I have never yet won a Pick 3, but if you have had two winners, you watch the third leg of your bet with extreme attention and terrific optimism … just as if you were actually going to have a good day.

I saw a notice stating that: 'Will Run has been scratched.' That cheered me a bit.

When I bet in denominations other than sterling, I tend to feel that the money is unimportant, bet more heavily (in Turkey, a million lire is about 1/9d in old money) and in view of my comparative ignorance of the local form, I am influenced by factors that are largely irrelevant. In a valuable handicap over one mile on the turf, runner number two was favourably drawn on the circular course, showed the letters GB after her name, was by a GB stallion out of a GB dam bred by a GB breeder – the only GB horse on the card and I seemed to be the only GB punter on the track.

I should have let it go at that, but my youngest grandchild had the same name as the horse and the jockey wore dark blue and orange silks (my colours are black and orange) and he was supported by one of the *Form*'s four experts. 'Primed for upset' was the brief comment.

The morning line had the mare at 10-1, and she was backed down to 8s, and the nap selection of one of the tipsters.

Now if all that is not an omen, I would like you to tell me what is.

I backed her across the board, which means win, place and show, and I put her in mixed exactas and trifectas with the first two in the betting; she was also the sole middle leg of my Pick 3, which was still alive.

'Primed for upset': the author of the pithy three-word comment turned out to be absolutely correct. She finished tenth, never ran as if she was going to be in the shake-up, not even when the jockey was moving faster than his mount. And I was upset, just like the man said.

I notice the dollar is getting stronger – not that I have very many left.

*

In June 2006 Royal Ascot returned to its Berkshire home on completion of the massive reconstruction programme which had caused the royal meeting to be relocated to York the previous year.

MAGIC AND MYSTERY OF THE PRE-ASCOT EXPERIENCE
14 JUNE 2006

YOU READ A lot about ski and après-ski, the latter involving quantities of hot sweet wine consumed as you tell monstrous lies about achievement on the slopes. Pre-ski never gets a look-in.

A lot of Royal Ascot concerns pre-Ascot. The topper to polish, the shoes to shine, morning coat to go to the cleaners – almost exactly where its wearer is likely to be taken over the next five days. I used to select five shirts and five ties – just as if anyone cared a costermonger's jockstrap what I wore to cover my upper body or wind around my neck.

I knew a Greek ship-owner who wore different gold and diamond watches on each day of the meeting; out of my league, that, but I do get different daily button-holes from the lady at the entrance to the No. 3 car park. She looks at the colour of my tie and decides. As my morning coat is made for me by a small tailor in Hua Hin, a man who is not particularly good but very inexpensive, the jacket has no designated place for the stem of a rose; luckily, lady at car-park entrance has pins.

Waistcoats are important. There is a shop in the hinterland of Savile Row in London that makes them from whatever materials you choose for only a few hundred pounds. They line them as you desire – mine is lined with my racing colours – and this perks up your appearance no end. Do remember to leave the bottom waistcoat button undone.

Getting to the track is an art form. Over the years I have found that the M4 to the Windsor turn-off and then taking the road past Legoland is steadily the most congested. I now use the M3 and turn north at exit 3, but there are cleverer ways. A chauffeur once took me from central London to the track in under an hour on Ladies' Day using minor roads and rat-running through villages where they had not seen cars, ever.

I understand that there are people who live west, even north of Berkshire, for whom the travel information provided in the previous paragraph is unhelpful; I wish them well, regardless, just hope things get better.

Let us move smoothly to the matter of 'chancing your luck', what we call 'investing our money'. It is very simple: if you mind losing more than you enjoy winning, do not bet.

Try never to bet within your limits. If it is not going to hurt to lose what you have lost, it is very, very unlikely that the amount you stood to win would have been sufficiently uplifting to have brightened your day.

Have two wagers: one for £10, which you can show people who observe your pleasure or ask why you are singing and jumping up and down, and another for the serious transaction that will enable you to upgrade your Bentley – which has nothing to do with anyone else.

Ascot has changed. £200 million has been spent on pulling things down and putting other things up, so forgive them their trespasses and I apologise for being unable to direct you to the places you should not miss. If you do come from London, it might be a good idea to stop at Lidgate's, 108 Holland Park Avenue, whose pork pies from Melton Mowbray are as good as any I have eaten and outperform most provender that is disgorged from the boots of cars in No.1 car park.

Derek Nimmo, whom I miss, used to invite me to partake of the contents of his hampers there.

'Champagne?', he once asked me.

'With a glug of fresh orange juice,' I replied.

'It is Krug vintage,' he said, petulantly. 'I hope you know what you are doing.'

Nimmo had a driver-butler, an elderly, white-haired, distinguished ex-actor who appeared at Ascot wearing a mauve cloak with gold buttons bearing an insignia.

'Is that your insignia?', I remember asking my friend. 'No,' said he, 'it is the butler's, he comes from a very good family.'

The meeting is called Royal Ascot, because Her Majesty is present. She is driven in a carriage from Windsor Castle, waves as she passes the cheering crowd, and every now and then leaves the box where she and her guests consume luncheon and afternoon tea to make her way to the parade ring, which is now new and beautiful and adjacent.

Should you make eye contact, you bow and raise your hat, unless you are female, in which case keep your hat on and curtsey. Do *not* say, 'Haven't I seen you on television?'

What this column would dearly like to do is advise a horse at long odds who will entertain you by being backed from the 20s you obtained to the 9-2 starting price next week ... and then win. Should you know of such a contender, do not, after the race, go around telling folk that 'that was the best bet of the meeting.'

I have suggested to the Jockey Club that such behaviour deserves a lifetime ban from attending racecourses, which might be mitigated on appeal to attending occasional midweek and evening meetings at Folkestone and Leicester, provided it is raining.

TAKE OFF YOUR HATS AND RAISE THEM TO THE NEW ASCOT

21 JUNE 2006

THE QUEEN WORE royal blue, the grass was verdant green, the champagne acceptably pink, and in the first race the favourite won, which always makes it look as if the game is as impeccably straight as we all know it is not. Nevertheless, it would rightly have pleased the organisers, who deserve great credit.

If I had a racecourse and £200m to spare, I doubt I would have done nearly as well in creating a Berkshire pleasure-dome on the outskirts of Windsor. From the road, it does look a bit like a very upmarket public bath, but once in, there is a great deal to admire: elevators, lifts, the occasional loo, instant Polish plumbers to repair what goes wrong even while you wait and on this, the first day of the royal meeting, my 20-1 'good thing' came second, beaten as comfortably by Takeover Target as is possible when the verdict is a short head.

It was the first day – and of course things go wrong on the first day – like the 'guides' who don't know anything and the doorman who pushed at a door marked pull and said 'Have a good day' with, I think, a Latvian accent.

There were rumours: like 'They have forgotten to install toilets: you'll have to go out and queue at Budgens in the High Street.' Untrue. I found a toilet, after a while: it was large, clean and gracious and had an attendant dressed in gold and scarlet who would, I am almost certain, have seen to the lowering and readjusting of my zip – had I asked.

Like the new-style Las Vegas, where food and wine and entertainment are no longer subsidised by gambling, Ascot has gone for beauty of design and magical views and the abolition of tunnels (in which, on dank, dark afternoons, people reputedly had a terrific time) and deserves ten out of ten for this.

Gamblers at this new venue have a hard time of it. It is my belief that those who chance their fortune should be high up in any authority's consideration. On Level 02 – where the new Royal Ascot Racing Club club is situated – the Tote had broken down and there was no facility closer than two floors away for doing one's dosh.

'We are', explained the Commanding Officer of Her Majesty's Course, 'looking at the next 50 years.' Well, me too, but though I eagerly anticipate my 132nd birthday celebration in half a century's time, I am also looking at the next four days.

They need more barmen, or someone to organise the queue of drinkers. I am told by friends in the royal enclosure that no-one can see anything – which might be an overstatement but could have about it an element of truth. We in the Royal Ascot Racing Club received brilliant food and drink, though if forced to nit-pick, the thickness of the bread around my smoked salmon sandwich could do with readjustment.

Something has happened to hats: milliners appear to have gone for feathers and wisps of spare cloth that confuse the atmosphere and tickle your ears. There was one woman who balanced on her head a purple pillowcase stuffed with whatever is used to make pillowcases look comfortable; I presume she came in a stretch limo, on her own.

Oh yes: I won significantly on race four. 'Stewards' inquiry,' they announced, and I know how important it is not to change a result when you are into the 'We are new and wonderful' business, so I bet that the result would not be overruled. They showed us the picture of the stewards deliberating while the 'interference' was flashed up over and over on another screen until the stewards gave in.

So take off your hats and raise them to the new Ascot: not only does it work for the masses, who came to gawp and left to contribute to a genuinely high-class traffic jam, but over the years what a prime location for a quiet Mexican wave on a twilight evening; or a gay wedding celebration, even divorce.

THIS OPERA HOUSE OF A GRANDSTAND

22 JUNE 2006

GOOD, BEAUTIFUL AND orderly ... but cosy the new Ascot isn't, not even on the second day. The great new stand – monarch of all it surveys – continues to make you feel it was going to be something else: a Scandinavian airport, even though one knows that Heathrow wouldn't have allowed it and they would be pushed to find staff. No Scandinavian au pair could afford to give up her domestic job.

But the more you look, the more you find, for it is a genuinely gigantic opera house of a place. On Royal Hunt Cup day, I discovered a Shore Bar that sells good fried fish and needs a stronger extractor; a Winners' Bar and a Losers' Bar; many places where one can sit comfortably, although few with good sight lines, and should you be blind, the sound system is not yet quite as I am sure it will be.

What will interest you is that on every floor there is a notice bearing the word 'Condiments'. I asked a passing woman whether she knew what the word meant, and she hit me. Condiments (which, of course, you knew) is the collective for salt and pepper, vinegar, spice, Worcestershire sauce and tomato ketchup. Here it is nicely arranged on a table under an umbrella, and if you're smart, broke and unfussy, you might like to bring your own biscuits and have a free meal, the attractions of which will depend on the quality of your choice.

Do not, as I had intended, tell anyone that you will meet them at the condiments stall; many people have done that, which is why there are, around the sea salt and the peppercorns, lost souls waiting to be claimed.

From an equestrian point of view, I had an interesting time of it: lost on the first race, lost on the second race, lost on the third race and in race four noticed a horse called Akona Matata and remembered that one of my sons once had it off with someone of that or similar name. A nice man from Sunderlands offered me 25s; I plunged. It came third. People around me nudged their neighbours and said: 'He knows.'

I wrote early in the week about the problems that occur when too many cars make for the same place at around the same time, and a man wrote me a helpful letter: Leave the M25 at Junction 13, pursue the A30 in the direction of Basingstoke and shoot down the A429 when you finish up in Ascot High Street.

'Dear Sir: I followed your advice. It took 1 hour and 55 minutes from the time I reached the A429. Further, better advice would be appreciated. Tomorrow I may come by train.'

Yesterday evening, leaving the course at around 6pm, hearing the songs and the thumps that came from the newly located bandstand, I stood in a crowd waiting for the police to stop traffic and enable us to cross Ascot High Street.

It was a long wait, but the atmosphere, hot, humid and happy, was extraordinary: most of the people around me were women, most were youngish and attractive and pissed, and wore what in the 1960s we used to call eff-me shoes (which are high-heeled slip-ons). A strange aura of sexuality charged the air.

To my left, an elderly teenager with bare feet snogged indiscriminately with adjacent mouths, while in front, a young woman stroked the back of the policeman blocking the crossing and asked if they could have sex. The policeman next to him explained that his friend had to stay on duty until late.

What it shows, and what must please the great and good organisers of Her Majesty's racetrack, is that, despite the futuristic architecture, down on the ground, all is as it was and as it should be.

SIR GERARD DID NOT NEED THE WHIP – AND SO NEITHER DID I

23 JUNE 2006

THERE IS A story about a man playing golf, lining up a long putt on a green adjacent to the road, when a funeral cortege drove by. The golfer laid down his putter, took off his cap and stood silently as the hearse drove past; he then returned to the job in hand.

'I'm very impressed,' said his partner. 'It was the least I could do,' said the man, 'she was a damn good wife and mother to our children.'

I thought of that yesterday afternoon as, on my arrival, I watched a tow-away van remove a 15-seater minibus flying St George for England flags. Was that an omen? Should I have called it a day and driven back to London to eat halibut at Sheekey's, which is what I used to consider doing when witnessing fatal accidents on the way to racetracks? I have given up superstition, so the answer was no, the way it had always been, and especially no for it was Ladies' Day, and I had this sizeable punt on Sir Gerard in the Britannia.

There is an interesting innovation at Ascot. Standing against a wall behind them between the entrances to the Silver Ring and the Royal Enclosure was a young man and two women of tender years and gentle expression. On the wall was fixed a placard stating, 'They say whipping does not hurt. Come and try it.' One of the girls had a whip and the other's upper body was tastefully tattooed. A policeman stood nearby – possibly in the queue.

I asked the girl with the whip how trade had been to date, and she said: 'We've had one or two very satisfied customers, would you like a few – on the house?' I declined – but this could run and run.

The new Ascot is into safety barriers. If you happen to walk on the wrong side of a row of these, you could be in for a major hike before a gap occurs enabling you to return from whence you came. Strangely, it doesn't make you feel safe, just bloody angry, especially if you are lame.

The great Sir Peter O'Sullevan, having parked his car near the eastern roundabout, approached an entrance marked 'security'. He was dressed in his finery and sported enough accreditation to be waved through the gates of Fort Knox.

Sir Peter explained to 'security' that he was 88 and undesirous of walking the 200 yards to the Royal Enclosure entrance and then back. 'No joy,' said security. Had he worn a yellow jacket or a chef's hat, they would have swept him in.

A friend did the journey from London by helicopter. I asked whether his trip had been a success, and he said, 'Up to a point; the flight took ten minutes and then we spent 20 minutes getting from where it landed to the racecourse.' 'Ho,' I said, repeating the syllable several times like a sozzled Father Christmas.

There is, in the corridor outside the Racing Club, a table attended by men resplendent in green velvet. The notice nearby states 'meeting point for heads of missions'.

To date, they don't appear to have had a customer. I do hope the world outside and all its missionary heads are in good order; in the club, everything flourishes. I had really good shepherd's pie for lunch – made with real shepherd.

The Britannia Stakes came and went – to Sir Gerard, which was extremely fortunate, for I had considered, on departure, stopping at the whipping post, confessing to losing more money than it behoves sensible people to lose, and being punished for my trespasses.

If you think that good fortune is a one-off occurrence, do stop reading now. On the other hand, if you believe that good luck brings more good luck, pawn the wife and children and shovel all you can get hold of on Glistening in the 4.55 on Saturday.

IF THERE IS AN AFTERLIFE,
I HOPE IT HAS CROWDS LIKE ASCOT'S
24 JUNE 2006

I TEND TO leave south-eastern racecourses after the fifth: no queues to get out of the car park, home in time for a bath before dinner and leisure to consider the lies I tell about where I spent the afternoon.

'Oh really, the museum again?'

'No, different museum,' is how the conversation goes.

I stayed on at Ascot on Ladies' Day and realised what I have been missing. Racecourse crowds are just the nicest, warmest, sweatiest, drunkenest people you could meet anywhere, and I had an extremely happy time mingling, agreeing that I was what they accuse me of being and gently refusing the contents of hip flasks containing warm liquid.

In Germany they have found and accepted that English football fans are top people, while we continue to believe Germans put their towels on the deckchairs which we want to occupy.

Our race crowds sing and dance and wave flags; they sit on the grass talking into their mobiles and continuing their conversation with whomever, stumbling out still talking, still waving and just occasionally falling down. No trouble to anyone, except possibly that great band of Ascot racecourse employees armed with hardware that enables them to pick up objects not meant to be there.

W.C. Fields, the American actor, was once given a glass of water. Asked what he thought of it, he replied: 'I don't know what it is, but it won't sell.'

He was also the first person to maintain that life was 5 to 4 against. I don't know what the odds are against the existence of an afterlife, but if it contains Ascot-like crowds I am a buyer.

I read in a paper with which I have considerable empathy, because both our circulations are poor, that there was fighting at the races. I have not met anyone disturbed by this but understand it took place in one of the car parks, around upmarket picnickers, and was caused by an assertion that Taittinger champagne was drier and more desirable than that from the house of Bollinger. A classy fight, you would call it.

On the fourth day the Queen wore appropriate garments of turquoise, and Prince Philip, who hates racing, sat next to her and smiled. He seems of late to be happier. The carriages were down to three and I suppose in a real democracy they would have been followed by the 100-plus white stretch limos wherein, behind darkened windows, all sorts of interesting things occur.

It must be very difficult if you have left your partner in one of these to find her again, though as with identical council houses, much involuntary wife swapping goes on.

The best outfit of the day (on a day on which I saw no hats of distinction) went to two Chelsea pensioners dressed in their impeccably laundered red uniforms.

In the 1950s, when I ran a nightclub in Sloane Square, red-jacketed pensioners were a common sight.

I remember once sitting next to a brace of ex-warriors on a park bench. One said: 'Do you remember those pills they gave us during the world war to take our minds off women?'

The other nodded his head and the first one said: 'I think mine is beginning to work.'

The most interesting conversation of the day came when I presented a substantial Exacta Tote ticket to the lady behind the counter in the Racing Club and she looked at it and said, 'I don't think we have enough money to pay this.'

Should I have said, 'Just pay me what you can afford'?

The trouble is that any hold-up at a Tote window causes the natives in the queue to blame the man at the front – in this case me.

Do not forget Glistening in the 4.55 this afternoon. If he fails to win, there will be all sorts of bargains on offer in Marylebone – like my house, my car, my wife …

In his column on the following Wednesday, Freud had to relate: 'Glistening, the horse I backed to win the 4.55 at Ascot on Saturday, the horse I advised you to back, the horse I told my friends to back and on whom I invested money on behalf of my grandchildren, the daughter of our Portuguese Maria who comes four days a week to rearrange the dust, also Willy the most wondrously helpful porter in Marylebone, lost. He failed to win. Did not succeed in coming first. Ran in a manner that caused the racecourse announcer not to mention his name when calling the first past the post.'

*

IF ONLY THE TIP HAD MATCHED
THE MAJESTY OF THE SURROUNDINGS

19 JULY 2008

THEY ASKED WHETHER I preferred flying from Stansted or Luton, which is a bit like, 'Would you rather have leprosy or syphilis?' As my destination was the kingdom of Kerry and I was a guest of the Killarney Race Committee at their July festival, I left the arrangements to my hosts. Killarney – though this is of no more than academic interest to me – has just closed its only sex shop.

The festival lasts four days: three evening meetings followed by Ladies' Day on the Thursday, when there is a sell-out crowd of 5,000. It is scenic – the most scenic racecourse anywhere, they tell you, with mountains that put those at Bangor-on-Dee to shame. There are also multitudinous lakes, some with islands, on one of which I saw sheep.

Queen Victoria came to Kerry in the 1890s, the biggest thing that has happened to the kingdom. The point from which she was shown the lakes is called Ladies' View; this is now a big tourist attraction with a sizeable car park, a café and a 'Presents From' shop where one buys postcards, embroidered oven gloves and DVDs of trendy Irish singers with silver studs on their eyebrows. The racing is mixed: hurdles, chases and Flat. The tote pools are modest – no-one managed to get the Tricast of the handicap hurdle, so there was a carry-over to the next race of €167.

And all the best people were in attendance: Tommy Stack the trainer, Ruby Walsh the jockey, Sean Graham's son the bookmaker, and John Buckley, distinguished local estate agent, auctioneer and chairman of the race committee – my host. Also there was John O'Donoghue, Speaker of the Irish Parliament, who is the Member for Kerry and is treated there as is the angel Gabriel in heaven, though I am not sure Gabriel worried about getting re-elected.

The track is oval, about a mile in circumference, and you can see nearly all of it from the stands. The commentator is excellent, yet gets no mention on the racecard; there are 40 or more bookmakers, a lot of elderly folk to make me feel at home and as children are let in for free, many children in gaggles of half a dozen or so, watching, eating chips at €3 for a modestly filled saucer. It is a Murphy's track, no Guinness, which grieves me, for I find Murphy's has a sweetness I can do without.

Killarney, with nine meetings a year – though more soon, for nearby Tralee racecourse has been sold and there will be meetings going spare – prospers. The fees from TV coverage, food franchise, stout exclusivity and race sponsorship all do their part. Each race was sponsored, unlike those at some of our all-weather tracks, like the Eat A Prawn Cocktail In The Fourth Floor Bar Maiden Fillies' Claiming Stakes.

On day one, I failed to find a winner but only bet sparingly, the way you do with funny money. On day two I had a substantial trixie on Ruby Walsh's three mounts, but alas, only one winner. I abstained in the four-runner 7.30 when I met Ted Walsh, Ruby's trainer father, and son of old Ruby Walsh, whom I had known in the early 1960s.

We talked of the old man who trained and lived in Kill on the road to Punchestown, and as I was moving off, Ted mentioned that Collingwood in the handicap was a goodish thing.

I had been going to back Majestic Concorde and Total Eclipse in the 8.00, but kept my powder dry for the handicap (my first choice actually beat my second choice). A tip from a successful trainer, moreover one offered voluntarily, is what going racing rather than watching At The Races is all about, so I had decent bets.

Mr Graham offered me 8-1 plus fractions. Five minutes later I had another bet at 12s, before he went back to 8-1. I had intended to back Maximo, Maundy Money and Master Marvel, so had three savers: Collingwood to come second to each of my original choices. I passed the Collingwood information to the people at my table – we ate terrine, lamb or salmon, tiramisu – and they were really grateful. A tip from Ted Walsh, who is known to keep information close to his chest – moreover a tip proffered without prompting – wow, that's 'well worth the journey', as the *Michelin Guide* puts it when there is something good at the end of the line.

Collingwood finished fifth, my three were first, second and fourth, and after a drink at The Laurels in the town centre – a pub you would be foolish not to patronise – it was back to my hotel, where they had put a square of chocolate and a bedtime story on my pillow. It was an odd choice of bedtime story: Middle Ages. This woman had sworn not to make a noise regardless, but saw her own child lying dead on a table, screamed, with which her husband, as well as his horse, his table and his library, were sucked out of the window never to be seen again, though rumoured to be at the bottom of the lake, turned to stone. Ah well. Goodnight.

As for the hotel, they give you paper napkins with breakfast. Had there been a king in the kingdom, I would have mentioned this to His Majesty.

*

CAMELS, ROBOTS AND RICHES IN THE NEW DUBAI

25 OCTOBER 2008

THERE WERE A number of reasons why I went to Qatar last week: first the bite-sized Arabian country, as sponsor, presents the weather on Sky News as frequently and as accurately as anyone, for which it deserves praise; then Qataris showed they were goodish eggs by sponsoring the Prix de l'Arc de Triomphe, not just this year but until after the 2012 Olympics (which will cost them £20 million), though not perhaps outstandingly terrific eggs, else they would have invited me.

The third determining factor for my visit was that in late October the sun beams down on the Gulf at 40 degrees, and though my social ambitions are limited, I read in a glossy monthly that Doha, Qatar's capital, is 'the new Dubai' and the Four Seasons Hotel there 'the place for wannabes'.

I wannad to be warm and get a suntan in time for Doncaster this afternoon. The flight took six and a half hours, cost anarmenaleg, but had both *Gone With The Wind* and *The Great Escape* in its armoury of on-board films.

You will notice when there that the people smoke a lot, use their mobiles unceasingly, do not drink, wrap their women in black garments leaving no more than a thin slit for the eyes, do not gamble and adjourn for prayers five times a day: sunrise, sunset, noon, and twice when you don't expect it. What is unarguable is that someone up there is listening: 600,000 citizens employing 700,000 foreigners to do their work have a national income of £100 billion: that is one hundred thousand million pounds sterling, give or take a fiver because currency goes up and down, ours mostly down. We call it 'fluctuation'; they 'flucteuropeans'.

Qatar sits on the biggest gas reserves in the world, is building the biggest mosque in the world and is on the shortlist of hosts for the 2016 Olympic Games. A total of 450 new vehicles are registered daily, which may have something to do with having to wait up to three hours when you order a taxi.

The Racing and Equestrian Club is three miles (55 minutes through the traffic) from my hotel. Meetings take place on Thursdays, nine contests an evening; races for Thoroughbreds and Arabian horses, races for Qatar apprentices and amateur lady riders; minimum prize-money to a winner, £5,000; crowds of around 2,000 on ordinary nights. The track is a verdant green thanks to the brilliance of a South African groundsman. No means of betting, but racegoers can fill in a forecast sheet, pray facing east on hallowed ground by the paddock and win a Land Rover.

The Club is luxurious with VIP rooms in which you are seated on extra-comfortable sofas and receive cups of hot, sweet flavoured teas and coffees. The men are dressed in formal dish-dash with white headbands secured with black cords and tassels. They greet each other sometimes with between two and four kisses on each cheek, often by touching noses twice in quick succession like woodpeckers, otherwise by shaking hands, always standing up for greetings, so that walking along a row of spectators takes a while and wholly obscures vision to those in the row behind.

This year the season began a week late because of the many who had been at the Arc, so I went camel racing, out in the desert. I had witnessed this pastime in Dubai: big, hairy, evil-smelling, khaki-coloured beasts with long necks stretching from humped backs running great distances at considerable pace, encouraged so to do by ten-year-old Pakistani jockeys carrying sticks with which they beat their mounts' genitalia. It is a measure of camels' intelligence that the more their private parts were beleaguered, the faster they ran.

That has all got much more civilised: as a consequence of outrage by childrens' and camels' charities, the jockeys have been replaced. Robots are secured to the camel's hump and wield their sticks, hither and thus, harder and softer at the behest of their trainers' hand-held radio-controlled device. The course is fenced-off desert, the going predictably steady, for the entire nation's rainfall is 80mm a year, roughly what Worcester gets on an average Tuesday morning.

The crowd and the trainers and the stewards and the VIPs follow the camels, shouting encouragement, pressing 'hit left buttock 80 per cent hard' buttons, talking into their mobile phones, boasting of the value of their beasts.

His Highness the Emir pays for it all, patron of all that goes on. Small price to pay if you consider the worth of their oil and gas.

*

Clement Freud's final dispatch from a racecourse – though not his final day at the races – was from his beloved Cheltenham Festival in March 2009.

PLACE TO BE – UNLESS YOU DESIRE TO REMAIN SOLVENT
14 MARCH 2009

THERE WAS I on Wednesday afternoon at the exit gate of Prestbury Park: dressed in a medium green suit beset with appropriate badges, iridescent with the silver lining of failure, in fact glowing with a successlessness that the normally sighted could have spotted from any precipice in the West Country.

'Hurry, hurry for Today's Special,' was writ on the billboards. 'See Freud and his Amazing Diminishing Wallet.' Actually, you would not have had to hurry a lot, for diminution was slow, ongoing and unrelenting.

Selections got stuffed as if they were aubergines. Advice, purchased regardless of expense, some from men with hyphenated names wearing Harris tweed capes managed to underperform even my sub-six-year-old grandchildren's hunches. Tips from a normally dependable source who uses the innards of farmyard chickens which, up to the time of their humane slaughter, had led largely contented lives never caught the commentators' attention.

As for my nap, my bet of the meeting, the horse I had told waiters, shoe-shine boys and taxi-drivers to plunge on since ceasing to tip them on Valentine's Day ... he is now a statistic: the seventh favourite to have been pulled up in 19 years.

Until around 1.30 on Tuesday afternoon, it had all been terrific. I had ante-post vouchers the way other people have mice. For a fortnight, instead of backing brutes to win claimers and sellers at Southwell, maiden chases and novice hurdles at scenic locations

181

from Exeter to Kelso, I had a massive 33-1 punt on Golan Way to win Cheltenham's opener, shovelled money on Gone To Lunch from 14-1 down to 8s, and obtained proper odds against Wind Instrument, Casey Jones and The Polomoche.

A bookmaker who asked me not to mention his name laid me 10-1 against Venetia Williams wearing a purple hat on Wednesday, I had sixes against Ruby and AP falling off their horses in the same race and 100-1 Gordon Brown to accompany the Queen on Gold Cup day.

The second day of the festival, that which stars the Seasons Holidays Queen Mother Champion Chase is my day.

As Wednesday's card was cancelled last year, I tried to make up for the disappointment via a superior helicopter sporting a cabin bigger than my box, a luncheon of wondrous quality: handsomely potted shrimps, white asparagus, glazed slow-cooked mutton with finest caper sauce, Lincoln Poacher cheddar, raspberry pavlova, all accompanied by wines from Rheims in France, Marlborough in New Zealand, Valpolicella in Italy, Sauterne, France again, and a pear distillery in Holland. Wines that were sparkling and still, dry and sweet, from gentle nectars to killer spirits.

Cheltenham is absolutely the place to be ... unless you manifest some small desire to remain solvent. The course is replete with kindly readers of the *Racing Post* who have news of sure-fire winners, given to them in confidence by no less than the cousin of the stable groom's best friend's hairdresser, who is only telling me this because: 'Aren't you what's-it who writes that column on a Saturday? Let me shake your hand.'

Everybody knows something, except the man at the information desk, who was ignorant of the location of the nearest gents. When I finally found one, it was impeccably clean, with enough spare rolls of soft loo paper to make me worry about the future of rain forests.

6

THE PUNTER

❛ Alas, bookmakers no longer accommodate wagers on the 2.30 when you ring at 6pm, not even if you are well known and promise that you haven't seen the result ❜

DREAM TICKETS ON
THE CAMPAIGN TRAIL
13 OCTOBER 1999

THROUGHOUT THE 1950s, I ran a London nightclub which provided me with all the gambling opportunities a man needs. I gambled on whether to buy this wine or that; on whether to get enough ducks for 60 portions of *canard à l'orange* when only ten might be ordered; on whether to employ Rolf Harris or Nicholas Parsons in cabaret; and almost hourly, I assessed the odds against admitting or refusing entrance to customers on the borderline of inebriation.

I did gamble a bit on shares, because my clients tended to work in the City and brimmed with ideas on turning fast bucks.

Over the years, I worked out my own system: I had discovered that when I bought an equity, the ones alphabetically above and below mine went up in value, so I bought 'shares and their neighbours'.

My accountant once remarked how strange it was that all three of my holdings began with the letter Q. I told him I hadn't noticed.

In the 1960s, I lost the lease of my nightclub, became a TV cook, wrote children's books, embraced journalism and reopened dormant accounts with those nice men who trade on the rails of British racecourses.

One of my cricket clubs chartered a plane to take a party of us to Longchamp for the Arc of 1965 and I went along laden with money – I fancied Sea-Bird a lot. I considered him virtually invincible.

Before plunging on, I went to the parade ring to ensure that my fancy was in good shape and found that he was not. He was a dead ringer for a giant shaving brush. Half a ton of horse covered in lather: sweat ran down his neck, litres of what looked like Greek yoghurt oozed from beneath his saddle, his rump was awash.

I know a bit about horses: when they deploy enough energy to produce a bathtub-full of white froth, the likelihood diminishes of their retaining sufficient verve to beat two dozen of the best Thoroughbreds in the world over 12 furlongs.

I passed the queues of bettors at the tote windows, returned to my party and offered to lay Sea-Bird at Pari Mutuel odds: 'Save you queuing to get on and I pay out more quickly than the Gauloise smokers behind the windows.'

I wrote the bets on the back of my racecard: £50 Fred. £65 Angus. £40 Charlie. £3 Charlie's girlfriend, on and on. As Sea-Bird paraded in front of the stands the sweat glistened in the afternoon sunlight; when he cantered to the start, specks of white foam flew into the air. I nodded smugly.

Sea-Bird won rather comfortably, but I was absolutely right – the people who had not bet with me spent an age waiting to be paid.

In 1973, I fought a by-election for the parliamentary seat of the Isle of Ely, the contest occasioned by the death of the sitting Member. At the general election in 1970, it had been a straight fight between Tory and Labour. Tory had won, as they had every election since 1945. We were in the dark days of Ted Heath's premiership and Harold Wilson's crap opposition. I had the substantial advantage of not being a member of either main party: a lifelong anti-Conservative who could not join Clause 4 Labour, I was only just a member of the Liberals; by nature I am not a joiner.

Ladbrokes, advised by a man called Ron Pollard, priced the by-election 6-1 on Conservatives, 7-2 Labour, 33-1 Liberal.

Odds of 33-1 against a trier looked absurd. So I backed myself. Decent bookmakers accept £10,000 to £300 and I had several of those, as a consequence of which my odds tumbled to eights.

Eights is credible: 8-1 the outsider of three lets you hold your head up, and I was fortunate in that the political editor of the *Daily Telegraph* covered the Isle of Ely by-election and wrote: 'The clever money seems to be going on Freud.'

It was actually the Freud money that had gone on Freud, but there was a fair amount of activity and, when I won the seat, some said that it was only because so many people had backed me and wanted a return on their investment. One of my punts had been at Ladbrokes in High Street, March, in my constituency, and they deducted tax from my winnings. I pointed out that this was an on-course wager. I lost that argument. For the record, when I was defeated five elections later, I was 5-1 on.

Fortune smiled on my political bets. Had to smile, to pay for the many good four-legged brutes that failed to do what I predicted. I accept that bookmakers know more than me about horses. But the reverse is true when it comes to politics.

In 1979, Corals laid me 11-2 against retaining my seat and let me have a Super Canadian with five other Liberals – two at 10s, one at sevens, another at fives and Emlyn Hooson at even money to retain Montgomery, a constituency Liberals have held for the entire century.

Hooson, alone, lost – cost me half a million – but my bets, prudently placed in small denominations so as not to exceed maximum payouts, still yielded six figures. Since then, no sane bookmaker takes multiple bets on members of the same political party.

Sadly there were no racecourses in my constituency, so I couldn't go to a track and pretend it was business. After a while it seemed prudent to eschew betting shops also. Tell someone what you are backing and you are on a hiding to nothing. If it wins – 'Why didn't you tell everyone?' If it loses – 'You daft bugger. Next election I'll vote for the other chap.'

When Simon Hughes stood for Bermondsey in February 1983, I thought he was in with a squeak. Ladbrokes offered 16-1. I blessed Ron Pollard and took £1,000 to £60, decided to put my mouth where my money was and went canvassing in Bermondsey.

A few days later I felt our campaign was making progress and had another £100 on Hughes; the odds were 5-1 and, as canvass returns looked better and better, I had £700 to £400 and said to the Ladbrokes man, 'I feel this is very close to insider trading.' He said: 'Nonsense, people always tell lies to canvassers.'

So the next day I had £600 at 6-5 on. Hughes gained a landslide victory. Had spread betting been around, I would have done even better, as third party winners always seem to romp away with the votes.

Martin Bell, the Mr Clean candidate who stood against Neil Hamilton in Tatton at the last election, is a case in point. Bookmakers made them joint-favourites at 5-4 on. Spread firms let you buy Bell's majority at 400 votes, sell at 50. I bought. Bell won by over 11,000. Spread betting when you buy and it goes your way is joyous; selling tends to make more sense, but wholly louses up enjoyment.

For the last couple of years I have consistently gone short on England Test match runs and, while this was a sensible and profitable course of action, watching cricket and saying 'hell' and 'damn' and 'bum' each time England scored or the opposition bowled a wide is just no fun. Betting should be fun.

I am sitting on a 'sell' of the maximum winning margin of any Rugby World Cup game. I went short at quite a lot of money per point at 113 ... believing that, when one team is 60 or so points ahead, they will go easy, not rub in their superiority nor risk injury to their players.

The oddsmakers' belief is that when a team is 60 points up, they rest the star players and field substitutes hell-bent on making names for themselves.

We shall wait and see; whatever is the outcome, this is unlikely to be my last wager.

*

TAKEN FOR A RIDE

10 NOVEMBER 1999

I WAS 16, standing in a queue at Stamford Bridge dogs waiting to be paid for a 2/- forecast when this man caught my eye and bowed. Some minutes later, while I was watching the dogs parading for the next, the same man approached me and apologised, saying: 'You bear this striking resemblance to the Duke of Kent. I used to work at Buckingham Palace and mistook you for His Royal Highness; now I see that you are younger. I trust my earlier familiarity caused you no distress.'

I told him that, on the contrary, I was rather flattered. We chatted and he told me that it was his job to ensure that Tote odds and bookmakers' odds were similar; if he noted a significant difference in the Tote price of the dog that was to win, he had money to put things right.

'So you always know who is going to win?', I asked.

'Ninety-five per cent of the time,' he replied.

We had a cup of coffee and he said that, as he had embarrassed me, he would make up for it by letting me put a tenner on the next winner. I had not got a tenner. After some discussion he consented to let me put on the 30 shillings I did have and we agreed to meet in the coffee bar after the race. The winner was returned at 5-1 and I hurried to our rendezvous and waited and waited.

It was not for some time that the unlikelihood of the Duke of Kent standing in the cheap enclosure at Stamford Bridge dogs on a Tuesday afternoon occurred to me.

I backed Purple Flash to win a big handicap at Kempton – £5 on the nose at 8-1. Purple Flash won and I went to the bookmaker who said: 'They haven't weighed in yet.'

After the weigh-in I gave him my ticket and he shouted: 'No wonder you were in a hurry to get paid, you were on Blue Legend.'

We abused each other for a while and a ring inspector was summoned. He suggested I take the man to the authorities and gave me names and addresses to which to write.

About three weeks later I was called to attend a meeting of the Tattersalls Committee in an upstairs room at the Café Royal, near Piccadilly Circus. Some serious-looking, elderly men asked me to state my case. The bookmaker was there to state his. He had £45 ready in his hand, paid me and disappeared into the London afternoon muttering: 'I didn't think you'd bother to go through all that for a miserable £45.'

In Martinique, at a Mardi Gras fair I was so spectacularly ripped off by a practitioner of the three-card trick that I congratulated the card-sharper and told him it had been a pleasure doing business with him. On a bench behind us, a young Creole girl fondling a grandfather figure told him it had been a business doing pleasure.

*

AGE IS NO BAR TO A GAMBLER
17 NOVEMBER 2004

I FELT BADLY last week, turning on the morning news and consistently hearing that Yasser Arafat was not dead. I am not dead, they didn't mention that. As a representative of those on the crematorium side of 80, I feel our voice should be heard positively. The sadness of our inability to perform as effectively as we did is made up by the niceness of those who recognise our maturity. A man of 70 got up to offer me his seat on a bus the other day; not infrequently do I hear the words: 'Can't be Freud, he's dead – innit?'

The fact is that we of four-score years and some can still do pretty well everything we did before. We run – more slowly. We jump – less high. We swim – along the bottom of the pool, and if we are lucky enough to get a proposition we just have to consider this carefully. 'Will you come upstairs and make love to me?' was once answered in the affirmative with alacrity. Now I tell them, 'One or the other.'

Fortunately, age is no trouble to a gambler. Had I been a bus conductor (my first career choice until I discovered that they did not get to keep the money they collected) I doubt I would still be in work. Bus stairs take an age to climb and having to hold on with both hands while the vehicle negotiates a bend is unconducive to the sale of tickets.

But gambling has no upper limit; rather the reverse. Investment in contests of chance actually benefit from the fact that after an elongated span of pitting your wits against dealers and wheelers, your next of kin has ceased to expect much from your ultimate betting slip – the one that begins with 'Being of sound mind I bequeath ...'

It is odd, is it not? That with folk living longer and governments ever eager to appear to show concern for the needs of the aged (my friend Bev washes old people for a living), no-one considers the hardship of a gambler denied access to his passion.

Watercolour painters on the verge of falling off the perch are taken to comfortable day centres where they can mess about with brushes and canvas; lovers of books who have lost their sight and some of their hearing have 'readings'; and for the halt and the lame sitting in lounges of old people's homes there's always Richard and Judy.

I have spent the last two weeks in a clinic in southern Austria, a land of calm and beauty. I lived on the shores of a large blue lake surrounded by nicely kept mountains, down which you steadily expected to see Julie Andrews and those awful children singing, 'The hills are alive with the sound of music.' The natives were friendly, wore lederhosen and played glockenspiel – also said 'Gruss Gott', which is like 'good day' involving Him.

No gambling. A TV channel showing you the same football match for a week at a time; the news, the weather, the state of the stock market and any number of films in which Anthony Hopkins, Julia Roberts and Maggie Smith spoke fluent German. Nothing for a man for whom even simulated dog racing from Monmore would have been a relief. While enemas were available around the clock, there were no playing cards and the backgammon board lacked dice.

And then, after a week, I saw an advertisement for a casino in a nearby village. I asked reception whether this would be open in winter. Reception said: 'Yes.'

Do they have roulette and blackjack? They do.

At home I can take or leave casinos. Going racing entails a mixture of skill and luck, and I regret the absence of skill in roulette. The house has a three per cent pull and is obliged to stay and take bets, while you the punter can leave at any time you want. In casinos there are no 'experts' who sidle up to you with information like 'No. 36 at the roulette table by the window is really hot; did some terrific work in front of the cleaners this morning, will not be beaten.' I miss that.

As we are about to be swamped by casinos and there are not – yet – specialist roulette columnists, let me explain the game.

Thirty-seven numbers from which to choose, each paying 35-1 for a hit. On a well-balanced wheel, between now and infinity, each number will come up an even number of times. If you were to take 37 chips, say £50 chips because we don't mess about, and pick a number such as 24 and play that at each spin of the wheel, there is a very strong likelihood that it will come up before you have lost all your ammunition. Go home, gloat, tell them gambling is easy.

It isn't quite like that. It takes a man of iron will (and unparalleled tediousness) to spend an hour at a roulette table placing a single chip on the same single number while all around are varying their bids, multiplying them and occasionally whooping with joy.

The man must remain at it, even while 5 and 16 – the numbers either side of 24 – come up; and because infinity is a long way off, there is as little reason for 24 to come up in an evening as there is for a coin to come down tails when it has come down heads 12 times running. We have a law of probabilities which favours tails. The law of averages remains at evens.

The casino to which I went wanted me to wear a jacket and I paid €40 to borrow one of theirs. They asked for €21 entrance fee – for which they gave me €25 of chips, and when my number came up at roulette and they paid me, the croupier stopped the wheel.

What goes on?, I asked.

You have not yet tipped us.

How much do you expect?

One chip of your 35.

I asked what would happen if I lost – did I get a tip? They looked horrified.

I took my winnings to a blackjack table, played one box for €100 chips and got two eights against the dealer's 5. I split the eights, got a 2 on one and a 3 on the other and bought a card for each. The dealer bust, as dealers with a 5 tend to do, and I left a tip, cashed in my chips, gave them back their jacket, drove to the clinic and the next day I switched on the television to learn that Yasser Arafat was dead.

*

EASIER TO GET TO THAN THE TRACK AND THE PEOPLE ARE NICER
26 JANUARY 2005

TESCO RECENTLY ANNOUNCED that, out of every £8 spent in the United Kingdom, £1 ends up in its tills. Hurrah for Tesco. There was a time when £2 out of every £8 I spent ended up in a bookmaker's satchel, but that sort of thing is all over. For the last 40-plus years betting shops have featured in my life – they were easier to get to than racetracks, were closer to the kind of restaurants I like to visit and on the whole had a nicer clientele: you very seldom met pushy, bowler-hatted, ex-cavalry people in betting shops.

Readers would have to be over 60 to remember the early days of legalised offices, as they called them (staffed by turf accountants).

In the beginning they were anonymous – not permitted to have signs over their doors or shop windows through which you could see what was happening inside. The law that permitted licensing these establishments was explicit in demanding that only those people with a real need to gamble would be patrons. So, no carpets, no chairs, no beverages and, of course, no television sets depicting the action; just a screen showing the odds and a race commentary via a sound system.

The Rothschild report had decreed that there must be nothing, absolutely nothing that could be termed as 'attractive' or a 'come on' to the innocent. 'What larks,' as Joe Gargery used to say to Pip in *Great Expectations*.

My favourite location – until it closed some ten years ago – was a William Hill in Soho, very near one of my favourite restaurants, The Pavilion, at 15 Poland Street.

The shop had a regular *dramatis personae* of two – a yellow-jacketed City of Westminster dustman who quietly contemplated life in one corner, and an elderly, red-haired bag-lady with a penchant for oranges, which she peeled and ate in the other.

We, the irregulars, wondered whether she wanted to be mistaken for a latter-day Nell Gwyn. She had been a prison officer in Glasgow, possibly the best screw north of the border; she was then almost certainly the best-smelling bag-lady in London W1.

When the shop closed, I took my Soho custom to a nearby Coral shop where business was brisker and among the punters was a mean-looking man with a Birmingham accent who would watch the action on the screens, then move to the doorway and shout four-figure bets into his mobile telephone.

'It's me, Graham. Let me have a £3,000 win on the four dog at

Monmore.' We watched the odds for that race and, regardless of the amount of Graham's bet, his selections never shortened in price.

I went there last week after a sensational lunch at The Pavilion and Ron Atkinson, the failed diplomat, would have been surprised – sitting in post-meridian occupation of the two roulette machines were a brace of really beautiful Chinese girls.

They played 20p three-number lines; watching them was much more fun than the racing from Wolverhampton. It took them several hours to lose their tenners.

*

IT'S NEVER TOO LATE TO HAVE A BET – EVEN IN THE POST-PAGET ERA
5 OCTOBER 2005

I THINK A lot about the late Dorothy Paget. In the 1930s and '40s, she was subject of much attention and endless discussion in racing circles. Golden Miller, the Arkle/Desert Orchid/Best Mate/Red Rum of his day, was owned by Miss Paget, who was excessively fat, stupendously rich and became famously eccentric.

While she continued to own horses, she lived a life of considerable indulgence which included staying in bed until late afternoon. Then would her butler bring the morning papers and a light meal: perhaps a brace of roasted woodcock, some scrambled eggs to accompany the Reform lamb cutlets and a toasted brioche with caviar – whatever – and shortly before the evening news, she'd telephone Mr William Hill and place her bets on the afternoon races.

Alas, bookmakers no longer accommodate wagers on the 2.30 when you ring at 6pm, not even if you are well known and promise that you haven't seen the result, which, of course, Miss Paget had not. But Mr Hill trusted Miss Paget and he became rich, and like Hilaire Belloc's heroine, 'bought a house in Berkeley Square and was accepted everywhere'. (Actually I think it was a stud farm in Hampshire, but you get my drift.)

I am once more in an Austrian clinic where UK newspapers arrive a day late. Horseracing does not feature in the lifestyle of the land of my fathers; television sport consists of old and recent football matches with occasional visits to bouts of kick boxing; no mention of Longchamp.

Some months ago, Johnny Murtagh opined that Motivator was an Arc horse and I placed a sizeable bet on that happening; a bet that would, if successful, permit a dozen dinners at Gordon Ramsay's in Chelsea's Hospital Road, accompanied by wines appropriate to the man's culinary genius. To put it another way, I would be shit-high up the creek if Motivator lost.

In 1835, the people of Birmingham got to know the result of the St Leger five and a half hours after the race. A judge had been retained to confirm the document listing the order of finish and the information was galloped to its destination by a messenger who changed horses every 15 miles.

Communication has improved. We have telephone and radio, television and computers, though not in the Austrian clinic where a nice woman in a white coat has just brought me a linen bag of hot dried herbs and attached it to my lower body where my liver is meant to be. I do have a mobile phone, but listening to a commentary on a telephone with no-one to cheer or commiserate provides minimal pleasure. 'The loneliness of the long-distance bettor' I seem to recall was the name of a film ... or possibly not.

On Sunday morning, the *Frankfurter Allgemeine* is the only paper in the clinic to mention the Arc – which they do in an article on the Aga Khan and his Shawanda. There is not a word about Motivator, though most other runners are mentioned as possible dangers.

I ring my friend Andy, co-owner of Orpen Wide, and ask what the Sunday papers are saying about the race at Longchamp. He tells me

Motivator is being backed: from 5-1 overnight to 5-2 favourite –
roughly a quarter the odds at which I backed him in June.

'Will you be able to watch it?' I say: 'No – send me a text if it
wins.'

I was watching a repeat of the Luxembourg women's tennis
quarter-final on my television set when the phone rang. Andy
said: 'The last few horses are going into the stalls, I'll put the
phone by the TV set.'

As I listened to the commentary, which was nice and clear as
the pacemakers did their job, it became thunderous gibberish as
the field entered the home straight, and I was left clueless as to
the result, but pretty sure that the volume of noise could not have
come as a consequence of an English horse's victory on French
turf.

I put down the phone, determined to read Tuesday's UK papers
with care, did so and bang went lavish dinners in Chelsea. I did
decide that when I got home, I might buy a cut price grouse in
Marylebone's Sunday market, stuff it with sea salted butter and
grated lemon rind, cover it with slices of streaky bacon, bake it in
a hot oven for 28 minutes and allow it to cool for ten.

It is best served with toasted breadcrumbs and bread sauce
made with cream, flavoured with ground mace. Spinach, topped
with an anchovy scented hollandaise sauce, would be a good
accompaniment ... but Gordon Ramsay will have to wait for my
custom.

*

BOOKMAKERS RUN FOR COVER
AS 'QUIET COUP' NETS A FORTUNE
12 OCTOBER 2005

I UNDERSTAND FROM the bookmaking industry that the victory
of Orpen Wide in the Royal British Legion Handicap at 25-1 last

Sunday over the round mile at Newcastle will go down as 'a quiet coup'; the sort of thing Iain Duncan Smith, had he been a punter rather than a Conservative politician, might have engineered. I was proud.

The three-year-old gelding had previously won twice over five furlongs and twice over six. It was at Windsor at an evening meeting in early June, in a race in which he finished in 12th place with a fair amount of shrewd money on him to get closer, that his trainer Michael Chapman – the Sage of Market Rasen – laid him out for this event. 'We'll run him at Newcastle on 9 October in a Grade 6 event over a mile,' he said. 'The track is round so we shall need a low draw.'

I was impressed. I nodded agreement.

After he had been drawn 16 out of 17, I phoned the trainer on the morning of the race and asked what he thought.

He replied: 'It will help his odds. Drawn nearer the inside rail, he would be shorter.'

The 5.15 race was priced up at noon; Orpen Wide was 25-1 everywhere, just as if there were no Monopolies Commission to ensure proper competition. I began my peregrination after a late-morning croissant at Patisserie Valerie in Marylebone High Street. Then, armed with a 5cm (2in in old money) wad of £20 notes, a hat pulled over my eyes, wearing a scarf that covered my chin, I spent the afternoon visiting those inns of ultimate unhappiness labelled Ladbrokes, Coral, etc.

I mingled, if there was anyone with whom to mingle (it *was* Sunday), had a read of the shop's *Racing Post*, now and then put a pound coin into the roulette machine, and wrote out my betting slip; £20 win Orpen Wide, or £19 when my bet on 24 at roulette had achieved no result. I did not take a price.

I drove towards King's Cross, stopping where there was a betting shop, repeating the routine, moving on through Islington, Old Street, Waterloo – where number 24 came up and I increased my bet to £36 – Kennington, Brixton and Clapham. In a Battersea shop there was so much trade I slipped in a couple of extra £15 win bets without the man behind the counter taking notice.

By 4pm I had run out of money, but carried in my pockets some 80 betting slips.

I returned home for Earl Grey tea and a Bakewell tart, which I brush with double cream, anoint with caster sugar and briefly crisp under a hot grill. The afternoon had gone well.

Orpen Wide, since his last win in May, had been a disappointment. He had run without success at Windsor, Beverley, Redcar, Ripon, Newmarket and Leicester; he had sunk in the handicap from 71 to 64. 'Others preferred' had been the summation of the tipsters. On Sunday his price remained steady, and I waited until the horses were behind the stalls and some of them were in before I telephoned my bookmaker and had a proper bet on account.

I was never in much doubt. The stalls opened, Paul Eddery jumped him out nicely, got a position on the rail after about three furlongs, lay a handy third or fourth until the two-furlong post and coaxed him home with a comfortable length to spare, returning the fastest time of the afternoon.

Although the commentator mentioned that the winner was carrying my colours, the response from the crowd was muted, the way it tends to be with winning outsiders; in fact, only one horse was returned at longer odds than Orpen Wide. He came last. I hope his owner had a more relaxed Sunday afternoon than me.

When the race was over and the trainer had received a framed photograph of our horse as a mark of the Royal British Legion's approval, he and I had a conversation about our equine hero's future.

'Did the jockey suggest we supplement him for the Cesarewitch?', I asked.

Chapman said no, but he did say he hoped he would feature favourably in the Wednesday column.

No question of that: congratulations to the trainer, the stable, the jockey, the handicapper, the groundsmen, the stalls handlers, not forgetting the bride's mother. There.

Now – before you accuse me of including you out of my big afternoon – let me tell you what actually happened on Sunday.

We were having tea with my younger daughter and her children in Notting Hill, got home just after 5pm and the phone rang. It was Michael Chapman, who said: 'Your horse has just won the 5.15 at Newcastle.'

Well, I said, I'll be buggered ... although I am not sexually that way inclined; it is a form of speech denoting surprise.

*

RUN FOR IT

23 NOVEMBER 2005

I SHALL NOT forget Sir Winston Churchill's grey horse Colonist. In 1951, I took my new wife to Royal Ascot and backed him each-way in the Gold Cup.

Colonist came second among muted cheers and V-signs and the queues at the Tote payout windows were so long we decided to have a shilling glass of wine, and wait to collect later that afternoon. When the queues were small, I joined one, shoved my ticket under the glass screen and the tote woman said: 'You *have* done well.' A few moments later she added: 'I make that £123, 12 shillings and sixpence,' counting the money with care before passing it towards me. I was expecting £9 and I started to tremble: my legs were quivering, my hand shook as I gathered the white £5 notes, my eyes fixed on the race 3 printed on my ticket as she paid on an outsider in another race, who had the same number as Colonist had carried.

I got about two paces from the window when she noticed, called out 'Excuse me, sir', then 'You there' as I was running away at my best speed.

'You must give it back,' said my wife when I told her. I explained that no-one would be the worse for the Tote woman's mistake; there were hundreds of people who lost their tickets or simply did not claim their winnings. Later, when I met a friend who asked me how I was doing, I told him I had backed Colonist and won three months' wages; he was very impressed. 'Didn't know you bet so heavily,' he said. 'You will come to a sticky end.' I still feel a bit guilty.

*

THE BEST 25 MINUTES
I'VE HAD IN A LONG TIME
29 SEPTEMBER 2007

MY FRIEND COUNCILLOR Wright and I went racing the other day, not for any good reason like owning one of the runners or having privileged information about who might win, but because we enjoy gambling; especially do we enjoy the idea of doing serious damage to the profitability of bookmakers. Not for us the fiver each-way bet on an 11-2 chance when there is an odds-on good thing; more like all or nothing, with the outcome usually the latter. We each picked a horse in the first four contests and placed 16 (2x2x2x2) £10 accumulators.

The councillor's selection won the first race at 7-1, mine took the second at 14-1, and bugger me with a garden rake if we did not have £1,200 going on two horses in the third race. We sipped glasses of the widow Clicquot's sparkling wine, and he thought we might lay off some of our bet. I considered ringing the Problem Gamblers hotline for advice, then realised that I would sooner be in line for winning a five-figure sum than going home £150 up.

I suppose the difference between gamblers and shrewd punters is that 'they' would ensure ending up with a profit regardless of the result; we did sums on the back of the racecard, finally decided to sit it out. Our horses were 4-1 and 6-1, to reward us with £6,000 or £9,600 going on to our selections in the fourth race. This was of academic interest, for our horses finished second and third.

'What sort of time did you have?', asked the dread Lady Freud when I got home, and I told her that I had had one of my most uplifting 25 minutes for a long time. I spent this awaiting the culmination of a high-class dream, watching the changing odds of two horses carrying four-figure investments.

I read somewhere that the difference between heaven and hell was minimal; both involved being dead, although apparently the quality of heaven's sweet trolleys was superior. What concerns me as my age moves from ancient to past-it is what will remain available to gamblers embarking on what Shakespeare called the seventh age of man – sans teeth, sans hair, and quite especially 'sans anything'. It must be a bit like being Belgian.

With a son of the manse ruling us from Downing Street, the likelihood of the government sponsoring old peoples' admission to places where we can dream – like a racecourse, dog-track or casino – is remote.

I quite often give up gambling, sometimes for as long as a week, but need to know that it is out there if I have need of it. There is a Ladbrokes at the end of my street; I have been known to go in, feeling that I won't much miss £20 but would be hugely chuffed if I won £300, so I play roulette on a machine. Do I win all that often?

Possibly not, but on Wednesday afternoon I had gone to the Post Office to send a birthday parcel to a New York-based grandson, passed the corner premises and went in having decided to have one bet.

I looked at the list of numbers that had featured on that wheel over the last 20 spins (as if that made any difference), placed a tenner on 29, which came up, instantly making me feel a whole lot better – pains gone, mobility restored, even my problems re which buttons to press to receive a voucher for my winnings overcome.

I collected £360, thereby saving the NHS serious money that it would have cost you, the taxpayer, on making me better.

*

MY MOST MEMORABLE BET

13 SEPTEMBER 2008

THURSDAY'S *POST* CARRIED a ten square inch front-page box headed 'Having Trouble Getting On?' I, who also has trouble getting off, turned as was suggested to pages 6 and 7 to find it not to be advice on instant dating, how to use chat-up lines, in front of which pictures to wait for proposals in art galleries. Nor were the pages remotely helpful to those who can sweet-talk women into submission, then have terminal problems with zips and buttons. It was about bets: getting a bet on.

As a Member of Parliament some 30 years ago I was responsible for bringing into our legislation a law that made it illegal not to state on the cover of a map the date when the information contained therein was valid. My private Dating of Maps bill, opposed by Ordnance Survey, who found it profitable to print in huge quantities, eventually rose from its humble beginnings to becoming an Act of Parliament.

While the law is busying itself interfering with what can and cannot occur in betting shops, I want to see the implementation of compulsory displays of the amount they will accept on over-the-counter bets before head office is rung for confirmation, during which you stand and wait to the fury of those in the queue behind you and the odds change. Good bookmakers already do this. It should be general. Last month I went into a betting shop in Grayshott, told the woman behind the counter I was backing a particular horse at its current price of 5-2, wrote out the betting slip, which she took and then said, 'It's now 9-4.'

The horse won, the way horses do when I have not backed them. I shall not go back in case the woman is still there.

People are frequently asked about their most cherished bet and relate stories of final legs of accumulators winning after the horse in front was disqualified.

My most memorable and successful bet was in a shop at Royston in Hertfordshire many years ago. I was driving from Westminster to Ely, where I had a meeting, on an afternoon when my horse Escarole was running in a race I did not expect it to win. Passing through Royston around the time my colt was to run, I went into the betting shop to watch the action. I was the only customer. With a few minutes to the off the manager – possibly owner – said, 'This is a betting shop, not an effing viewing parlour; either you have a bet or you piss off.'

The screen showed an open race from an afternoon greyhound meeting and I wrote 'Monmore 3.41, £20 Trap 2 to beat Trap 4' and put the slip and the money on his desk. My birthdate is 24/4/24. I tend to order number 24 in Chinese restaurants and back 2 and 4 in forecasts, which really do come up a lot (while the actual statistics are about once in 30 races, one forgets when it does not). On this occasion the dog in the blue jacket beat the one in black, both were at very long odds, my winnings came to over £1,600 for which I had to wait while the foul-mouthed one went to the bank blaspheming all the way.

My least favourite bet was at Cottenham point-to-point. My eldest brother, who is extremely knowledgeable about hunter chases, advised that an outsider had shown considerable form before his injury and two-year rest, and could be returning to winning form. I found a bookmaker away from the main ring who showed the horse at 20-1, accepted £50 to win, and when I returned to collect, he burst into tears.

*

HAPPINESS IS HAVING A BIG BULGE IN YOUR TROUSERS

4 OCTOBER 2008

NEWARK NORTHGATE STATION must be one of the very best railway terminals in Britain. A wondrously courteous, amazingly helpful, impressively uniformed staff abounds – even the man who sweeps the floor of the waiting room was dressed as if Her Majesty was due in on the 18.34.

When I arrived there from Southwell, after the last race and the Friday traffic jam, the man at the barrier, noticing I was past the first flush of youth, showed me the location of the lift that saves the halt and the lame from the rigours of the footbridge stairs.

I pressed the requisite button for the elevator to permit my entrance, noticing the impeccable spotlessness of the interior and, once inside, with the gate closed, pressed the button pointing upwards. 'Keep calm,' said a voice. 'Help is on the way.' So I pressed the other button that pointed upwards and we (the lift and I) ascended, then came a short walk, a descent that was all you could desire, and arrival at Platform 2 which, were it possible, seemed even more attractive than the one on the western side at which I had arrived earlier in the afternoon.

Announcements of a quality superior to Radio 4 provided almost non-stop entertainment. 'The London train due to arrive at Platform 2 is running 12 minutes late. An express train is about to pass Platform 1 at great speed, please stand well behind the yellow line. The service for Cleethorpes will leave from Platform 3, calling at Lincoln.' Hardly a dull moment. The evening sun bathed us in its amber light, the quality of the waiting passengers was unblemished – nobody smoked, sang or threw up – and there were welcoming, nicely maintained benches all along the platform, which is more than you get at King's Cross. As a station, King's Cross sucks.

I wallowed in contentedness, tried to think back to when I last felt as happy, even though there was one element of discomfort about my person. This was caused by an unyielding lump in my left trouser pocket, and yet it was this very lump that made for my euphoria: the consequence of having placed £50 each-way on Last One Standing at 50-1 in the bumper.

Since I began my gambling life with a bet of two pence each-way on a 7-2 shot at Buckfastleigh in the early 1930s, I must have backed something at 50-1, although I certainly don't recall winning anything at that attractive price.

Last One Standing, who had never before seen a racecourse, whose only trip in a horsebox had been the previous week when her trainer drove her to an adjacent roundabout as an introduction to travelling, won nicely. Mark Goldstein rides well, is worth his 5lb claim, while the talented trainer, Sheena West of Lewes, is one whose horses always deserve an extra look.

Had I attended another meeting, or taken my business to Hill's or Chandler's plush betting offices in Mayfair, I would have received my winnings in three sealed packages of £1,000 plus two £50 notes. Not at Southwell, I did not.

Michael Cannon – A Sure Fire Bet – with whom I transacted the speculation asked me to wait a few minutes, and then handed me this massive bundle that began with five Scottish £100 notes and followed, via two £50 notes, with more £20s and tenners and fivers than you can shake a stick at, all wrapped – at my request – by two ultra-strength rubber bands. What is more, the bookmaker was really nice about paying out, said: 'Well done.'

*

ONCE AGAIN THE JOY OF SIX HAS BEEN DENIED ME
22 NOVEMBER 2008

THERE ARE THOSE who think that interesting things stop happening when you are old. Not so. At 3.30pm last Saturday, for an investment of £96, I was the holder of one of the 19 tickets that survived the first five Scoop6 races, was in line for winning £3 million.

My bet had consisted of three bankers at Cheltenham: Pricewise's selection in the handicap chase at 2pm, Spotlight's nap in the Paddy Power Gold Cup – about which my knowledgeable friend Marten Julian had also been extremely confident – and the very good thing, tipped by Topspeed, Postdata, RP Ratings and Spotlight, in the novice handicap hurdle.

For the other three races I had supported the diverse selections of that valiant quartet of my collegiate equine advisers, providing me with four runners in the 2.55 at Wetherby, three (Topspeed and RP Ratings had both gone for the same brute) in the 3.25 and four in the 3.10 back at Cheltenham. Hence my 48 lines at £2.

'Sitting pretty' is not a phrase I like, but it is hard to think of other verbiage to describe a recumbent posture when within shouting distance of weekly deliveries of truffled goose liver and enough dosh to shower in Krug champagne for the rest of one's life.

Fifteen minutes before the final leg, both England and Scotland were in contention in their respective rugby internationals, so I watched them for a while, then switched channels to a really interesting programme from Japan featuring some entirely naked ladies, with which I had a glass of very cold pink Sancerre and a dish of warm, salted, buttered cashew nuts.

Reading the Sunday paper the following morning, I turned to the sports pages and observed that no-one had won the Scoop6. That included me. What a shame. It does mean that the Tote, which is quite close to many of our hearts, will get interest on the millions that were carried over, seven per cent if they invested with Anglo Irish Bank.

In the beginning, betting shops had to abide by the most dire rules to deter any but the most dedicated punters. By law shops were allowed no sign outside the door, no chairs, no carpet, no pictures on the walls, no food or drink.

The laws have been relaxed, and if you look around there are now some quite agreeable betting shops that will give you cups of instant coffee, the occasional biscuit or sandwich, cake on high days and holidays.

I have not examined recent legislation pertaining to these inns of ultimate unhappiness, but I doubt it would be outwith the law to give punters things they wanted to eat. When it became common knowledge that a particular chain of shops provided some desirable gastro item, I believe they would flourish. Ladbrokes for lozenges, Paddy Power for pork scratchings, Chandler for cheese straws.

7

THE COLUMNIST

❛ My memory is beginning to go a bit, also my memory is beginning to go a bit ❜

The piece opposite was the first Clement Freud column published in the Racing Post *under the heading '80+', with a 'shoutline' proclaiming: 'Sir Clement Freud casts an experienced eye on events in the racing world.' Within a few weeks the shoutline had become 'Another week older and deeper in debt', reflecting two of the regular preoccupations of the column, and a third staple theme was suggested by the line used from May 2008 onwards: 'Good to soft, firm in places.'*

Appropriately for a man whose grandfather wrote the ground-breaking psychoanalytic study Jokes and their Relation to the Unconscious *(first published in 1905), Clement Freud was a dedicated connoisseur of jokes. They would be seamlessly woven into his writing, and before long the '80+' column was featuring a weekly joke. Far from remaining aloof from his readers, Freud supplied his email address so that they could send him their own favourite jokes, and he received several a day. Occasionally a joke was not understood by everyone, and the story about the four bee-keepers on pages 252–3 baffled many readers. Freud himself, who did get the joke, was highly amused by such bewilderment, and insisted that the story should be included in this book.*

WHEN A STRANGER GIVES ME
A RED-HOT TIP, WHAT ELSE AM I TO DO?

13 JULY 2005

TIPSTERS ARE BELIEVED to be the third oldest profession – right up there behind prostitutes and bookmakers. When Goliath, the great Philistine, was generally quoted at 1-5, there was a fair amount of clever money on David at 11-4, advised by a service in Bethlehem.

A shrewdy from Byzantium had his clients in at 6-4 against St Paul's letters to the Romans getting delivered within a week ... and so it has gone on.

A newsletter from Auchtermuchty recommended backing the Scots to win Bannockburn (England were 4-9) and there was something of a coup in the Lowlands when an 'adviser' suggested a Lucky 15 on Salamanca, Victoria, Toulouse and Waterloo all going to us rather than the odds-on French; Napoleon was ever a popular favourite.

An antecedent of Paddy Power offered 28-1 against Bonaparte ending his days on St Helena (Orkney was 5-2 favourite) – a hot tip believed to come from the Admiralty caused layers serious damage.

The trouble about tipping is that, as with the oldest profession, some people do it because they enjoy doing it, for free, for the feel-good factor. Unlike prostitution, there is often nothing in it for the receiver.

In my youth, Prince Monolulu, wearing his tall, feathered head-dress, paraded outside racecourses selling his tip sheet to the cry of 'I gotta horse.' Damon Runyon, the American author whose *On Broadway* was the non-Bible, non-Shakespeare book I took to my Desert Island, related the story of The Lemon Drop Kid: a tipster who, in an eight-horse race, would tip a different horse to eight punters and collect from the one to whom he had given the winner.

On racetracks, if you have a public face, the number of people who ask you for a tip is exceeded only by those who tell you 'So-and-so is a sure thing.' What I really dislike are people who come up after a race and tell you, 'That was the best bet of the week, I hope you were on it.' I have written to the Jockey Club suggesting that those folk should be barred from racecourses for life. I am also wary of men in gents' toilets leaning towards my stall, dispensing or requesting information. Nanny's advice is best: 'Look down, don't speak to anyone and remember to wash your hands.'

There is a story about a theatrical impresario who put on the musical *Tales from the Vienna Woods* at the Alhambra Theatre in Bradford and, after a couple of nights, he phoned his front-of-house manager to ask how things were going at the box office. The man was hesitant, and opined that business was probably no worse than *Tales from the Bradford Woods* would be in Vienna. Which brings me smoothly to last Friday evening, when I was doing my one-man show at the Rosehill Theatre in Whitehaven on the West Cumbrian coast.

The audience was just under 50 per cent capacity; I am not big in Cumbria – more forced to tour than tour de force – and to emphasise my standing the manageress was AWOL, having taken the evening off. Around 10pm, after the show, which had gone well, I was sitting in the foyer signing my autobiography for a goodly number of buyers, wishing someone would bring me a drink.

'Will you write "To Jackie with love" – two Qs in Jaqqi?', asked a woman wearing a lilac wig; then the man behind her shook my hand, gave me a tenner for the book and said: 'Michael Dods's horse in the 4.15 at Beverley on Tuesday.'

I asked whether he was sure it would win. The man said it had worked brilliantly on the gallops after not having shown much for a while on the course.

I took stock: man I didn't know, but who had the sense to see my show and the wherewithal to buy my book, had stood in a queue for

15 minutes to tell me that he in Cumbria felt that a horse trained in Durham would win a handicap in South Yorkshire in four days' time – clearly a man to be trusted.

I looked up the race in Saturday's *Post*: Class 6 sprint over the minimum distance, 71 entries, with Dods's horse sufficiently high in the handicap to be assured of a run.

On Sunday I phoned Mr Dods, apologised for the intrusion, explained where, when and how I had heard about his 'good thing', and asked whether he felt it had a squeak. 'Needs fast going and a high draw,' the trainer said, sounding optimistic. I thanked him.

On Monday at 11am I gleaned from page 581 on Channel 4 text that the horse in question, Betty's Pride, was drawn 18 out of 20 and Beverley's going was good with good to firm patches, which is also known as 'fast'. The jockey was P. Makin, claiming 3lb; a jockey who had ridden Orpen Wide for me when he won on the all-weather. A jockey I respected. Odds were 16-1 others.

In the morning post, which arrives at lunchtime, I received a four-figure cheque from William Hill in respect of a fortnight's betting and, looking at the 25 transactions listed on my statement, I thought back to why I had backed the horses involved. Some I backed because they had no form and a reputable tipster had selected them; some because I had noticed them in previous races; some whose odds had contracted sharply in the ten minutes before the off; others because they were not only in with a shout, but because Jeremy Noseda – for whom I have the greatest respect – trained them. And a couple because the races were genuinely poor, but my selections were ridden by jockeys of quality, like D.R. Dennis and Mr T. Greenall. Some had won, some not; on balance I was ahead.

So there I was yesterday morning, a man with a genuine tip in respect of a horse that lurked among 20-1 others, until I got the *Racing Post*, who forecast her odds at 8s. I had not had a bet on Saturday nor on Sunday, not even on Monday, when I fancied Scriptwriter in the second race at Windsor; no-one had told me it would win, though it did – with a bit in hand – at 15-2.

Which brings us to Tuesday, the day of the race. The bookmakers who advertise in the *Racing Post* put 'early prices available' on some races, and the 4.15 at Beverley was among those. The previous evening's *Evening Standard* had given the runners and riders for Beverley and I noted that in my 4.15 their man had napped a horse with no form either; no form, not in the betting but drawn number 20. Could the tipster have been somewhere, met someone, heard something?

As I write, it is noon on Tuesday and I have to go to a luncheon party for my son-in-law's mother's 80th birthday. I have negotiated six sizeable win bets and perhaps my most interesting ones are Betty's Pride to finish second to the top five in the betting. As you read this column, turn to the results page and you can rejoice – or mourn – with me.

Betty's Pride started 7-1 third favourite, and finished ninth.

*

THIS WOMAN SAID to her husband of long standing: 'When I die, will you marry again?'

He said: 'Of course not, not ever; you're probably going to outlive me anyway. You're not to talk like that.'

'But if you did marry again, would you bring her to live in this house?'

'This is a silly conversation. You're not going to die; for the record I like this house, always have.'

'Would you let her sleep in our bed?'

'Stop this; you're not going to die. I am very fond of our bed, so I'll go on sleeping in it.'

'Would you let her use my golf clubs?'

'Good heavens no; she is left-handed.'

*

WE NEED MORE LEGENDS IN THE SADDLE
20 JULY 2005

IT WAS SATURDAY night at the Arena in Bolton and the man with the microphone asked: 'What will you do next?' – a question beloved by journalists after an auspicious event. Amir Khan, who was not old enough to vote at the last election and has yet to pass his driving test, replied: 'I want to become a legend.'

He had just dispatched, if that is not too moderate a word to describe his 90-second demolition of his first professional opponent, a journeyman boxer from Fulham, and had become the No. 1 Muslim in Britain. He is bright, presentable, nicely spoken and has promised to retire when he is 25. There's no question that he is a great prospect with quick hands that throw powerful, accurate punches, and he has an athleticism that serves him well.

I just hope he has the right back-up to realise his ambition. It is some time since I attended fights for a living, but I remember Frank Warren – Khan's manager – of whom *The Times*'s correspondent once told me: 'He protests his honour too much.' Nevertheless, putting your about-to-lay-golden-eggs goose into the ring wearing shimmering silver knee-length shorts more suited to Liberace than a pugilist pointlessly diverts attention from a man whose talents might do untold wonders for the sport.

The following day, Tiger Woods, wearing the acceptable clothing of a genuine legend, showed us the stuff that established stars are made of. He is quite simply the best player of golf there has ever been. There were previous golfing 'legends', from Bobby Jones, through Arnold Palmer and Jack Nicklaus and Nick Faldo, but none has the genius and the consistency, the total yiplessness and the impeccable manners of Woods. When asked after winning his second Open at St Andrews what victory there meant to him, he paused, then said: 'It is very special.' You could sit up all night, search through a mountain of books on manners, and diplomacy, and not come up with a more apposite statement.

Golf, for some reason, has produced extraordinary characters: introverts like Faldo, control freaks like Goosen, sartorial role models like Payne Stewart and Ian Poulter, not to mention Lee Trevino – probably the smartest, jokiest golfer of them all. When Trevino was first drawn to play young Tiger in the 1990s, he looked at him and said: 'I've got things in my refrigerator older than you'; watching John Daly drive at a par-five hole in Texas, he remarked: 'I don't go that far for my holidays.'

Amir Khan is right about wanting to be a legend, for legends, though rare, are essential to the wellbeing of a sport. Legends get talked about, bring in the crowds. The presence of Stanley Matthews when he finished his football career at Stoke increased crowds by 10,000; George Best made Old Trafford the place to go, and in cricket, Denis Compton filled Lord's while Viv Richards, Ian Botham and Fred Trueman steadily merited taking a day off work. Jonah Barrington's brilliance on the squash court made him a legend and brought the game into European prominence, and just imagine what Wimbledon would be had Henman done what his fan club on the hill prayed for him to do.

The fact that I make no mention of the heroes of Formula One, rugby, hockey, athletics, darts – all the way to curling – is due only to space. I have marginally upwards of 1,000 words a week and the perspicacious reader will have noticed that I am over halfway there, and I have yet to mention racing.

Nobody has decided why racing has of late become so very successful. Despite the fact that last Monday evening's Windsor bread-and-butter card was bulging to the gunwales with humanity, there is no questioning the fact that the presence of a legend would have increased even that crowd. Legends are a huge help when it comes to bringing folk through the turnstiles.

Currently we have Frankie Dettori and Best Mate; we had Arkle and Red Rum and Lester Piggott and Desert Orchid, the presence of any of whom made clerks of courses rub their hands with glee.

Who next? There will always be horses who catch punters'

imagination, who cause crowds and television audiences to blossom, but where is the next Lester? We need a few more legends in the saddle. Jockeys about whom you can tell stories – not just of their prowess in the saddle, but their eccentricities out of it. There are no hard and fast rules: crookedness is appealing, shiftiness is not. If you are mean, be really mean like Piggott was mean: he once asked a friend to drive him from Brighton to Newmarket (to save petrol), got him to make a two-mile diversion to a shop in Hove and emerged with an ice cream. 'Couldn't you have bought me one?', asked his chauffeur. 'Didn't know you liked ice cream,' said Lester.

The trouble is that a jockey's way of life, working from dawn to dusk, driving a zillion miles a year and existing on a diet that Lester once described to me as 'a cigar and a dry retch for breakfast and not a lot more for lunch' makes folk look as if they have had a charisma bypass.

There are jockeys that you can admire, think well of, respect, even look up to, but none now comes to mind when you are carrying your grandchild's autograph book and are looking for an *oooh* or an *aaah* when you get home and they work out the signature.

It was different before the communications revolution. Sir Gordon Richards was a statistical legend – 'So many winners in so many years, so many times champion jockey ...' – but a real legend needs to perform before and after as well as excel during; and a legend must not be too approachable. A legend is ... how can I best put this? Special.

*

I WAS TELEPHONED by a broadsheet newspaper last week and asked what was my favourite joke. The story that I had to tell myself several times before I could relate it without cracking up concerned a lush: a drunk who, when he started to drink, could not stop. One day, his wife told him that if he came home drunk one more time, she would leave him. He went to the pub, got plastered, threw up down his shirt and trousers, recovered and told his friend: 'When I come home like this, my wife will leave me.'

His friend said: 'This is what you do: put a £20 note in your jacket pocket. When your wife accuses you of drinking, pull it out, explain that someone in the pub vomited over you, and gave you the money to have your suit cleaned.'

He came home, his wife looked at him, and said: 'That's it.' He explained what had happened, and showed her the banknote. She looked, and said: 'You've got two £20 notes there,' and he gulped, but finally managed to say: 'I was given the second one by the man who shat in my pants.'

*

AS I WAS SAYING ... OR WAS I?

19 OCTOBER 2005

WHILE WE OF the fourth estate bask under the title of 'journalist', some of us, those who concentrate on a specific subject – architecture, education, finance or sport – bask that much more. We are specialists, recognised for our knowledge on garden sheds, university entrance, hedge funds or real tennis, are justified in holding up our heads higher than the rest of the herd and attend award luncheons with our acceptance speeches rehearsed in front of the bathroom mirror.

Now and then there comes to us 'specialists' an event of such great pith and moment that the fact that we are hacks persuades us to forget our own subject – in my case, racing.

Such a happening overrides current job specification, and such a happening occurred last Friday, persuading me to abandon my intended musings about Motivator and Lasix and how much more honourable would be victory by our undrugged horse, how much more explicable defeat by equine junkies.

What happened to me on Friday did not come unexpectedly, out of the blue. It is something I have been considering for over ten years, about which I have deliberated since the beginning of the millennium and finally embarked upon after consultation with family and friends. Let me provide readers with the background.

My life is not dissimilar to that of other octogenarians spared the effects of mental disintegration – though my body has been less fortunate. Today when I bend down to tie a shoelace, I remain down in case there is anything else I can do in that position.

I am no longer able to run, which is why the announcement of London hosting the Olympics in 2012 gave me pleasure. I shall need all of seven years to achieve the required fitness – and remember fondly the words of Baron de Coubertin, who reinvented the Olympics in 1896: 'Competing is more important than winning.' His sentiment is echoed by all of us on the crematorium side of three-score years and ten.

My Toyota permits me to obtain access and egress with facility; if I go shopping at Waitrose and see no adjacent parking place, I leave my car on a single yellow line, placing a note 'Have run over cat, and placating owner' under the windscreen wiper; this with the crutches and clerical collar I leave on the back seat ensures that only the meanest parking attendants issue tickets. Sadly, mean is the quality that commends these yellow-hatted swine to the local authority or their sub-contractors.

I have had my moments: I recently saw the film *Kinky Boots*, two hours of feel-good, which would have felt even better had there been an hour and a half, but on my way out I overtook a man going upstairs: first time I've done that for a while. And the man past whom I surged was really nice about it: lifted up both his walking sticks to make way.

Then I went to a restaurant, was seated at a table where I couldn't read the menu because the lights were so fashionably low, was told by the waitress about the specials, which I couldn't hear because the noise was too great, then realised I had not brought my credit card and only had £65 in cash, which at least ruled out having to ask for a torch to study the wine list.

My credit card is becoming a bit of a gamble: NatWest are so concerned that someone might have stolen it that substantial amounts are not honoured, just in case. A fortnight ago in Austria, I invited three people from my clinic to join me in a casino outing, stood in front of them like a lemon as the cashier was denied confirmation of my card. As this – my attempt to obtain credit on my card – had occurred as recently as August in a casino in Barcelona and resulted in a fulsome apology, I had supposed the next time I went for a modest four-figure withdrawal, lights would flash in their offices and the word 'Yes' would illuminate the walls in coloured lights. Not a bit of it. While for all I know my number – 24 – kept coming up on the roulette wheel, I drove elsewhere to obtain money, for I no longer feel secure about the blue plastic that I used to trust. I saw a TV commercial for another card, one which gave you interest and a fortnight's holiday in Tenerife, all in (presumably the state in which you return) if you become their customer. By the time I had raced to my study to get pen and paper and write down the telephone number, *The Bill* had started – actually it had been on some time. This must be one of the longer build-ups to an event – I speak of that which happened on Friday, which I have not yet specified (could I be getting wordy in my old age?).

Let me explain. It was noon, give or take. The mail lay on the floor on our side of the front door. Royal Mail say they save money delivering it four hours later than they used to, and it hardly took any time for me to sit on the floor and go through the assortment of envelopes, one of which (I think it was the seventh, a strong envelope with voluminous content) contained documentation to affix to the windscreen of my car and identify me as a person with disability – empowered to park almost anywhere, though not on a pavement or a double-yellow line. And I think it gives me the right to shout at traffic wardens.

There has been much rejoicing, and when I told trainer
V. Williams – who deserves to be sent some high-quality jumps
horses, for she has great talent – she said: 'Oh good, now you won't
have to limp any more.' That too.

*

A MAN WHO was very unhappily married and did not have
enough money for a divorce from his wife asked a friend for
advice. The friend told him to get an inexpensive hitman to
take her out.

So the man went to a pub where he was told of a cut-price
hitman named Arti, who charged £1 a time because he enjoyed
the work so much. The man told Arti his wife was in her fifties
and came to Tesco every Friday at 11.30am wearing an off-
white raincoat and black and yellow head scarf.

At the due time the woman entered the store. Arti
followed her into a corner, strangled her and hid the body
under some cardboard boxes. He was making his escape when
he saw a similarly dressed woman make her way in. To be on
the safe side Arti strangled her also and was hiding her body
when the police arrived and arrested him.

The next day's front page told the story under the heading,
'Artichokes two for a pound at Tescos'.

*

A DAY'S RACING DONE AND DUSTED IN TIME FOR LUNCH
26 OCTOBER 2005

MY WIFE, THE dread Lady F., said: 'You promised you would come
to Charlie's birthday party.' I explained that there was nothing but
goodwill between me and my about-to-be four-year-old grandson,

other than that it is plain inconsiderate to celebrate things on a Saturday afternoon. 'You know what it is like if I have a whole week without going racing.'

'You save money,' she said.

So there was conflict between my instinctive liberalism, which gets me my own way, and my grand-paternal duties: conflict unexpectedly resolved by Wolverhampton, where racing started at 11.15am and kicked out around the time an average man expects to sit down for luncheon.

Odd thing that: in the Far and the Near East, also on the sub-continent; in Africa and both North and South America, on the islands of the Indian Ocean and the Caribbean as well as all over Europe, racing takes place in the afternoons and, natural or artificial lights permitting, in the evenings. At Wolverhampton they do it in the morning.

This means, if you live in London and don't want to miss the first race, getting an alarm call in the dead of night – like 7am – being at Euston station by 8am, purchasing a cheap-day return ticket and upgrading to first class at a tenner a journey and arriving at Wolverhampton station at 10.20.

Wolverhampton, home of the Wanderers, with a thin, unfurnished metal horse sited on platform 3. I found a taxi outside: Black Country, black cab, Indian driver, £5 including the tip and I was there.

I spent my initial 20 minutes trying to coax a bacon sandwich out of a surly woman who operated from behind a counter marked 'Food' and was devoid of a sense of priority, never asking who was next, serving whomever she fancied, which excluded me.

Wolverhampton, named after Wulfruna, sister of Edgar II, is an overall welcoming place; they used to make bicycles there, but have stopped.

The spirit of friendliness extends to Dunstall Park where the winter sun shone on the Polytrack oval and the crowd, which I thought would be sparse, achieved a volume of total respectability which kept the six on-course bookmakers nicely heeled for the week to come.

The races were Class 7, sums exceeding £1,100 but not quite reaching £1,200 were credited to the accounts of winning owners, and one forgets that regardless of the quality of runners, you can still lose serious dosh backing the wrong horse. I did. Over and over, for age is no bar to backing losers.

I went to a funeral last Thursday and when it was over, the undertaker looked at me and said: 'Hardly worthwhile going back home.'

Race one was for horses who had not won a race and been sold as yearlings at auction for less than £2,000. It went to Soviet Legend at 20-1, a colt who had shown admirable consistency in that he had finished out of the first ten in his last six races. There were not enough layers to raise a proper cheer, but their smiling faces informed us of their contentment.

I adjourned to the Zongalero restaurant on the third floor (they have a lift), where a nice waitress called Lisa gave me a hug and called me 'darling'.

I was going to back Ragasah in the third, but a man whose advice I respect said that in banded races horses never win twice running. Ragasah came fourth, a length ahead of my selection.

And the outing was a success in that I came home in time for Charlie's tea party, although my natural cheerfulness was affected by the news about Motivator and Well Chief: I had them in a double to win their respective races. Is there perhaps a bookmaker who refunds ante-post doubles on two non-runners? He would get my business.

The most intriguing thing about Wolverhampton's meeting had been the presence of some ten under-30 women roaming hither and thus, wearing pink Stetson hats; a bit early for a hen party, neither fit nor numerous enough for a lady's rugby team.

I suppose they were just lucky there was something going on where they could show their finery.

*

THIS CAPTAIN WAS posted to a barracks in the Iraqi desert, went for a tour of inspection, noticed a camel tied up outside the men's barracks, asked a passing soldier for the reason. 'We have 250 men and no women here; now and then we get urges,' said the soldier.

A few weeks later the Captain got an urge, found a ladder, put it up against the back of the camel, climbed up, dropped his trousers, felt better.

'Is this how you men do it?', he asked a soldier who was standing nearby.

'No sir. We ride him to the brothel in the next village.'

*

I'M A CELEBRITY ...
GET ME IN THERE
2 NOVEMBER 2005

I AM A member of a gaming club called Aspinall's – a luxurious establishment where glasses of champagne and butterfly prawns are on offer on the ground floor, which is as lavishly appointed as God might have done, had He the money. There are heavy carpets, flat screen televisions and every newspaper, though the *Racing Post* has pride of place.

You can sit on a plush velvet seat as you travel to the first floor in the lift; there you find the stunning casino and a dining room of quality: caviar comes in 100gm tins and is, of course, Baluga; when you order lobster thermidor, they don't quibble about size; you get a whole beast and they do the work keeping the shells, leaving you with the contents of tails and claws garnished by egg-yolked, buttery, spiced, herbed sauce and Jersey Royals and peeled broad beans. Also warm, home-baked bread. The membership is of some class: only about half the shortlist for the Conservative Party leadership would get in.

And it came to pass that the great and good management of Mayfair's, Aspinall's decided to open some provincial casinos and they started with one in Newcastle.

They had invited me to last week's opening and as they sent a first-class rail ticket, had a car to meet me at the station and booked me into a grandish hotel, I accepted with gratitude and alacrity to ensure they will ask me to witness further openings in Sheffield, Cardiff and possibly Skegness – or is it Cleethorpes? Maybe both.

I spent much time in Newcastle in the early 1960s where my networked cookery programme was filmed and have kept an occasional eye on the city – from racing at Gosforth to football at St James's. It has changed ... or perhaps I never knew it. It is now a proper city with a fancy port and huge modern buildings housing museums, art centres, exhibitions, banks and – only some minutes by taxi from my grand hotel – the new casino, called Aspers.

Rather as at Hollywood premieres, there is a red carpet and one walks from the street to the entrance through the cheering crowds; we had many, many hundreds of fans gawping at the celebrities who made their way from pavement to front door. Look, they said, 'It's Abi Titmuss innit?' Not a name I knew, though perhaps related to a Middlesex spin bowler called Freddie who lost several toes when, on a West Indies tour I covered for the *Sun*, he got too close to the propellers of a boat. I walked some 70 yards along the carpet before I had my own moment of fame. 'Oh look, it's Sigmund,' shouted a kindly housewife jumping up and down while her voluminous upper body shook in harmony.

It was the first night. The doors had opened at 7pm, I got there at 8.15pm, passing many people who asked whether I had my invitation and what was my name; there were many others who said: 'I know who he is,' and invited me to walk through. There is a huge escalator, which they had stopped for security reasons; I asked whether they might turn it on again for my lameness reason and they did.

Upstairs is enormous, Las Vegas-like: acres of one-armed bandits, roulette machines, poker machines, blackjack machines and beyond them roulette and poker and blackjack tables serviced by croupiers wearing my racing colours, which I appreciated. There are bars, a beauty shop for massage and manicure, and a restaurant which was not open on that first night. The mezzanine floor was guarded by minders and for the use of VIPs like Abi Titmuss. I also saw James Hewitt and Paul Gascoigne.

I did a circuit of the premises and sat down at a roulette machine, pushed a £50 note in the appropriate slot and the amount appeared on the screen as 'credit'.

On the first day in the life of a roulette machine, I thought zero was an appropriate number and put £30 on it. The machine showed my investment on the screen but I was unable to find the 'play' button or lever or light; I asked passing people. So there was I: glass of champagne in hand, sitting at the machine and stopping passers-by for information. They looked, examined, shrugged shoulders, sympathised and it was not for quarter-of-an-hour that I found a man wearing badges of authority and received the information. The machines don't start until after the speeches at 9.30. He pressed 'cancel bet' then 'cash out' and soon after passed me a slip which the machine had disgorged from its interior which I was to take to the cash desk. The cash desk said it was not yet open, come back after the speeches around 9.30. This was the longest I have remained even in a casino for more than 50 years.

After an hour of sitting in the mezzanine lounge talking to people who were not Abi Titmuss I returned to the roulette tables, backed my number and its neighbours. The croupier spun the wheel as if his life depended on it spinning for ever, then hurled the ball in the opposite direction. I considered going out for a meal but the crowd was so great I stayed and waited until the wheel slowed sufficiently for the ball to come to a rest. I repeated the process three times. Some good canapés came along, my number did not come up, a lot of local beauty adorned the premises.

As my bedtime approached and such luck as hung over the premises remained rightfully with the proprietors, I walked out over a glass floor beneath which goldfish were dancing the tango, passed a queue of some 500 people waiting to get in – one of whom looked me in the eye, asked whether I was on the telly. 'Friend of Abi Titmuss,' I said, and got into a taxi.

When it all settles down, this will be a great casino and make a lot of wealthy people a whole lot wealthier.

*

THESE TWO WOMEN acquaintances met at the pearly gates. 'What brings you here?', asked one. 'Froze to death, how about you?'

'I broke my neck; believed my husband was cheating on me, told him I was going out for the night, came home to find him sitting reading the papers, searched everywhere in wardrobes, under the bed, in the attic, was going to the cellar when I slipped and fell down the stairs.'

'You should have looked in the freezer; then we would both have been alive.'

*

LAS VEGAS: TIME GOES BY – BUT PLEASE DON'T TELL ANYONE
16 NOVEMBER 2005

I CAME BACK at the weekend having had three days in Las Vegas, which is about the right length of time. I stayed at the Wynn Hotel, which opened recently, has 2,750 suites and a casino that keeps itself to itself, unlike the many other hotels on The Strip.

In this new emporium you can walk from the entrance hall to your room – a quarter of a mile away – without having to vault over fruit machines, or squeeze past the crowds at the blackjack/roulette/baccarat/poker tables and have to play keno (a sort of bingo) in the snack bar before they bring you a cup of coffee.

Vegas is no longer as aggressive as it was. Some 40 years ago, I attended a launch of an airline's direct London–Vegas flight: me and 30 other hacks and photographers. On arrival, waiting to check in, one of them put a quarter into a one-armed bandit and there came a ringing of bells and a flashing of lights; as he was scooping up the 500 silver dollars that spewed from the machine, he was seized by a scantily dressed 'hostess' who asked whether they might not celebrate his win in his room. He returned a happier man about 20 minutes later, and looked slightly embarrassed as he asked me to lend him a tenner.

At the Wynn casino I sat down at a blackjack table before noticing a sign stating: 'Minimum bet $1,000, maximum $20,000.' I got up; I was out of my league and thought about Kerry Packer, who once walked into a casino in Florida and was asked to go elsewhere. The conversation apparently went like this:

Man: 'This is the private room, reserved for high rollers.'
Packer: 'That's okay by me.'
Man: 'You want to go and play the tables over there; this is out of your league.'
Packer: 'What's your league?'
Man: 'I'm worth 60 million bucks.'
Packer: 'I'll toss you for it.'

I watched a blackjack player take a seat at the $1,000 table, put the minimum on two boxes. He got a 6 and a 9, then a 6 on his 6, and a 2 on his 9. The dealer showed a 5. The punter split the sixes, doubled the 11, and the dealer gave himself a 6 and a picture.

A man who was watching and did not understand gambling said to me: 'For that $8,000 lost in under a minute, one could have flown first class from London, had a six-room suite at the hotel and eaten lobster three times a day.'

A gambler going to Las Vegas is akin to a Catholic visiting the Vatican, a Muslim making the pilgrimage from Mecca to Medina. Where we of secular pursuits score is in not having to wait for high days and holy days, because our chosen destination boasts the ultimate in timelessness.

What you do not find in the jewel of Nevada's prize city is any sort of reminder that it may be time to go home. (No-one 'lives' in Vegas. The population of one million is there to look after us visitors.)

The casinos have no clocks, the artificial light is set for the Lotus Eaters 'who came unto a land in which it seemed always afternoon' and the temperature remains constant.

When Blackpool becomes our first major resort city there will be much to learn from the way Las Vegas has changed; from picking your pockets to giving you diversions, before, during and after which you can lose your money in style.

Now you come home remembering the food and drink, the shows and pools and health resorts, the girls wearing amazingly well-cut dresses that only cover the essentials who give you very significant choices of drink. I was quite taken with Mojitos: white rum and mint and syrup and ice and soda water ... agreeably lethal once you get into double figures.

*

THIS DEEPLY RELIGIOUS, recently married man was concerned about having sex on Sunday. If it was work, it was surely forbidden ... but what if it were play? He asked around: Presbyterian, Wesleyan, Plymouth Brethren, Church of England, Greek Orthodox, Roman Catholic, but received no definitive answer until he came to a synagogue.

The Rabbi's reply was unequivocal: sex was 'play', no question of it.

'How do you know for sure?'

'If it were work, my wife would get the maid to do it.'

*

SEX AND RACING – IT'S THE WAY FORWARD

1 MARCH 2006

I WAS LISTENING with half an ear to the BBC news bulletin when I heard the announcer say that 'the World Cup will be a boon to the sex industry.'

I had not thought of that. I mean, why? Why will the presence of football fans clutching tickets for the Estonia v. Togoland match enrich the hookers who pursue their trade in the vicinity of stadia of German cities where you would have thought they had their own working girls? Could it be that *Footballers' Wives* is being taken seriously?

If there is a connection between football and prostitution, why don't we work harder to extend this to other sports? Specifically, is it not time the Department of Culture, Media and Sport commissioned a paper on 'Sex and Racing'?

What we need to liven up our sport is to make attendance irresistible to the oldest profession, and for us to find another, even better, reason for going racing other than reading form and pitting our wits against those of the bookmakers.

Currently the question 'Why do you go racing at Yarmouth?' tends to bring the pathetic reply, 'I take my summer holidays in East Anglia and there is not much else to do.' Just think what effect the sex industry could have. We would go to the track only partly because of the seven-furlong seller and because the wife likes us to be out of harm's way. We would also be there because of the mixed sauna at the back of the parade ring and the fact that they have the best lap-dancing east of Market Harborough.

In fact, racecourses, their boards of directors and the suits they employ are scared of sex. I once mentioned to the head man at Ascot that I much admired the white stretch limo in No. 3 car park that regularly bounced up and down when the engine was off, and from which I had heard a pleasant female voice say, 'It has been a business doing pleasure with you,' as an elderly man crept out of the rear door. Was it, I asked, part of the service at the royal meeting, or had private enterprise stolen a march? Also, was I, as a boxholder for many years, eligible for a discount? He became apoplectic.

The fact is that things change, and it will not be long before two- and three-women brothels will be legal and eligible for government start-up schemes. And where better to site these new enterprises than in reconstructed London double-decker buses conveniently parked at racecourses on racedays? To comply with the new laws, patrons will not be allowed to smoke upstairs.

Everyone will benefit. Courses will charge for the parking and get extra revenue advertising the facility on their racecards; what the BBC called the international sex industry will be kept that much more fully employed (though I personally cannot imagine that there are too many Estonian blonde hookers hell-bent on plying their trade at Bangor-on-Dee); for punters, there will finally be an acceptable reply to, 'I have had five losers on the trot – what on earth can I do now?'

It has long been my belief that in this world of ours, no-one actually gets what they want. Men want women, women want children and children want hamsters. As for the belief that if you give up drink, tobacco and sex you live longer, let me advise you: it just seems longer.

There are things you can do, even if you have achieved a venerable age – like looking forward to a mammoth double on Chris Huhne to become leader of the Lib Dems and Racing Demon to win the Arkle – but if this fails to make one rich and famous you, like me, will just have to wait for the greater benefits of living with new knees. Begin on the lower deck of the bus.

*

WITH ALL THE sadness that currently fills the pages of our papers and occupies radio and TV news bulletins, it is worth reflecting on the recent demise of a very important personage, which went largely unnoticed.

I refer to Larry LaPrise, who wrote 'The Hokey Cokey', and died peacefully at the age of 93.

I understand that the most traumatic part for his family was getting him into his coffin.

They put his left leg in ... and then the trouble started.

*

AGE SHALL NOT WEARY US – WELL, NOT MUCH

26 APRIL 2006

I SEND LOYAL, belated congratulations to Her Majesty – because I don't have a column on Fridays – but no less sincere good wishes on achieving the age of 80, which is excellent and, as Maurice Chevalier explained in his birthday party speech in 1978, beats not being 80.

Having reached the four-score figure some years ago, I welcome You to octogenarianism, which is an honourable state although one, perhaps especially One, in which changes are noticed. 'They' who used to do as they were told, now try to organise things for you, make decisions on your behalf which are 'good' rather than apposite – like telling you which hat to wear.

In my case, and I accept this would occur less frequently to Your Majesty, people who look older than me get up and offer their seat on a bus. Also 'they' speak in front of you as if you were elsewhere, as in: 'Has he lost his bus-pass again?'

I very much hope that with Your Majesty at the helm, the octogenarian decade will become the wannabe age for lame, halt, hard-of-hearing folk around the world. As with the men who fought at Agincourt, at 80 they will strip their sleeves and show their scars (and their birth certificates) and wallow in pride. Living for three score years and ten is for sissies – long live us.

Eighty is important, as is the last furlong of a race, the final ten minutes of a football match. With some notable exceptions – in which the House of Windsor excels – it is likely to be the last decade in which the word 'useful' is likely to apply to what we do; that is not our fault but 'theirs'. 'They' simply don't go out of their way to include us in and give us the good time we deserve.

Why do football teams, like Chelsea and Liverpool last Saturday, run on to the pitch from the tunnel holding by their hands some innocent anonymous cherub dressed in their colours, instead of trotting out with John Mortimer, Denis Healey or me, who have actually done something? I'll tell you why: we are in our eighties.

Tennis fans complain about short matches, games that are all serve and smash; they don't realise that if there were ball-men and ball-women instead of boys and girls, contests would last longer – much longer – and add an extra dimension to the entertainment; Sir Donald Sinden would do the job with aplomb.

In my own line of business, occasional opportunities do come up. When Dame Thora Hird died, there was a vacancy for someone to ride the stair-lift in the TV commercial giving that special 'Look at me, it's all so very convenient' wave, which I had been practising. They said they would let me know. The swine.

The fact is that with the exception of Class C celebrities urging us to take out full life insurance that would help our loved ones to pay for our funerals (make up your mind within 14 days and we will send you this attractive carriage clock), models on screen and in magazines are youthful, lissom and not-far-from-naked as they lie beside a Ferrari.

Also, there is no-one to protect us the way younger people are protected. Film censors announce the recommended ages at which films can be viewed, PG, 12, 15 or 18 – never 'unsuited to over-80s', which so many films are.

At crossings on main roads they signal 'walk', and when halfway across it changes to 'don't walk'. We live in a young people's world and have to put up with it.

This column is not all whinge. It was recently announced that at 80 we don't have to pay to get a new passport. I think it's a bit like patting a turkey on the head in November, akin to saying, 'Thank you for getting that much closer to when we grab your inheritance tax.'

In Chairman Mao's China, 80 was when you started to climb the political ladder; in the East, age is accorded great respect. It would be such a good thing if we in Britain had a substantial four-score bonus: perhaps cheaper peerages, a badge giving old drivers 20 minutes free parking anywhere but on double yellow lines; half-price rail-fares, and a significant contribution for those confined to non-travelling lives.

Let me end on an uplifting thought: the lifespan of a mayfly is 24 hours – mostly, I suspect, spent at other mayflies' funerals and memorial services.

*

IT WAS THE occasion of one of Her Majesty's scheduled visits to the London Zoo. The head keeper lined up his men and allocated to each an area that they would represent, and about which they could respond to questions Her Majesty might ask.

'And you,' said the head man to an egregiously incompetent warden, 'sod off and look after the porcupines.'

By a strange and unfortunate coincidence the Queen chose to visit the porcupine enclosure. The keeper was presented to her and she said: 'Tell me about your charges.'

'Well,' said the man. 'What can I say? Porcupines: they live to a ripe old age and their pricks are about eight inches long.'

The Queen went a paler shade of pale and moved away. The head keeper turned to the oafish man and said: 'You damned idiot, fool, moron. Their quills are about eight inches long. Quills.'

The keeper said: 'Leave it to me; I'll make it all better.' He raced after the Queen and reintroduced himself, saying: 'It's me from the porcupines, Ma'am. I made a mistake, Ma'am. Porcupines: their quills are about eight inches long. Their pricks are hardly any size at all.'

*

THANK YOU, RACE CALLERS: CONDUCTORS OF OUR ENJOYMENT
10 FEBRUARY 2007

WELL OF COURSE there are disadvantages to being on the crematorium side of 80, like the seeing and the hearing, not to mention the running, not being what they were, nor likely to get better; but where we score over the opposition is that they haven't been around that long, and have to confine themselves to relating what happened last week or last year. Not me; I was at Buckfastleigh in 1933, cheered Steve Donoghue riding at Epsom for the old Aga Khan while at preparatory school, and watched Battleship win the Grand National.

Given half a chance, I mention these and other happenings. Let me take you back to late 1945: Field Marshal Montgomery was visiting the HQ of the British Army on the Rhine and my commanding officer told me to organise some suitable post-

dinner entertainment. I was a very junior officer and said, 'Yes Sir.'
I seem to remember that I spent most of my time saying that.

I went to the mayor of the Westphalian town where we were
based and asked him if there were perhaps some local German
equivalent of Edith Piaf or the Beverley Sisters who could regale an
audience of senior British officers on the appointed evening.

He said: 'You want Herr Plattenkopf.'

I explained that I did not want Herr Plattenkopf or any other Herr.
I wanted something as close to glamour as was available in those
immediate post-war times, ideally a singing or dancing act, though
conjurers, if of high quality, might be all right.

The mayor called in a deputy, they discussed my request,
agreed there was no-one they could recommend except Herr
Plattenkopf.

And so it came about that at the end of the formal dinner –
vegetable soup, stewed beef, apple crumble with condensed milk – I,
who was far too junior to have been invited, walked on to the stage
and announced that I had tried hard to discover a local entertainer
of beauty and talent, but was persuaded by the citizens of this town
with whom I was authorised to communicate (the fraternisation
ban lasted until 1946) that the local star entertainer was none other
than Herr Plattenkopf.

The applause was subdued, more like non-existent, and on came a
small, middle-aged, bespectacled, shabbily dressed German carrying
a bulging pillow-case.

He said 'good evening' in reasonable English, walked up to a
Brigadier General at one of the top tables and asked: 'What your
name?'

You could see the Brig wondering whether to shoot the man
himself or order him to be taken away, but it was entertainment – it
said so on the menu – and he mumbled his rank and name.

'No, no, I mean first name, like George or John,' said the
entertainer.

'Humphrey,' said the General.

'Good,' said Herr Plattenkopf, taking a pipe out of his pillowcase. 'Here, Humphrey, when I call your name you blow into the pipe; is good, Humphrey?'

It didn't look good to us.

He had seven more pipes; he gave them to seven other senior officers, a couple of whom became apoplectic at being called by their Christian names by a German civilian; the German then approached a waiter, a Lance Corporal in the Army Catering Corps, and asked him the name of his favourite song.

'The Blue Bells of Scotland,' said the soldier and Plattenkopf announced: 'When I call name, you blow pipe.' The room was eerily silent, I considered having him arrested and doing my rendering of 'Albert and the Lion', but Plattenkopf remained upbeat, called out, 'Percy, Percy, Humphrey, Jack. Donald, Humphrey, Victor, Victor, Gervase, Matthew, Matthew, Jack', and the officers blew their pipes and we got a brilliant if stuttering rendition of the song, followed by sustained applause and at least a dozen more songs by request.

I thought of that when I heard the stunningly fluent, impeccably accurate commentary on a 23-runner steeplechase from Punchestown last week, and wondered whether we make enough fuss of men who are able to translate the shape of a horse and the colour of a jockey's silks to a name, get it right and then do it again half an hour later in respect of a couple of dozen different horses and colours.

Like Plattenkopf, whom I should have brought back to the UK to achieve fame and fortune, we don't make enough fuss of these talented men, without whom TV racing would fail to be compulsive. Perhaps we should start an appeal to raise enough money to buy them honours. Commentators deserve our gratitude for their brilliance, and the long hours they spend making it look easy. They certainly have mine.

*

LET ME TELL you a story about Mrs Thatcher. A bright June afternoon in 1983 and she swept out of the door of No. 10 having decided, on a whim, to walk to the Palace of Westminster, whither she was pursued by startled minders, police, secretaries, advisers, her chauffeur and a Japanese TV crew. Marching down Whitehall, clutching her handbag, she noticed in the distance a beggar standing on the pavement. Thatcher loathes beggars, they are simply not ... Thatcher. Passing him, she noticed out of the corner of her eye that the beggar was holding up a sign saying 'Falklands War Veteran'. Thatcher thrived on the Falklands war, but for the success of which she would never have won a second term. She stopped, opened her handbag, gave the man a £50 note.

He said: 'Muchas gracias.'

*

IN SEARCH OF ADVICE ON BUYING MY LAST CAR

7 APRIL 2007

I TELEPHONED MY bank the other day to ask them to send me a new cheque book. They explained they would have to go through security clearance first:

'What was your first motor car?'

A year ago Coutts had decided that verifying my identity by asking for my date of birth, account number, sort code and mother's maiden name was not enough to be absolutely certain I was not an impostor; they asked me for the make of my first car, my favourite school subject and the name of my first house. Had I rung them to ask for half a million pounds in used fivers to be delivered in a plain brown envelope to a numbered cubicle in the gents at Tottenham Court Road underground station I would have understood their concern, but 'Please send a cheque book to my home address' is a harmless request from which no impersonator could benefit.

My first car had been a Singer, bought from a man in my village with whom I had played football for the Walberswick Under-11s, therefore thought he was straight. The car used as much oil as it did petrol and lasted a fortnight. I unscrewed the number plates, left it in a street in Holloway and bought an ex-London taxi that had spent its working life as the property of Stanley Baker's wife's uncle.

The purchase of one's first vehicle depended entirely on price – one's ability to pay. Now, approaching my 83rd birthday and actively skiing (spending the kids' inheritance), I am told by my youngest son, who is knowledgeable about life, that it is time I had a new car … which is likely to be my last.

I drive a Toyota RAV4, which I like. Nothing goes wrong with it, except when I drive it into other cars; it is easy to enter, unlike my son's Ferrari – access to which necessitates lying on the pavement and easing forward, feet first.

My car permits me to sit some ten inches above other drivers, which is handy, and when I leave it in racecourse car parks I find it again quite quickly, thanks to its height. (I never used to be able to find my cars, and would very much like to have back the time I spent wandering around the car parks of the world looking for the vehicle in which I had arrived.)

My last car, then: priorities are facility of getting in, sturdiness of body for when in an accident, individuality of shape or colour to enable me to locate it, and limited length – to make it easy to park. I am not terribly worried about the environment, pollution or having to pay a high road tax … age does that to a chap.

I suppose there is an argument for making your last car double as a hearse; I thought about that, but rejected the idea. Somewhere among my papers is a policy bought many years ago to provide for funeral expenses; on reflection the upper payout limit is £250.

If anyone has a good idea, I would like to hear from them. If Mr Clarkson wants to invite me on to *Top Gear* to discuss this, I suggest we do so before I drive a circuit of his track, which, until the car turns over, I expect to do considerably more quickly than did Simon Cowell.

*

THIS HORSE WAS going easily, several lengths in the lead coming to the four-furlong post, when he was struck by a side of smoked salmon, making him stumble and get overtaken.

The jockey settled him and regained the lead when, a furlong and a half from the line, the horse was hit by a roast turkey, veered to the right and lost his position.

He was coming back to win the race when a plum pudding knocked him sideways and he featured in a photo-finish, which went against him.

The stewards called in the jockey, asked for an explanation of his erratic steering … and he replied: 'I was badly hampered.'

*

HAMBURGER HEAVEN

12 MAY 2007

WHILE I WAS watching Chester races on television, a commentator informed viewers that the Roodee provided 'the best hamburgers of any racecourse', though Wincanton, where they used fresh meat, came a close second. What an interesting occupation would be official BHB hamburger taster: plying one's trade at each of the 59 British tracks and designing a league table that would change every few months, requiring constant work.

There would be two divisions: fresh and frozen. The inspector, unless already significantly overweight, would become very fat, and would have to take into account the asking price; freshness, warmth and desirability of the bun; time-lag between cooking and selling; provision and quality of tomato ketchup, brown sauce and mustard

(Heinz, HP and Dijon are best), as well as the availability and efficiency of napkins.

Then he would have to wait around to see how long a hamburger remained on the grill before being dumped. Wendy's, the US franchise, when they opened up many years ago, undertook to translate every item into chilli con carne after eight minutes, which is a lovely idea, but does require a predictable number of customers for each product. This could work at metropolitan courses, but I doubt whether demand for Mexican-style dishes is very large in places like Bangor, Newton Abbot and Wolverhampton, but you never know – just as you don't when backing horses with high draw numbers in sprint races at Chester.

For the very best product, stand over the butcher as he finely chops Aberdeen Angus rump steak, hung for 45 days. To 500 grammes of meat, add one egg yolk, a tablespoon each of plain yoghurt and soft white bread-crumbs, and a few twists of white peppercorns, and blend with your fingers. Shape into four patties, cook for 20 seconds a side over fierce heat to seal in the flavour, and give another half to two minutes per side, depending on whether you like them rare or well done.

Do not forget to heat the plates and buy warm, soft baps, such as they sell at supermarkets with their own bakeries; as you have gone this far, serve with absorbent napkins of frequently washed Irish linen, dyed in your racing colours.

*

THIS MAN HURRIED into a hotel lift as the doors were closing, accidentally thrusting his elbow into the breast of a woman, startling both. He apologised, said: 'If your heart is as soft as your breast you will forgive me.' She replied: 'If your willy is as hard as your elbow, I am in room 426.'

*

PROTECT YOUR HOME
FROM THE THREAT OF CAULIFLOWER

20 JUNE 2007

I LEARNED FROM a tabloid newspaper lying in a doctor's waiting room last Monday that cauliflower is no longer the big seller it was. Due to an unprecedented lack of demand caused by non-advertising, farmers are grubbing up cauli-fields and replanting them with trendy crops like Japanese broad beans and passion fruit, while the Common Agricultural Policy, as is its wont, is paying farmers not to produce, thus avoiding the creation of a cauliflower mountain.

When I was in Parliament, constituent farmers used to come to me for advice on these matters. There was the not-rearing pigs grant when a bacon glut faced the country.

Pig farmers were paid not to rear pigs and bombarded me with enquiries on how best to benefit therefrom. 'What breed of pig did I suggest they do not rear?', was one question, then 'If I buy an adjoining piece of land for not rearing pigs, how many pigs per acre can I claim for, how do I prove my non-pigs to the agricultural department's inspector, and might there be a way of forming partnership with neighbours who get paid for not producing crops that my non-pigs could have eaten?'

Until contemporary Nigellas, Delias or magazine columns devoted to readers' health proclaim that, 'For firmer breasts, more luminous hair, longer penises and relief from athletes' foot, three portions of cauliflower cheese a week is beneficial', it will be goodbye cauli, also au revoir choufleur, auf wiedersehen Blumenkohl, and arrivederci cavolfi.

I suspect that the ever-increasing TV programmes about buying and selling houses are partly to blame. They advise you to present a sweet-smelling property to potential purchasers, and the odour of a boiling cauliflower has put paid to many a deal that had looked promising. This advice may be on the late side, but a crust of bread, any bread, placed on top of a boiling cauli does eliminate the stink.

And if you are seriously selling a house, place some coffee beans under a low grill and create a genuine 'This is a place I must buy' smell, or the right atmosphere for serving Nescafé to visitors.

*

THIS POSTMAN HAD served his years working for the Royal Mail and it came to the day before his retirement. As he delivered letters to a house where he was on chatting terms with the owners, the woman asked him in, told him that she had prepared for him a dish which her mother used to make, which she was sure he would appreciate. She took from the oven a bowl of delectable strips of braised fillet steak, sliced new potatoes and broad beans cooked in double cream, and offered him a plate.

He liked it a lot and the woman said:'I don't suppose you get to see beyond the ground floor in people's houses,' and took him up to the bedroom, where they had a truly amazing time. When they were back downstairs, she opened her handbag and gave him a pound coin. He looked at it with some puzzlement, and said:'You cook me a fantastic stew, take me to your bedroom and we have nearly half an hour of terrific sex, and now you give me one pound. I don't understand.' She replied:'I told my husband you were retiring, what should we give you as a farewell? And he said, "Screw the postman, give him a pound." The stew was my idea.'

*

THE NIGHT DYLAN THOMAS WAS SICK ON MY CARPET

22 JUNE 2007

LAST YEAR, AN alternative rock band called The Slip released a song that contained the words, 'It is the day before the rest of my life, / And I feel like Dylan Thomas.' They were referring to the Welsh poet rather than the then three-year-old Danehill colt who this week got stuffed by a German-bred, French-trained five-year-old, but they were not alone in 'feeling like Dylan Thomas'.

He had been a friend, inasmuch as one can have friends who drink a bottle of spirits a day before they settle down to get drunk.

We had met at the Wheatsheaf pub in Fitzrovia before I went to war, and then again in 1950, soon after I married my first wife. I found him slumped in a corner of the Windsor Castle, my local pub in Regent's Park, and at closing time I took him to my home, for he had nowhere intelligible to go.

We took off his shoes and laid him on a downstairs sofa. In the morning he had gone, leaving a pile of vomit on the drawing-room carpet. Jill cleaned up the mess and I suggested getting the carpet cleaned. She (we remain married, I call her my 'first' wife to keep her on her toes) said, 'We'll keep the stain', and while we remained in that house, people who looked at the patch of discoloured Axminster, as well as those who did not, were told its history.

During the last years of his life, Dylan went on speaking tours of the USA, where he drank Bourbon whiskeys before reciting his poetry. He told me of one occasion when he had been met at an airport by a gushing blue-rinsed matron who led him to the Rolls-Royce, driven by a man the back of whose neck had many rolls of surplus fat.

'Mr Thomas,' said the woman, 'I just love your poem *East Coker*.'

'That was written by T.S. Eliot,' said Dylan. And the bulging neck turned round and said to his wife: 'You been had again, Emily.'

Dylan Thomas died in 1953, the year Pinza won the Derby; he was

39, cause of death was officially pneumonia, but not many of us believed that. He left a wife and three sons. His four-legged namesake is likely to be even more fertile, very much less of a lush and, while I admire him a lot, if I did find him slumped in a corner of my local saloon bar, there is no way I would take him to our fourth-floor flat, where the carpet is and shall remain a uniform shade of light brown – dung-coloured, you might call it.

*

THIS MAN WAS driving to an appointment that could make a huge difference to his life. He arrived in good time, drove around looking for a parking place … in vain. He drove round and round, getting ever more desperate as the minutes ticked away.

With appointment time approaching, he looked up to the heavens and mouthed: 'Dear God, if you find me a parking place I will never miss another Sunday Mass for the rest of my life and absolutely promise to stop drinking Bushmills whiskey after dinner.'

Miraculously a parking place appeared. He said: 'Never mind; I've got one.'

*

NET-CORD JUDGE –
A JOB I WOULD VERY MUCH HAVE LIKED
30 JUNE 2007

I MAY BE a Luddite, but for me Wimbledon is simply not what it was. I liked the Centre Court before its re-invention, I thought the absolute power of umpires was appropriate, and I really miss the presence of net-cord judges.

There was a time when this was the job I wanted to pursue, as it required neither terrific eyesight nor hearing, and to the best of my knowledge, there was no retirement age. Unlike most jobs, you knew when it started (when a player served) and finished (after the player had served), and you could then watch the rest of each point at your leisure – having got in for free, and possibly even been paid. It was a job that involved some danger, for you were sitting right in the midst of things, unable even to strike back if a player hit a ball at you, but then danger is an integral part of favoured employment.

It was an extraordinarily pointless function to rest your finger on the net-cord and shout 'let' when you felt the merest of tingles which made no difference to the flight of the ball, but the presence of net-cord judges determined the importance of the tournament.

I remember seeing one on *What's My Line?*: when asked to make a gesture such as he used at work, he extended his left fore-finger, then withdrew it. The panel was flummoxed. There were no famous net-cord judges, no judge of the year, nor is there a record of anyone saying: 'This is probably the least competent net-cord man I have ever met.' And no-one knew their names. They thrived on anonymity. I wonder, is the world ready for an autobiography? *Confessions of a Judge* should be a big seller.

*

JACQUELINE AND HER husband Gavin went for counselling after 25 years of marriage. When invited to explain their problem, Jacqueline went into a passionate tirade, listing every tribulation that had occurred since their wedding day: neglect, lack of intimacy, emptiness, loneliness, being unloved, unlovable … She went on and on and on – an entire laundry list of unmet needs she had endured for a quarter of a century.

After allowing this to go on for long enough to justify his fee, the therapist got up, walked around his desk, bade Jacqueline stand up and remove her blouse, then embraced her, fondled her breasts and kissed her passionately; Gavin looked

on with raised eyebrows. When this was over Jacqueline sat
down, buttoned herself up again, sat as if in a daze.

The therapist turned to Gavin and said: 'This is what your
wife needs at least three times a week. Can you do that?'

Gavin thought for a few moments before saying: 'I can drop
her off here on Mondays and Wednesdays, but on Fridays I
have golf.'

*

I'M NO STRANGER TO SEVEN DEADLY SINS
1 DECEMBER 2007

THE OTHER DAY one of my grandchildren asked me how many
of the Seven Deadly Sins I had yet to commit, and it took me a
while to work out that the answer was 'arguably one', mainly
because I was not entirely certain what exactly 'sloth' involved. To
go nit-picking, I do not accept that 'pride' is a sin. How guilty
should you feel of being seriously proud of five children and 16
grandchildren? (I accept that under the circumstances my
ownership of a miniscule share of a Derby winner has about it a
touch of sinfulness.) But the ability to cook impeccable pizza
crust makes up for that.

I plead guilty to coveting my neighbours' wives, but then we have
moved houses a lot. I consider envy and lust to be a part of
covetousness, far too serious to count three times separately. I get
angry, though not as angry as I used to get, while gluttony, in which I
indulge a lot, fails to feature in my sin list. It may be a heartless
confession but I have yet to shed a single tear for an oyster that
slipped down my throat pursued by chilli vinegar, or mourn the
passing of a partridge – which I eat plainly roasted with bread sauce
and crisply fried rashers of rindless, smoked, streaky bacon.

Is owning horses 'sinful'? Now there's an interesting question. You
could argue that we owners pay trainers in order for them to

persuade horses to run faster than they want to run, or is it every Thoroughbred's ambition to run faster than its peers, the way all six-year-old children try to win the egg-and-spoon race? Were that the case, it's hard to justify the use of the whip, or do Thoroughbreds change to a higher gear for the reward that comes the way of winners ... or are they deterred by the 'punishment' that is meted out to those who fail?

Perhaps it is sinful to pay one trainer twice as much as you would pay a rival? Subjecting the poorly endowed racehorse to less comfortable quarters, cheaper food, lads with too much to do, therefore insufficient time to glean meaningful bonuses to enable payments for high-quality legal advice when the fuzz comes to call on them ... which they tend to do even before first lot.

Please do not write accusing me of fallacious reasoning. From time to time when there is nothing more compulsive than a West Country Racing Club after-dinner speech to prepare, I have agreed to answer questions for which the audience would like answers. Then do I stand by the top table of a Totnes hotel, announce that question time had come around and promise I would do my level best to satisfy the assembled crowd's lust for information.

'Could you tell me the best way to get to Sidmouth?', asked a man with a speech impediment. I seemed to be the only man who did not know: know what he had asked or had even a rough idea of how one went there.

So I asked whether anyone knew the direction and advised the questioner to follow him.

*

THIS MAN WAS having dinner in a small but quite pretentious restaurant when an attractive woman came in and was seated at a corner table on the far side of the room. The man called over the waiter and asked him to take a bottle of good Claret to the lady with his compliments. Waiter did what he had been asked and explained it was from 'the man over there'. She looked at the bottle for a while and without turning, wrote a note: For me to accept this bottle you need to have a Mercedes in your garage, a million pounds in your bank and seven inches in your pocket.

The waiter delivered the note to the man, who wrote back: Things are not always what they seem. I have a Ferrari and an Aston Martin in my garage, houses in Aspen and Monte Carlo, a large ranch in Idaho, in excess of £20 million in my bank. However, not even for a woman as lovely as you would I cut three inches from what I have in my pocket; please could I have my wine back.

*

MR JAY-Z, I HAVE PROBLEMS YOU CAN'T IMAGINE

5 JULY 2008

TO ME, THE word festival conjures up Cheltenham, Punchestown, Galway and Killarney. Last week, almost twice the number of people who went to Epsom Downs on Derby day attended the Glastonbury Festival, where the presenters bewildered viewers – certainly this viewer – with words that had wholly unexpected meanings.

I thought 'set' was to do with beavers; it now has everything to do with Amy Winehouse. And 'wrappers', whichever way you spell the word, was what you put around sandwiches to preserve freshness and stop butter from staining your jacket pocket. Now, a rapper is one who sings lyrics that neither necessarily rhyme nor scan and at Glastonbury was cheered by 80,000 people.

Mr Jay-Z, who is American and angry and talks about himself disparagingly, has a number called '99 Problems'. Audiences call for this refrain as they used to demand that Vera Lynn sing 'There'll be Blue Birds over the White Cliffs of Dover'.

The words of Mr Z's oeuvre are: 'I got 99 problems but a bitch ain't one / If you having girl problems I feel bad for you son / Hit me.'

Well, I wanted to hit him; sadly there are not yet buttons on my television set (I mean 'set' in its old sense) that enables activation of such measures.

Giving the matter thought, I too have problems, and 99 would be a conservative number: there is my age, my health, both my knees, my hearing, the size of my waist, disappearing hair, and the fact that my Portuguese Maria is going on holiday next week and I will have to make my own bed, are just starters. There are my bookmakers' bills, ante-post vouchers on non-runners, the form of my horses, the dearth of summer jump meetings (nothing within 100 miles of London this month) and my elder brother's outpourings to the *Daily Mail* to take us into double figures. Then there is the Tote, which I would like to buy but can't afford because of my limited fortune (big problem), and the Lib Dems who aren't going anywhere and the Conservatives who are, and my one-man show on Monday in Buckingham which is not yet sold out.

Don't hit me.

It has become trendy for broadsheet newspapers to show off the versatility of their hacks by sending the theatre critic to cover darts, the rugby league man to do the House of Lords, the travel editor to assess the Royal Academy Summer Show. I have not yet seen an opera critic at a racecourse, but it can only be a matter of time ...

In the parade ring, Pipedreamer looked *allegro* and his *bravura* stood out *deciso*, while the group around him was genuinely *animato*. I thought Multidimensional appeared *agitati*; this could have been the tongue-strap, but you don't want your horse to manifest *forte-piano* before the music starts lest *rallentando* occur in the final act. Mount Nelson had been my bet '*ma non troppo*', I told the bookmaker, giving him a £2 coin.

The conductor dropped his whip, *prestissimo* went the horses – except for Campanologist who went *fugato*, almost *grave*, while Maraahel was *staccato*.

Over the three movements, what they call ten furlongs, it was Phoenix Tower who ran *suave, con brio, con anima* and, with only a movement to go and the man in the saddle giving every sign of *rigoroso*, he slowed down to *andante*, finishing *largo*, what we call *morendo* in my trade . . . or did I forget to mention that I usually write about musical events?

*

THIS YOUNG CHINESE couple got married. She was a virgin and he had never been with a woman, though he pretended to be worldly. On the wedding night she lay under the sheets as he undressed in the dark, then joined her in bed.

'I love you,' he said. 'I will do anything you want, anything at all, you just say it.' There followed a longish silence before she said, shyly: 'My girlfriend says that 69 is very nice.'

An even longer silence before he asked: 'You want garlic chicken with cauliflower?'

*

MUSHY BEES:
THE ULTIMATE URBAN TONIC
20 SEPTEMBER 2008

IT IS A while since I have written about my bees. The involvement started when the dread Lady F. and I got this flat with more rooms than we needed and it occurred to me that as we both liked honey, I could embrace apiarism. I examined the freehold of our apartment and found nothing therein about not keeping bees. I went for it.

At first I bought a single cedar hive, a khaki protective suit and veil, a single swarm of Araminta Ambers and two dozen Queens for rearing and mating.

Opportunities for pollination are sparse in London W1, but we grew some heather in a window-box and I applied to join BKASE, the Beekeepers' Association of Southern England. They asked me to send a sample of my honey. I went to Church Street market and bought a jar from an Indian gentleman minding a stall, and posted it to BKASE HQ in Catford.

They were not impressed, and suggested I purchase a hand-held heather-loosener replacement wire from a specialist supplier in Okehampton, along with an extracting filter unit and Apidea mating hive for Queen-rearing and marking.

I declined, became what was probably the first wholly independent metropolitan apiarist, and have not looked back. We now have three hives, two in a spare bedroom separated by a gauze curtain, the third in an out-of-use bathroom. When the neighbour in the flat on my left complained about the bees humming around our window-boxes – by then we had three, all growing heather – I decided to keep the windows closed, and daily provided the hives with bunches of Galloway heather from a garden centre in Little Venice, a part of Maida Vale by the Grand Union Canal.

In the beginning, I liquidised the honey in a blender at a low speed, increasing this until I had a pulp which I rubbed through a sieve, clarified with egg-whites and shells, dribbled into labelled jars and sold to our corner shop as Marylebone Parish Honey. Then I bought a Wilbraham centrifuge which revolutionised the business. The rest is, of course, history; I am told there is a distinct chance of a Royal warrant.

*

IT WAS THE annual dinner of the United Kingdom and Ireland Apiarist Society, and the 300 beekeepers had an ordinary dinner, listened to some ordinary speeches, then adjourned to the withdrawing room to get plastered.

A quartet of men but for whom there would be no honey for our tea were assembled in a corner behind the bar, chatting, when one of them said: 'Let us introduce ourselves. My name is Michael, I farm in west Devon, mostly acacia, have about 20,000 bees, 34 hives.'

The next man to speak was called Rory, came from Renfrewshire, his bees, of which he has 45,000, feed on gorse. He had 40 hives. The Welsh beekeeper had massive hedges of heather around Carmarthenshire: 35,000 bees, intense cultivation with 50 hives.

They looked at the Irishman in their midst and said: 'Your turn to tell us.' 'Well,' said the Irishman. 'My name is Patrick, I come from Tralee, grow clover and borage, am a bit bigger than the rest of you with a million bees, no hives.'

'A million bees, no hives,' Rory mused. There followed a silence which Michael broke to ask: 'How do they manage?'

'Feck 'em,' said Patrick.

*

THE SIGNS THAT 'ELDERLY' IS A THING OF THE PAST

20 SEPTEMBER 2008

I HAVE BEEN changing my will ... a lot. This is a very pleasurable exercise for people of my sort of age, known in the trade as 'old' – not elderly, certainly not middle-aged, just plain 'You haven't long to go.' You tell people who invite you to parties to keep their eyes on the obituary column. In a nutshell, 'old' is when you are complimented on your alligator shoes when you are barefoot; when you are cautioned to 'slow down' by your doctor rather than the police; and when 'getting lucky' means finding your car in the car park. Particularly, 'old' is when you are not sure whether any of these are jokes.

*

A VERY LOVELY young redhead went to the doctor's surgery, told him that her body hurt wherever she touched it. The doctor told her that was not possible, asked her to show him. She touched her shoulder and screamed, touched her elbow and screamed even louder, touched her leg and yelled with pain, and when she poked her ankle she almost fainted.

'You are not really a redhead, are you?', asked the medic.

She looked surprised and said: 'No, I am actually a blonde.'

'I thought so,' said the doctor. 'Your finger is broken.'

*

HORSES AND RACING – WHAT ELSE WOULD YOU EXPECT?
20 DECEMBER 2008

THIS MAN CAME up to me at Sandown and asked whether I might consider making the odd mention of horses or racing or breeding or betting in my weekly 'joke column'. I was hurt; however, it being the season of goodwill to all men, it occurred to me that he might have a point and I will try to do better.

A mortician who liked going to evening all-weather meetings at Wolverhampton and Great Leighs was working late one night, as he prepared for cremation the body of an owner called Schwartz who had had a passion for jump racing, especially favouring Huntingdon, Fakenham and Towcester, where he had once famously landed a double at very long odds.

Looking down at the cadaver, he could not help noticing that Mr Schwartz had the most amazingly massive member, too rare a thing to push into the oven, so he cut it off, wrapped it in foil and placed it in his briefcase. When he got home, he told his wife that he had something remarkable she might enjoy having a look at, unzipped his bag, took out the huge willy and put it on the table.

'My God,' she said. 'Schwartz is dead.'

One afternoon, in a field of sugar beet at Walkington, which is just west of Beverley racecourse, the BHA official deputed to deal with the track's marketing and publicity was walking his Labrador and wondering why nothing exciting ever happened in his life other than the time an amateur jockey had weighed in 7lb light and been disqualified from fourth place. He looked up to see a hot-air balloon hovering some 10m above him.

The pilot leaned out of his basket and shouted: 'Excuse me, can you tell me where I am?'

The man below shouted back: 'You are in a hot-air balloon hovering 30 feet above this field.'

'You must work in IT,' said the balloonist. 'I do,' replied the man. 'How did you know?'

The balloonist said: 'Everything you tell me is technically correct but of not the slightest use to anyone.'

The man said: 'You must work in management.' The balloonist answered: 'Yes, how did you know?'

'You don't know where you are nor where you are going but expect me to be able to help; and you were in the same position as you were when we met but now it's my fault.'

This young man had been involved in a dead-heat on his second-ever ride: a hunter chase at Exeter over three miles on heavy going. He was dating a girl who rode out for a well-known trainer – who asked me not to mention his name lest it gave his yard a bad name, but told me he thinks he probably has the winner of the King George.

The young couple got on really well, and one day she asked him to come to her home, meet her parents over dinner, and go to bed together. He was very excited.

Being a virgin, apart from a single nocturnal grope in the stable lads' hostel at Taunton, he went to a local chemist to buy condoms and seek advice, coming away with interesting knowledge and a family pack of Durex.

On the appointed evening, his girlfriend met him at the door and took him into the dining-room where her parents were waiting. The boy kept his head bowed, asked if it would be all right if he said grace, and remained in the position of prayer for a very long time. After ten minutes, the girl whispered to him: 'I didn't know you were so religious.'

He whispered back: 'I didn't know your father was a pharmacist.'

In ancient Greece, Socrates was widely lauded for his wisdom. One day, the great philosopher came upon an acquaintance outside the local dice parlour who ran up to him excitedly and said: 'Socrates, do you know what I just heard about one of your students?'

'Wait a moment,' Socrates replied. 'Before you tell me, I'd like you to pass a little test – the test of 'three'. The first test is Truth. Have you made absolutely sure that what you are about to tell me is true?'

'No,' the man said, 'actually I just heard about it.'

'All right,' said Socrates. 'So you don't really know if it's true or not. Now let's try the second test, the test of Goodness. Is what you are about to tell me about my student something good?'

'No, on the contrary ...'

'So,' Socrates said, 'you want to tell me something bad about him although you're not sure it's true?'

The man shrugged, a little embarrassed. Socrates continued: 'You may still pass though, because there is a third test – the filter of Usefulness. Is what you want to tell me about my student going to be useful to me?'

'No, not really ...'

'Well,' concluded Socrates, 'if what you want to tell me is neither True nor Good nor even Useful, why tell it to me at all?'

The man was defeated and ashamed. This is the reason Socrates was a great philosopher and held in such high esteem. It also explains why he never found out that Plato was banging his wife.

No jokes this week, though a happy Christmas to all my readers.

*

THIS MAN (why is it that so many filthy stories begin with 'this man'?) was sitting in his study when his wife came in and hit him on the head with a saucepan.

He said:'Whatsematter?'

She said:'I went through your trouser pockets before sending them to the cleaners and found a piece of paper with the name Barbara Ellen, that's what.'

'It's the name of a horse I was tipped for Fontwell,' he said, being a quick thinker.

A few days later he was sitting at his desk when his wife came and smashed his head with a frying pan.

'Why did you do that?'

'Your horse phoned up.'

*

A FEW THINGS I WANT TO DO BEFORE I DIE
7 FEBRUARY 2009

MY ELDEST DAUGHTER said: 'I will get your watch when you don't need it any more ... won't I?' And I realised that she meant when I was dead and tried to remember whether I had made mention of this in my will. We were having dinner in a restaurant in Kensington and to make her feel that talking about my 'not needing things any more' was an accepted conversational subject – also because the plates had been cold, the meat overcooked and a 15 per cent service charge added to the bill – I said: 'I shall never come here again.'

Never?

With just over five and a half thousand days to go before I hit my century, maybe a thousand dinners while I still know roughly what I am doing, one can make these statements with proper gravitas. My friend Sir Peter O'Sullevan, who is 103, lucid, does 60 press-ups before breakfast and still drives to Newbury from London in 35 minutes, is a rare exception. My memory is beginning to go a bit, also my memory is beginning to go a bit.

Where old people get it wrong is in reminiscing: recalling the great moments of youth, when it is joyful anticipation of life after 80 that should feature.

Who cares a damn, let alone wants to hear, about teenage boxing careers? Too heavy to be a flyweight and too fly to be a heavyweight, I was made to fight friends with whom I had no argument: boring. In cricket, the year I kept wicket for my prep school, long-stop won the fielding cup. I played football when the W-Plan was the new thing, and rode horses against Lord Oaksey when he was Mr J. Lawrence (7).

I can hear readers shouting, 'Enough already', so will switch to a few things I would like to do before I die.

1. Buy a three-year-old who has won over a mile and a quarter on soft going at York, watch him win the Triumph Hurdle at the Cheltenham Festival having backed him at 50-1 (if a capable jumps trainer comes across a horse that has substantial juvenile hurdle potential he is going to offer it to one of his/her trusted, well-heeled owners who already has a dozen horses in the yard … which includes me out).

2. Find a talented helicopter pilot/bookmaker/chef who will fly me to Cartmel, Perth, Plumpton and Ffos Las, cook me great dishes

like glazed ham with Cumberland sauce, lobster thermidor, reform lamb cutlets while I sit sipping a magnum of Chateau Lafite and obtain best prices against my selections, winnings paid in freshly printed £50 notes (get real).

3. Attend an East Anglian point-to-point (which is what I do) where there is a bookmaker who will take serious bets and pay out – should I win – without making me feel that I have ruined his life, caused him to have to sell his house, rent out his wife and pawn his children (every hope of this happening, but betting with people who noticeably can't afford to lose hugely diminishes the enjoyment of winning).

4. Live long enough to witness the invention of the pill which causes you to lose weight on a diet of salted cashew nuts, oysters, smoked streaky bacon sandwiches, toasted cheese and sherry trifle with jelly and cream.

*

THERE ARE THOSE who believed that humour does not travel, that despite Eurostar and the stunning St Pancras station, where there is a champagne bar you would be foolish not to patronise, appreciation of our jokes ends at Dover. The following is believed to be the best joke to have emerged from Australia and I welcome it:

Charlie walks into his bedroom with a sheep under his arm, says: 'Darling, this is the pig I have sex with when you have a headache.'

His wife, who is in bed, says: 'I think you will find that is a sheep you have under your arm, you idiot.'

And Charlie says: 'I think you'll find I wasn't talking to you.'

*

This is the last Clement Freud column to appear in the Racing Post, *published one week after Mon Mome, trained by Venetia Williams, had won the John Smith's Grand National at 100-1.*

RON LIVING THE DOG'S LIFE THAT EVERY GREYHOUND SHOULD ENJOY

11 APRIL 2009

RON IS FIVE and a half years old. He was born in Ireland, settled in Tralee, came to England at an early age, the way so many Irish do, and had his odd moments of glory at Walthamstow and Wimbledon, on the flat and over hurdles. He was favourite to win an open race when he went lame and never quite recovered that form. His lifetime record is 50 runs, ten wins.

Amanda is about Ron's age, if you equate a dog year to seven human ones. She is an actress, had among her most memorable moments playing a mad doctor called May Wright, who was married to businessman Rob Minter, who was having it off with a barmaid in *Eastenders* a couple of years ago.

Today, Amanda stars in *Parlour Song* at the Almeida Theatre in north London, playing the wife of a demolition expert in a failing marriage. Ron, who is retired, whom she picked up from the Waltham Abbey Kennels when his owners put him up for rehousing at the end of his career, sleeps in her dressing room, takes her out for two proper walks a day. They are inseparable; both know how to look after the other.

Amanda Drew, daughter of a vicar, was brought up in Devon and Leicestershire, went to the Royal Academy of Dramatic Art (the year below Michael Sheen), gets work steadily on stage, screen and television, and one day received a pamphlet telling her of the cruelty accorded retired greyhounds, especially by the Spanish, who are particularly barbaric. She had always wanted a dog and, reading about the void that confronted retired greyhounds, became determined to provide one with a full life. She went to the kennels, met Ron, and they took to each other.

Ron is brindled, fit, clean, well-behaved, doesn't bark, eats two £1 bags of offal – a mixture of liver, lungs, hearts and lights – a day and has as his second home the back of Amanda's Rover convertible.

At their house in east London he stays away from noise, doesn't watch television, not even greyhound racing, just has 'a lovely temperament'. She calls him 'my 40mph couch potato'. He does not like birds, rabbits, cats or squirrels (probably realises the latter are just rats with good PR) and Amanda says: 'I don't like to hector him, I just talk to him.'

Her ambition is to have people realise that retired greyhounds are the best, loyalest, most rewarding pets to have; that good people should be queuing to offer them homes and save them from the cruelties that await those whose owners make no provision for their futures. Google tells you where the kennels are, or Amanda will guide you; go and see *Parlour Song*, which is excellent and funny and only takes an hour and three-quarters, and buy her a drink in the theatre bar after the show.

'Our next guest,' explained the question-master, 'requires no introduction' – which I have always felt to be a pretty dumb way of presenting visiting speakers … but this was in Pontefract.

He began by asking me in which age I would most like to have lived, and I went for the mythical Greek. It was the time of lotus eaters, when inhabitants of the shifting sandbanks near Carthage could suck at fruit whose roots drew water from the underworld, causing forgetfulness of the past as well as eliminating all concept of the future.

I want to forget the past, especially last Saturday.

Venetia Williams had advised me to have a little investment on Stan in the Grand National, which I did each-way at 100-1. And then I fancied Battlecry and Darkness and was pretty sure that Kilbeggan Blade would get round and run into a place, and when Pricewise selected Offshore Account there was only State Of Play to fear.

I backed them all; I had exactas and trifectas featuring the selections, executed a quick, late excursion from the Lord Derby stand to place a saver on Butler's Cabin and Parsons Legacy, because I would have been sick if they had won when I had taken such care to include all those with apparent chances. I want to forget Liverpool.

I want to forget what I could have bought with the money I left at Aintree: the bottles of Bollinger that would have lined the lower (cooler) shelf of my refrigerator, the eau de vie of Pear William that can lie comfortably in the freezer, it being too alcoholic to freeze solid. The supply of smoked eel fillets, horseradish grated into Cornish cream, potted goose liver, Melton Mowbray pork pies, pickled walnuts, turtle soup, Roquefort cheese, wild strawberry jelly.

*

The column concluded with the final joke:

THE OWNER OF a filling station was trying to boost sales, put up a notice stating 'Free sex when you fill your tank.'

A driver with a friend filled up, then asked for sex. Man said: 'Give me a number between one and nine.'

'Seven,' said the driver.

'Bad luck,' said the man, 'it was six.'

The driver and his friend came back twice, each time filling up, each time getting the number wrong.

'I think it's a racket,' said the driver to his friend as they drove off.

'No, it's not,' said the friend. 'My wife got it last week and the week before that.'

8

THE SAGE

❛ Small bets are a waste of time; if it doesn't hurt you to lose, winning cannot be sufficiently significant to cause happiness ❜

A HELPING HAND ON THE
LEARNING CURVE

17 NOVEMBER 1999

THE FIRST TIME I went to Huntingdon races was just after the war; a party of us had lunch at the Eel and Pike in the nearby village of Over, where they had a buffet of roast chicken, roast turkey and boiled ham, which were then wondrously bounteous. I expect I lost money – Huntingdon has never been a lucky track for me.

Last month, I was at Huntingdon and decided, for old times' sake, to stop at Over: there is now a menu outside, on which the most exotic item was Chicken Ping (put chicken in microwave and take it out when it goes 'ping').

At the races, I had a few bets and lost, and thought to myself, 'Should I not have learned something in all those years?'

On reflection the answer was: I have learned. I now go to Huntingdon with less money. I know a parking place from which I can make a quick getaway after the last. I discovered the stand which sells mulled wine in the winter and there is a Punch and Judy man in the autumn.

Moreover, the people who work at the Cambridgeshire track are so altogether pleasant that I would sooner lose there than break even at Plumpton. At Plumpton they treat punters with contempt; half the raceday trains don't stop at the racecourse station and the road to the enclosures is pitted, so that on a rainy day – just about every day they race at Plumpton is rainy – you get splashed by cars that explode the puddles.

It would not cost a fortune to sand the puddles or have someone welcome you on arrival, as they do at Uttoxeter, Brighton and Newcastle. Don't tell me I have not learned.

Perhaps lesson number one is that small bets suck (a word I learned from my children). Small bets are a waste of time; if it doesn't hurt you to lose, winning cannot be sufficiently significant to cause happiness.

If my grandchildren want advice on the subject of racing I am their man:

Try to become a journalist and get a press badge, which saves you paying entrance fees.

Resist ownership, unless you are very rich or slightly insane.

Avoid the Jackpot. While it is a better bet than the Lottery, you need to have your head examined if you buy Lottery tickets; if masochism rules, do a single-line Jackpot for a fiver and send another fiver to a good cause.

Drink champagne at York, where it is cheaper than anywhere else I know.

Take a shooting stick or chair to Bangor, for there is nowhere to sit.

Join the Royal Ascot Racing Club, the best-value outfit in the land. (I think there may be a waiting list; put your children down for it.)

Avoid Salisbury, unless you are a close relative of the gatemen.

Take a picnic and hip flask to Folkestone.

Resist the packed evening meetings at Ripon and Pontefract, unless you are agoraphobic or a pickpocket.

If you are into kilts, go to Perth. If you want a really good, honest dining-room luncheon, Kelso may be the place for you – though the Sandown/Epsom/Kempton/Newbury restaurant manager, whose name is Page Nine, or possibly Paganini, is a star and looks after you like a high-class nanny.

It cost me a lot of money to acquire all this knowledge. If racing grabs you the way it has grabbed me and so many readers of this excellent paper, participate fully in the action.

Don't just gravitate from bar to bookmaker to viewing point; observe the parade ring, watch the start, stand by the water jump at National Hunt courses, drink local beers and buy local cakes and fudge at the sweetie stand; take this home to your family – it beats £3.99 bunches of flowers from filling stations.

Listen to the buzz, what the Irish call 'the craic'; if you are over 40 and less than fat, wear jodhpurs and riding boots. This impresses people a lot.

About betting: if you embrace a system, re-evaluate it from time to time. While every system has its day, none works consistently. Backing the horse with the number 9 saddlecloth is guaranteed to lose you money in the long run. Grey horses do not win a disproportionate number of races. Look at statistics and you find that jockeys, however good, have poor strike-rates compared to top trainers.

The outsider of three wins less often than the favourite or second favourite.

The combination of black and white and red is elegant, but the colours of the jockey's silks have absolutely no bearing on the performance of the horse below.

The very best bet is when you have a gut feeling and this is supported by one or two reputable tipsters.

The going is the most important thing to consider when assessing the form of horses in a race; in sprints the draw matters greatly at some tracks, quite especially on the all-weather.

Do not proposition Mrs Pitman nor ask Sir Mark Prescott for a tip. Take into account the size of the pool when betting heavily on the Tote and remember, when totting up the expenses of a day on the track, how much it will have cost *not* to have gone racing.

The price of a decent seat at a West End theatre is £35; for the cost of six seats, you can have a goodish time on a racecourse and not have to talk to, or buy ice creams for, five people in the interval.

Vary your stakes; it is just plain dumb to have a fiver each-way on every race, hugely sensible to plunge a couple of times an afternoon and have, if you must, a modest interest in other events instead of which a glass of whisky mac is usually a good choice.

The plunge is what racing is all about: many years ago my eldest daughter phoned and said: 'Dad, I dreamed who won the Grand National and who came second and third; number 8 was first, beating 17 and 23; I've got a pad by my bedside table and made myself wake up straight away so I wouldn't forget: 8, 17, 23.'

I looked up the horses about whom she had dreamed and found none of them very appealing – but then Foinavon had not been very appealing, nor Tipperary Tim, who surprised both his trainer and his jockey when he won at 100-1 from the only other finisher, just before my fourth birthday.

Horse number 8 was 20-1; her dream second was any price and number 23 was around 16-1.

The nightmare scenario was that the dream would become true and she would have missed the opportunity of becoming seriously rich.

The obvious solution was to bet the horses in a tricast. The problem was that most bookmakers had a limit of £10,000 per bet and at 30,000-and-something to one it would be foolish to put on more than 30p per betting slip.

She managed one hundred bets, at 30p, never more than four bets in any one shop and, after an uplifting morning trawling the inns of unhappiness in Battersea, Clapham, Wandsworth and Balham, went home exhausted. She was actually asleep while the race was run. This did not, of course, alter the result: number 19 won, 4 came second, 6 was third.

Better to have played and lost than regret missing out on that million for the rest of your life.

INDEX